RASHI
the Man and
His World

Italian manuscript of Pentateuch with Rashi's Commentary (14-15th century).

RASHI
the Man and
His World

ESRA SHERESHEVSKY

SEPHER-HERMON PRESS, Inc.

New York, 1982

RASHI, the Man and His World

Copyright © 1982 Esra Shereshevsky

Published by Sepher-Hermon Press, Inc.
New York, N.Y.

Library of Congress Cataloging in Publication Data

Shereshevsky, Esra.
   Rashi, the man and his world.

   Bibliography: p.
   Includes index.
   1. Rashi, 1040-1105. 2. Rabbis--Biography.
3. Scholars, Jewish--Biography. 4. Bible. O.T.--Criti-
cism, interpretation, etc., Jewish. 5. Talmud--Criti-
cism, interpretation, etc.--History. I. Title.
BM755.S6S54 1982   296.8'2   82-10821
ISBN 0-87203-101-2

For M.H.

Contents

Prefatory Note

In a publication of this character I believe it is proper to begin with an expression of thanksgiving to the Source of all wisdom, Who has been my inspiration in this venture and Who has enabled me to complete it.

According to our tradition God has two partners in the creation of every human being: the father and the mother. I wish to record my gratitude to my parents, of blessed memory, whose constant nurturing care and guidance led me into the service of our people and its Torah. It was given to both my parents to be spared the horrors of the Hitler regime and to spend the final years of their lives in *Eretz Yisrael*.

My revered father, Solomon Joseph Shereshevsky, in addition to providing for the material needs of nine children, imbued each one of us with his own love for Zion and with his hopes for the rebirth of the Jewish people on its own soil. He was a respected and admiring friend to many builders of the Jewish Homeland. My beloved mother, Rachel Friedman Shereshevsky, reared us in devotion to Jewish scholarship. She was the daughter and niece of three brothers who were known in Lithuanian Jewry as the "Sages of Zhagare," and a granddaughter of Rabbi Shimon Hurwitz (1810-1900), a noted halakhic authority in Leipzig, the author and editor of major Rabbinic works. Rabbi Hurwitz prepared the first published edition (Berlin, 1889-93) of the *Mahzor Vitry*, the work of Rashi's disciple, Simha ben Samuel of Vitry. Thus my maternal heritage first inspired me with love and admiration for Rashi and his work.

It was also my mother who, following the rise of Hitler in Germany, directed my steps to that great citadel of Torah, the Yeshiva of Telz (Telsiai), Lithuania, where Torah was not only a subject of study but also a fact of everyday life. This yeshiva, one of the finest institutions of Jewish learning in recent centuries, was my *alma mater*, my spiritual "fostering mother," in the truest sense of the term. My late brother-in-law, Juda Ari Wohlgemuth, one of the early West European students at the Yeshiva of Telz and in his own life a splendid representative of the Weltanschauung of *Torah im Derekh Eretz*, led me with gentle words of warm encouragement into a world which was then completely new to me. Telz not only implanted in me the love of Torah but also developed in me the ability to understand a Rabbinic text and to delve deeply into its intricacies. To the Yeshiva of Telz, and to those who encouraged me to sit at the feet of its great Talmudic masters, I will always be grateful.

Accumulation of knowledge alone, of course, is no assurance of its full utilization. For the development of whatever sensitivity I have acquired to these hidden precious treasures of our classics I am indebted to my esteemed teacher, the late Professor Solomon Zeitlin, and to his disciple, my close friend, the late Professor Sidney B. Hoenig, who through their friendship, their guidance and their invaluable counsel have made their abiding presence felt in this publication.

The first draft of the manuscript for this book was read with painstaking care by the late Professor Solomon Grayzel, whose suggestions were most encouraging, and particularly enlightening where Rashi's comments allude to historical events of his day. I also wish to pay a tribute of thanks to my friend of many years, the late Elkan Buchhalter, one of the finest librarians I have known, who, with his intellectual integrity and wide bibliographical knowledge, gave me many important suggestions. His untimely death deprived me of a loyal friend.

My heartfelt thanks go to my publisher, Samuel Gross of Sepher-Hermon Press, for his kind encouragement, warm personal interest and invaluable counsel.

May I add a word of appreciation to Ms. Nadia L. Kravchenko, who with great patience and efficiency typed the first version of this manuscript. Though usually given so little recognition, such day-to-day chores are vital in the publication of any book.

This book is the fruit of many years of research. But the collecting of data produces only the raw material from which the author must then weave a smooth, harmonious fabric acceptable in both substance and form. This harmony could be achieved only through the intensive and enthusiastic collaboration of my editor, Miss Gertrude Hirschler. The editor and translator of classic works of Jewish history and literature, Miss Hirschler did not consider her task fulfilled merely by the superficial polishing of style or reformulation of ideas and concepts. She delved into the raw material and pursued its context and connection with Biblical and Talmudic texts. Her corrections and suggestions were astute and many questions that she raised stimulated new approaches and interpretations. I wish to express my sincerest gratitude to Miss Hirschler for her cooperation and assistance which made the publication of this book in its present form possible.

The ultimate purpose of this book is to motivate further studies in Rashi's commentaries and particularly to restore "Humash with Rashi" and "Gemarah with Rashi" to their rightful places as household words in the Jewish family. If my work will serve at all to help accomplish this objective I will feel richly rewarded indeed.

ESRA SHERESHEVSKY

Introduction

The true progeny of the righteous are their good deeds.

—Rashi, Commentary on Genesis 6:9

For centuries Rashi (Rabbi Shlomo Yitzhaki, or Solomon ben Isaac) was known — in an allusion to his initials — as *Rabban shel Yisrael*, the Teacher of Israel. But today there are surprisingly many Jews to whom Rashi's classic commentaries on the Bible and Talmud are literally a closed book and Rashi himself is an unknown figure. Only a few decades ago, when the great centers of Jewish learning spread their light into the remotest corners of the Jewish diaspora, old and young alike immersed themselves into Rashi's commentaries. The men gathered at synagogues, houses of study and at each other's homes to listen to discourses on Rashi's interpretations of Biblical and Talmudic texts. Meanwhile, the womenfolk enjoyed Rashi's wise and warmhearted aphorisms and parables which had been adapted especially for them in popular Judeo-German or Yiddish translations. Over the centuries Rashi was so inextricably a part of Jewish religious and cultural life that it was considered almost mandatory to study, before each Sabbath, not only the Pentateuchal portion that was to be read in the

1

synagogue that week but also the relevant commentaries by Rashi.[1] Where Rashi's commentaries were studied, ignorance could not long endure. With Rashi's explanations to guide the students through the complexities of the most intricate Biblical and Talmudic passages, a continuing supply of *talmidei hakhamim* — scholars of Jewish law — and hence the survival of traditional Jewish learning was assured.

Given Rashi's paramount place in the continuity of Jewish religious and cultural tradition, it is not surprising that seven centuries after his death the scholars of the 19th-century *Wissenschaft des Judentums* were eager to investigate the historical and spiritual conditions which led to the emergence of this intellectual giant. Monographs and biographies stemming from diverse viewpoints appeared, enriching not only Jewish lore but also general scholarship.[2]

Rashi's commentaries were known and utilized not only by his co-religionists but also in the non-Jewish world. In order to establish the correct text of the Old Testament to their satisfaction, early Christian theologians and churchmen had no other recourse but to turn to the original Hebrew text. Rashi's commentaries aided them greatly in resolving the many ambiguities presented by the original text. It is commonly acknowledged that the foremost Christian beneficiary of Rashi's commentary was the French Franciscan Bible commentator Nicholas de Lyre or de Lyra (1270-1349). In his *Postillae Perpetuae*, which he composed between 1322 and 1330, Nicholas makes frequent references to "Rabbi Solomon."[3]

However, it is apparent that Christians knew of Rashi's commentaries even before these were taken up by Nicholas de Lyre. The 12th-century Biblical interpretations of the Victorines in France[4] show many similarities to those of Rashi. They are introduced with the phrase *tradunt Hebraei* ("the Hebrews transmit") or simply *Hebraei dicunt* ("the Hebrews say"). Just which *"Hebraei"* were meant is not indicated. (Obviously, we cannot exclude the possibility that both Rashi and Christian theologians who were active during, or even after, Rashi's lifetime, used the same Talmudic and Midrashic sources for their Biblical comments). Peter (Pierre) Comestor (1100-1180), who, like Rashi, was born in Troyes and who served as Dean of the Cathedral Chapter of Saint Peter in that city from 1147 to 1164, shows his acquaintance with Rashi's commentaries in his *Historia Scholastica,* which purports to narrate religious history beginning with the Garden of Eden. Here, too, we find references to the *"Hebraei,"* with the verbs *narrant* or *tradunt* ("relate" or "transmit," respectively) frequently added. Comestor's expression *alii dicunt* ("others say") refers in most instances to Jewish informants. Comestor came under sharp criticism from churchmen of a later period, such as the Italian Cardinal Robert Bellarmino (1542-1621)[5] for his use of what Bellarmino called *parum firmatae narrationes* ("not quite confirmed legends") because these "legends" had been of Jewish origin. Comestor's *narrationes* show remarkable similarities to some of Rashi's commentaries.[6] However, Nicholas de Lyre was the only one to admit explicitly that he had been making use of Rashi's commentaries: he cites Rashi by name: *"Dicit hic Rabbi Solomon"* ("at this point Rabbi Solomon comments").[7] Indeed, Nicholas de Lyre seemed so dependent on Rashi that Jean Mercier (d. 1570), professor of Hebrew at the Collège Royal in Paris from 1541, nicknamed him *Simius Solomonis,* "the ape of Solomon."[8] A popular rhyme about de Lyre, *"Si Lyra non lyrasset, Lutherius non saltasset"* ("Had Lyre not played the lyre, Luther would not have danced"), would seem to imply that the influence of Rashi's comments may be detected in the works of a long chain of Christian Bible exegetes and that, in fact, his interpretations are reflected in many of the Bible translations which were important forerunners of the King James Version[9] — including, in all likelihood, the version of Martin Luther, who consulted de Lyre's *Postillae Perpetuae* when he composed his German translation of the Bible. The earliest printed Hebrew book showing a date of publication (Reggio, 1475) is an edition of Rashi's commentary on the Pentateuch. This edition was used by the German Lutheran Hebraist Johann Friedrich Breithaupt (1639-1713) for his Latin translation of Rashi's Pentateuchal commentary, which was published in 1710. The scholarly writings of the Buxtorfs (father and son) during the 16th and 17th centuries in Switzerland show a remarkable familiarity with Rashi's commentaries. Indeed, some acquaintance, though not necessarily first-hand, with Rashi's commentaries is reflected also in the works of non-Jewish Bible scholars of the early modern era. The Orientalist Theodor Noeldeke of Strasbourg (1836-1930) and the Hebraist S. R. Driver of Oxford (1846-1914) both acknowledge their indebtedness to Rashi. The scholarly significance of Rashi's commentary on the Talmud is far greater than that of his Biblical exegesis; yet it is his interpretation of Biblical concepts and ideals, which form the basis of Western civilization, that has accorded Rashi the honored place he holds among the immortals who have contributed unfading threads to the moral fabric of society.

Of course Rashi's impact was incomparably more profound upon the Jewish people, for whom his commentaries had been primarily intended. As a rule, spiritual and intellectual influences are not easily measurable, but this is not true in the case of Rashi. Until the 19th century, when Jewish enlightenment and the *Wissenschaft des Judentums* first set their imprint upon the world of Jewish scholarship, a knowledge of Rashi's commentaries — at least on the Pentateuch — was considered *the* criterion of Jewish culture and learning.

During the many centuries which preceded these modern movements — and in some circles into our own day — Jews saw no conflict between their commitment to Judaism shaped by traditional Jewish learning, on the one hand, and the practical demands of life, on the other. To the Jew, the sole objective of acquiring knowledge was to learn the art of living as a Jew.[10] The scholar, the "genius," was at the same time a pious, upright man. Ingenuity or brilliance did not constitute a license to deviate from the religious and moral laws and customs observed by the "masses." On the contrary, intellectual gifts served only to impose upon the "genius" more numerous and difficult moral and religious responsibilities than were placed upon those less endowed. Rashi's teachings as reflected in his commentaries mirror also the standards he set for his own conduct. There was no dichotomy in his personal life between "theory" and "practice." History tells of great minds whose intellectual gifts, unfortunately, did not shape their character or behavior. Not so Rashi. The simplicity and humility reflected in his style were part and parcel of his own life. On the eve of Jewish festivals he himself would chop the garlic and grind the pepper for the holiday meal.[11] If he was at a gathering where a meat meal was served to others and he chose to eat dairy dishes, he did not ask for a separate table or tablecloth but ate his food from a napkin placed upon his knees.[12] His humility and naturalness earned him the high regard of his disciples, who were convinced that "all his deeds were done for the sake of heaven."[13]

By writing his commentaries, particularly on the Bible, in a popular style, Rashi made them accessible to the less educated. At the same time, he interwove his notes with stimuli which guided the novice toward further study and inspired the scholar to delve into the basic sources for a deeper understanding of Biblical teachings. Thus Rashi satisfied the needs of layman and savant alike. By studying Rashi, even a neophyte in Jewish learning could clear himself of the opprobrium of ignorance, for one who could claim that he had studied "Humash with Rashi" could no longer be called an *am ha-aretz* (ignoramus).

No other medieval commentary on Bible or Talmud enjoyed such a wide readership or had such a notable influence as that of Rashi. Apart from his clarity of style, Rashi's apt selections from the vast treasure house of Midrashic and Halakhic interpretations helped introduce the student to much of the extant Hebrew literature on Biblical and Talmudic lore. But Rashi did not content himself with citing these interpretations verbatim. With a subtle change here and there, often no more than one seemingly insignificant word or phrase, he left the mark of his own warm soul and keen psychological insights upon the passages he quoted.[14] The many surviving manuscript editions of his commentaries, dating from before the invention of movable type, bear witness to the wide dissemination of Rashi's work. Once Hebrew printing was introduced, numerous printed editions of the commentary appeared, first without the Biblical text but later on as inseparable companions to the relevant Biblical verses. The "Humash with Rashi" — the Pentateuch with Rashi's commentary — became a basic text in the Jewish home and in the house of study. No other work of Jewish literature has ever been accorded such appreciation — one might even say has commanded so much respect — as have Rashi's commentaries. The foremost scholars of Bible and Talmud have turned to Rashi for their own elucidations of Biblical and Talmudic passages. More than 200 supercommentaries are known that deal directly with Rashi's commentary on the Pentateuch, supplementing and explaining the Rashi text, and at times even attempting to emend it,[15] for as the Rashi commentaries spread to ever-widening circles in almost all the countries where Jews had settled, Rashi's original text became corrupted by misreadings and copyists' errors.

The emergence of the *Wissenschaft des Judentums* in the modern era introduced a new approach to traditional texts. The founders of this important movement in Jewish scholarship brought modern philological and historical methods to bear upon the study of the Jewish literary heritage. Attention now was given not so much to the content of the text as such, and its various versions, as to the conclusions which the text might suggest. The scholar was invited to look not only *at* the material but also *through* it. The text was utilized as the raw material from which to extract information that the author mentioned only in passing.

All this does not imply that the founders of the *Wissenschaft des Judentums* made light of the painstaking labors of their predecessors who for centuries had studied, expounded and added their own contributions to the literary heritage of Judaism. The savants of a later period could not dismiss their debt to earlier generations of scholars who had supplied the soil, as it were, within which their own new approaches could germinate and bear fruit.

Leopold Zunz (1794-1886), the trailblazer of modern Jewish scholarship, was the first to construct a composite picture of Rashi's life. His essay entitled "Salomon ben Isaac, genannt Raschi" first appeared in the *Zeitschrift fuer die Wissenschaft des Judentums* in Berlin in 1822 (Vol. I, No. 2). Zunz gleaned his data primarily from the Rashi commentaries themselves, which reveal, here and there, some sparse details about Rashi's family, his teachers and his contemporaries.

Chronology provides an indispensable framework for placing the events of an era, or a life, into their proper perspective. However, in studying a figure such as Rashi, in whose day records of birth and perhaps also of death were of interest only to the subject's closest kin, even Zunz had no alternative but to rely on Rabbinic sources whose prime purpose had not necessarily been to record history. Thus, Zunz's source for the dates of Rashi's birth and death is the 16th-century Talmudic commentator Solomon ben Yehiel Luria (1510-1574), himself a descendant of Rashi,[16] who in his Responsum No. 29 gives the date of Rashi's birth as the year 4800 Anno Mundi; i.e., 1039/40 of the Common Era, and the year of his death as 4865; i.e., 1104/05 C.E. This would mean that Rashi died at the age of 65.

All subsequent modern scholarly works on Rashi basically follow in the footsteps of Leopold Zunz, though with varying emphases, depending on the authors' fields of special interest, personal temperament and, in some instances, emotional attitude toward the subject matter. Whatever importance one may ascribe to the various scholarly biographies of Rashi or to the many specialized studies devoted to his commentaries, in the final analysis it was Leopold Zunz who laid the groundwork for them all and motivated them by touching lightly upon various areas which he felt invited further inquiry. Zunz's essay was translated into Hebrew in 1840, with copious annotations, by Samson (Simson) Halevi Bloch (1784-1845).[17]

A *sine qua non* for any scholarly study is, of course, the availability of an authentic original text. In his own work with the Talmud, Rashi approached the text with a rather critical eye, eliminating errors and correcting readings which in his opinion required such emendations. Admittedly, the only manuscript text available to Rashi was that of Rabbi Gershom ben Judah (Rabbenu Gershom; see Chapter I, below). However, he consistently endeavored to ascertain the most nearly correct version of the original text. In 1866 Abraham Berliner (1833-1915) of the Hildesheimer Rabbinical Seminary in Berlin published a critical edition of Rashi's commentary on the Pentateuch.[18] Berliner compared the variants found in about ten different manuscript versions of Rashi's commentary — some of them dating as far back as the 12th and 13th centuries — and established a text from which he had eliminated, as far as possible, additions and changes resulting from copyists' errors. Berliner also pointed out the sources which Rashi himself used for his commentary. Almost 40 years later — in 1905 — Berliner published a new edition of his work, based on over 100 manuscripts and a large number of printed editions of the Rashi commentary that had not been available to him in his initial effort.[19]

It may not be a mere coincidence that, two years after the publication of Berliner's original critical edition, Arsène Darmesteter (1846-1888), professor of medieval French at the Sorbonne, began to research the French glosses in the Rashi manuscripts at Oxford, Cambridge and the British Museum. His objective was to clarify the phonetics and structure of Old French with the help of the transliterated Old French terms found in Rashi's commentaries. Darmesteter's findings, which represented a significant contribution to the study of the history and development of the French language, were published as early as 1872. However, his source material; i.e., a list of well over 3,000 Old French terms (le'azim)* used by Rashi in his

---

*When Rashi sought to "translate" difficult Biblical and Talmudic words or concepts for his readers and felt that even a simplified Hebrew explanation would not suffice, he used Hebrew transliterations of terms taken from the vernacular spoken in his day in Northern France and the Rhineland. Although the main component of this vernacular is Old or Medieval French, there are also a considerable number of German and Italian expressions. Rashi would identify these terms as bela'az (Cf. Psalm 114:1) where am lo'ez occurs in the connotation of "a people of strange language;" i.e., a language other than Hebrew). In his commentary on Isaiah 33:19, "Thou shalt not see the bold people...", Rashi notes that no'az, the Hebrew term used in this verse to denote "bold," is the same as lo'ez and he identifies the "bold people" as the Assyrians and the Babylonians "whose language is not the sacred tongue;" i.e., not Hebrew. In his commentary on the Talmud (Gittin 37a) Rashi notes, in connection with the term lel'uza that one who does not speak Hebrew is l'uza.

commentaries, was not published until 1909, two decades after Darmesteter's death.[20] In 1929 David S. Blondheim (1884-1934), professor of Romance philology at the Johns Hopkins University, became Darmesteter's posthumous collaborator, as it were, by publishing *Les Gloses Françaises dans les Commentaires Talmudiques de Raschi*,[21] which was based in part on Darmesteter's material. Blondheim himself later elaborated upon this material with his own lexicographic studies referring to a large part of his 1929 publication. These studies appeared as an Extra Volume in a series of the Johns Hopkins Studies in Romance Literatures and Languages published in 1937, three years after Blondheim's untimely tragic death.[22]

In an introduction to Blondheim's lexicographic studies, his sister, Grace H. Blondheim (d. 1976), noted that he had originally planned to pursue his study according to subject matter, beginning with botanical terms.[23] Blondheim may well have been motivated in this direction by Rabbi Immanuel Loew of Szeged, Hungary (1854-1944), whose article, "Pflanzennamen bei Raschi," had been included in the *Festschrift* honoring Berliner's seventieth birthday.[24]

Modern Jewish scholarship in Germany served as a stimulus for Jewish students in Eastern Europe, mostly products of *yeshivot* (traditional Talmudical academies), who were more thoroughly versed in Rabbinic literature than their Western counterparts. Indeed, this combination of modern German scholarly methodology and the phenomenal East European at-homeness in rabbinics produced some of the finest works of the *Wissenschaft des Judentums*. Thus, under the influence of Zunz and his school, Isaac Hirsch Weiss (1815-1905), a native of Moravia and a *yeshiva* student for many years, used his impressive Talmudic knowledge to write — among other works — a very detailed biographical sketch of Rashi, which appeared in Volume II of the monthly *Beth Talmud* founded by Weiss himself in Vienna in 1881.[25] Weiss shows the skills of a true navigator upon the "sea of the Talmud," intertwining his findings on the life of Rashi with a thorough investigation of Rashi's halakhic sources. Unlike the Rashi biography by Zunz, Weiss' work is not merely a historical study; it is, in fact, a Talmudic discourse written with warm admiration for Rashi, the great master. It seems, too, that Weiss had an advantage over Zunz in that he was able to draw upon other works, including a number of responsa, from the school of Rashi which did not come to light until the 1880's, six decades after the publication of Zunz's essay.[26]

In 1904/05 the first public observance of the anniversary — it was the 800th — of Rashi's death generated a number of popular biographical articles which are listed in the general bibliography appended to this study. In that year Maurice Liber (1884-1956), while still a student at the École Rabbinique (whose head he eventually became), published a book on Rashi and his time,[27] which is essentially based on the work of Leopold Zunz. However, unlike Zunz, Liber had access to *Sefer HaPardess, Sefer HaOrah* and *Mahzor Vitry,* works which deal with various aspects of Jewish law and ritual and which are attributed to the school of Rashi. Liber enriched his biographical study with engaging legends about Rashi and with some very human excerpts from Rashi's commentaries.

The outstanding book-length opus on Rashi's life and work was written by the noted educator and connoisseur of the Hebrew style and language Eliezer Meir Lipschuetz (1879-1946),[28] at whose feet this author sat in Jerusalem and to whom he owes his own deep admiration for Rashi. Lipschuetz's work, an exquisite literary monument to Rashi, leaves very little room for further elaboration on Rashi's life, activity and impact. As a pioneering Jewish educator, Lipschuetz had a special feeling for Rashi's method of exegesis, particularly his fine differentiation betwen *p'shat* (usually rendered as "literal" or "straightforward" interpretation) and *d'rash* (usually rendered as "allegorical" or "legendary" interpretation) in the explanation of Biblical passages. In his biography of Rashi, Lipschuetz understood how to blend his own vast Biblical and Talmudic knowledge, which he had accumulated in the *yeshivot* of his native Galicia, with the scholarly historical methodology which he had acquired during his years as a student in Berlin. At home equally in the Talmud and the Bible, and a master of the Hebrew language, Lipschuetz drew upon some of the most beautiful passages from Rashi's commentaries on Bible and Talmud to produce a fine portrait of Rashi, the man, the thinker and the teacher.

The year 1939/40 — the 900th anniversary of the generally accepted date of Rashi's birth (1039/40) — presented another occasion for scholarly studies on Rashi. It was symptomatic, perhaps, of the period — the outbreak of World War II — or of the fading interest of modern Jewish scholars in a field of medieval exegesis irrelevant to the criteria of the modern historical approach, that this anniversary year did not yield so much as one scholarly work on Rashi. True, in accordance with the custom then in vogue, *Festschriften* or anniversary volumes appeared which collated scholarly efforts of various periods and fields of interest. However, the publication of such works in anniversary volumes does not imply that their authors must of necessity be generally acknowledged experts on the life or the literary heritage of the person honored. Berliner in one of the lectures he delivered in 1905 — to commemorate the 800th anniversary of Rashi's death — deplored the gradual decline in familiarity with Rashi, whose commentaries had been household words in earlier generations.

With the destruction of East European Jewry the centers of Jewish learning were borne across the seas and reconstituted in the United States and in Israel. In 1955 Rabbi Judah Leib HaKohen Maimon (Fischman; 1875-1962), a religious leader and early member of the Israeli government, published in Jerusalem *Sefer Rashi*,[29] a collection of essays, some originally written in Hebrew, others translated into Hebrew from other languages. Fourteen years earlier, in 1941, the American Academy of Jewish Research had published a Rashi Anniversary Volume[30] in a similar format. The essays in these two publications do not concentrate on the person of Rashi or on his writings but utilize his commentaries as source material for a variety of disciplines. Generalities yield place to specifics. This trend is reflected also in two other scholarly studies, neither of them written with the intention of commemorating the birth (or death) of Rashi. Henry Englander dealt with the grammatical aspects[31] of Rashi's Pentateuchal commentary and in 1963 Herman Hailperin[32] traced the influence of Rashi especially on Nicholas de Lyre, whose interpretations were studied and utilized by later Bible translators and scholars, thus extending Rashi's influence on Bible translations into our own day.

The most comprehensive known study on Rashi, the monumental *Thesaurus Linguae Hebraicae — Auctore Rashi (Heikhal Rashi)*,[33] was published in 1949 by Isaac Avineri, a scholar who with acumen and diligence penetrated deeply into Rashi's world of thought. Only a man of exceptional gifts of mind and heart could have succeeded in producing so rich and valuable an encyclopedic work as did Avineri. His *Thesaurus* is not only a dictionary and concordance, an alphabetical collection of *bon mots* coined and used by Rashi, but also a comprehensive grammar with all its nuances to which Rashi was so exquisitely sensitive. It is an indispensable reference work containing all the contributions of Rashi's commentaries to the Hebrew language and its variegated usages. From conversations which I was privileged to have with Avineri, that humble scholar, during my annual visits to his modest home in Tel Aviv, I learned that his plans called for a thesaurus of five volumes; Volume Five was to deal with the cultural and civilizational data contained in Rashi's commentaries. Unfortunately, Avineri was able to complete only the first four volumes. But is was from these conversations with him that the plan for my own study on Rashi evolved.

With admiration for the illustrious scholars who gave of their talent and knowledge to pay their tribute to Rashi, I wish to express my humble gratitude for the opportunities left for me to shed additional light on the inexhaustible treasure hidden in Rashi's commentaries.

NOTES

1. *Shulhan Arukh, Orah Hayyim*, 285, par. 2.

2. Nehemias Kronberg, *Raschi als Exeget mit besonderer Ruecksicht auf das Sprachwissenschaftliche in seinem Bibel Commentar*, Halle a/S. 1882; Abraham Berliner, *Blicke in die Geisteswerkstatt Raschis*, Frankfurt a.M., 1905; Max Grunwald, *Etwas*

ueber Raschis Einfluss auf die spaetere hebraeische Literatur, Berlin, 1905; A.S. Onderwijzer, *Raschies Leven en Werken*, Amsterdam, 1901.

3. Herman Hailperin, "Nicholas de Lyre and Rashi: The Minor Prophets," in *Rashi Anniversary Volume*, published by the American Academy for Jewish Research, New York, 1941, pp. 115-47. See also A. Michalski, "Raschis Einfluss auf Nicolaus von Lyra in der Auslegung der Buecher Leviticus, Numeri und Deuteronomium," in *Zeitschrift fuer alttestamentliche Wissenschaft* (Giessen), 1915, pp. 218-45; 1916, pp. 29-63; 1921, pp. 300-7; F. Maschkowski, "Raschis Einfluss auf Nicholaus von Lyra," in *Zeitschrift fuer alttestamentliche Wissenschaft* (Giessen), 1891, pp. 268-316.

4. The Victorines were a canon regular of the Order of St. Peter, founded in Paris in 1110. Famous for its learning, the Victorine order became extinct following the French Revolution. See Beryl Smalley, *The Study of the Bible in the Middle Ages*, New York, 1952, III, and IV, particularly IV, 4, p. 156.

5. *Patrologia Latina*, CXCVIII, 1052.

6. E.g.: When Abraham's servant Eliezer wanted to take Rebecca home to her intended bridegroom Isaac, her mother and brother complied with his request only after they had consulted Rebecca (Gen. 24:57). Comestor infers from this that a woman's consent is required before she can be given in marriage. (P.L. 1107 C, *Et his primo legitur consensus mulieris requisitus*, which echoes Rashi's inference, "From this we may infer that a woman should be given in marriage only with her consent.")

Before meeting his brother Esau, Jacob divided his household into two camps (Gen. 32:8, 33:2), placing Rachel and Joseph into the hindmost position in order to afford them as much protection as possible in case his brother came with evil intentions. To this Comestor adds the words "... *ita tamen... tamquam chariores*" (P. L. 1120 C: "...because they [Rachel and Joseph] were the more beloved"). This corresponds to Rashi's comment, "The hindmost is the most beloved."

7. On the familiarity of Christian scholars with Rashi's commentaries and particularly the relationship between Rashi's commentaries and the writings of Nicholas de Lyre, see Herman Hailperin, *Rashi and the Christian Scholars*, Pittsburgh, 1963.

8. Hailperin in *Rashi Anniversary Volume*, p. 119ff. See also Moritz Guedemann, *Geschichte des Erziehungswesens und der Cultur der Juden in Frankreich und Deutschland*, Vienna, 1880, p. 16.

9. Erwin I.J. Rosenthal, "Rashi and the English Bible," in *Studia Semitica*, Vol. I (1971), pp. 56-85.

10. Talmud, Kiddushin 40b: "Study is important because it leads to action."

11. *Mahzor Vitry*, ed. S. Hurwitz, Berlin, 1893, 91, p. 290.

12. *Sefer HaOrah*, ed. S. Buber, Lemberg, 1905, II, 76, p. 205.

13. *Ibid.*, 75, p. 205.

14. Three examples that most readily came to mind:

a. Genesis 24:18: "And the damsel [Rebecca] ran and told her mother's house according to these words."
Rashi's comment: "A daughter confides only in her mother."
Rashi's source: "A woman is accustomed to go only to her mother's house" (Genesis Rabbah 60)

b. Isaiah 10:19: "And the remnant of the trees of his forest shall be few, that a child may write them down."
Rashi's comment: "There is no such thing as a little one who cannot write the little letter *yod*."
Rashi's source: "What figure can a child write? Ten (Sanhedrin 95b)

c. Avot 6:5: "Torah is acquired by forty-eight qualities... [one of them is] cheerfulness."
Rashi's comment: "The Divine Presence rests [upon man] not through sadness but through joy."
Rashi's source: "This teaches you that the Divine Presence rests [upon man] neither through gloom, nor through sloth, nor through frivolity, nor through levity, nor through talk, nor through idle chatter but only through joy in connection with the performance of a precept" (Shabbat 30b).

15. Aaron Freimann, "Manuscript Supercommentaries on Rashi's Commentary on the Pentateuch," in *Rashi Anniversary Volume*, pp. 73-114.

16. S.M. Chones, *Toledot HaPosekim*, Warsaw, 1910, p. 69a; I. Epstein, *Die Familie Lurie*, Vienna, 1901.

17. Leopold Zunz, *Toledot Rashi*, Hebrew translation by Samson Bloch, Warsaw, 1862.

18. Abraham Berliner, *Raschi (Salomonis Isaacidis) in Pentateuchum Commentarius*, Berlin, 1866.

19. Abraham Berliner, *Raschi: Der Kommentar des Salomo B. Isaak ueber den Pentateuch*, Frankfurt A.M., 1905.

20. Arsène Darmesteter, *Les Gloses Françaises de Raschi dans la Bible*, Paris, 1909.

21. Arsène Darmesteter et D.S. Blondheim, "Les Gloses Françaises dans les Commentaires Talmudiques de Raschi," I, *Texte des Gloses*, Paris, 1929.

22. D. S. Blondheim, "Gloses Françaises dans les Commentaires Talmudiques de Raschi," II, *Études Lexicographiques*, Paris, 1937.

23. *Ibid.*, p. 7.

24. Aron Freimann and Meir Hildesheimer, *Birkat Abraham: Festschrift zum siebzigsten Geburtstage A. Berliners*, Frankfurt a.M., 1903, p. 231ff.

25. Isaak Hirsch Weiss, "Toledot Raschi," in *Beth Talmud II*, Vienna, 1882, pp. 33-40, 65-73, 97-101, 129-38, 161-66, 193-206, 225-31, 257-64, 289-97.

26. *Sefer HaPardes*, ed. H. L. Ehrenreich, Budapest, 1924; *Sefer HaOrah*, ed. Salomon Buber, Lemberg, 1905; *Teshuvot Hakhmei Tsorfat veLothir* (Responsa of the scholars of France and Lorraine), ed. Joel HaKohen Miller, Vienna, 1881.

27. Maurice Liber, *Rachi, un Rabbin de la France du Nord au XIe siècle*, Paris, 1905. English translation: *Rashi* (tr. Adele Szold), Philadelphia, 1906, 1938, 1948.

28. Eliezer M. Lipschuetz, *Raschi, sein Leben und sein Werk*, Warsaw, 1914.

29. *Sefer Rashi*, ed. Rabbi Y. L. HaKohen (Fischman) Maimon, Jerusalem, 1955.

30. *Rashi Anniversary Volume*.

31. Henry Englander, in *Hebrew Union College Annual:* Rashi's View of Weak ע"ע and פ"ו Roots," Vol. VII (1930), pp. 399-437; "Rashi's Vowel Terminology," Vol. XII-XIII (1937-8), pp. 505-21; "Grammatical Elements and Terminology in Rashi," Vol. XIV (1939), pp. 387-429; "A Commentary on Rashi's Grammatical Comments," Vol. XVII (1942-3), pp. 427-98.

32. Herman Hailperin, *Rashi and the Christian Scholars*, Pittsburgh, 1963.

33. Isaac Avineri, *Thesaurus Linguae Hebraicae Auctore Rashi (Rabbi Solomon Izhaki)*, Vols. I-IV, Tel Aviv, 1949.

Part I

THE LIFE

CHAPTER ONE

Family and Mentors

Solomon ben Isaac was born in Troyes, the historic capital of the province of Champagne in the northeast of France. Most authorities accept the tradition that Rashi was born in the year 4800 Anno Mundi or 1039/40 of the Common Era. It is possible that this date was conveniently agreed upon by those who would accept 4800 also as the year of the death of Gershom ben Judah (or, as he is popularly known, Rabbenu Gershom, the "Light of the Exile"), to fit in with an oft-cited allegorical interpretation of Ecclesiastes 1:5, "The sun also rises and the sun goes down." This interpretation rearranges the verse to read "the sun goes down but the sun also rises," the intention being to assure the Jewish people in its exiled state that whenever one of its great leaders dies, Providence has already prepared another to take his place. Thus it is explained that the very year that Rabbenu Gershom left this world, an infant was born who in due time would assume that place of spiritual leadership left vacant by the "Light of the Exile." No matter what befell, then, the chain of Jewish learning would continue unbroken.

It is generally agreed that Rashi died in the year 4865 Anno Mundi or 1104/05 of the Common Era. This date was derived from a note found in a manuscript called *Siddur Rashi* (dated 5042 Anno Mundi or 1282 C.E). This manuscript was acquired by Samuel David Luzzatto (1800-1865), who mentions it in his letters. Another reference to the date of Rashi's death occurs at the end of a manuscript of Rashi's commentary on the Pentateuch dating from the year 1305 and discovered in the Parma Library:

> The Holy Ark [a play on the Hebrew word *aron*, which can mean either "ark" or "coffin"], the holiest of the holy, the great teacher, our Rabbi Solomon of blessed memory, the son of the *kadosh* [the holy one] Rabbi Isaac of blessed memory, the Frenchman, was taken from us on the fifth day [of the week], the twenty-ninth day of Tammuz 4865; he was sixty-five years of age when he was called to Heaven.[1]

The Hebrew month given in this passage would indicate that Rashi died sometime in the summer of 1105. In actuality, it seems that the only dates in this context which we have been able to establish with a fair degree of certainty are those of the death of Rabbenu Gershom and the death — as distinct from the birth — of Rashi. In the case of historical figures from an era before systematic registers of birth were kept, it is always easier to ascertain the *terminus ad quem* than the *terminus a quo*. The loss of a great man full of years may have had an impact on his entire generation, but the birth of an infant, no matter what his potential for future greatness, was important only to the child's immediate family; hence, dates of birth as a rule were not as widely known as dates of death. It is therefore not surprising that while scholars have managed to arrive at a consensus regarding the year in which Rashi died, they disagree widely when it comes to the age he had reached at the time of his death. Thus, the *Sefer Yuhasin HaShalem* ("Complete Book of Records," a history of the Jews outlining, among other things, the chronology of the Sages of the Oral Tradition), which was compiled in the year 1504 by Abraham ben Samuel Zacuto (1452-c.1515), contains a note to the effect that "the

great luminary who explained and commented upon the Talmud and the Holy Scriptures, Rashi, the French exegete, died
in the year 4865 [1104 or 1105, depending on the month in
which his death occurred], when he was *seventy-six* years of age"
[Author's italics].[2]

According to the historical-chronological work *Seder HaDoroth* by Rabbi Jehiel ben Solomon Heilprin (Lithuania; 1660-
1746) Rashi was born in the year Rabbi Hai Gaon[3] died, which,
according to the *Sefer Yuhasin HaShalem*, was 4791 Anno Mundi
(or 1030/31 C.E.).[4] Even if we were to accept the hypothesis
that Rashi was born in the year Rabbenu Gershom died, we
have every reason to rely on the accuracy of a statement in
Seder HaDoroth[5] to the effect that Rabbenu Gershom's death
occurred in the year 4788 Anno Mundi (or 1028/29 C.E.)[6],
which would be a full decade prior to the date generally
accepted for that event. In that case, given the year 1104/05 as
the date of Rashi's death, Rashi lived 76 years, not 65. We
would prefer to accept this additional decade for Rashi's life
span, for it would seem difficult to believe that even a man of
Rashi's attainments could have completed his monumental
commentaries, his numerous responsa and his other prolific
writings by the time he reached the age of 65.

Rashi's Family

Rashi came from a most distinguished family. According to
his own statement in his commentary on Tractate Shabbat, his
mother's brother was Rabbi Simon ben Isaac "the Elder" (born
c. 950) of Mayence,[7] an older contemporary of Rabbenu Gershom and one of the earliest German *paytanim* (liturgical poets).
This Rabbi Simon was known also as Rabbi Simon the Great,
son of Rabbi Isaac.[8] In his commentary on Tractate Avodah
Zarah[9] Rashi mentions the name of his father, Rabbi Isaac
(hence Rashi's cognomen Yitzhaki). Since the Parma manuscript of Rashi's Pentateuchal commentary[10] adds the appellation "the holy one" to Isaac's name, it is to be assumed that
Rashi's father died as a martyr "for the sanctification of the
Name of the Lord."[11]

Rashi inherited his own prodigious spiritual and intellectual gifts from a long chain of scholars going back to Rabbi Johanan haSandlar (Johanan the Sandal-Maker),[12] who lived 33 generations before him and was a devoted disciple of the martyred Rabbi Akiba. Rashi had no sons, but two of his three daughters married men who made their mark in the world of Rabbinic scholarship. One daughter, Miriam,[13] was the wife of the Tosafist Rabbi Judah ben Nathan (RIBaN), who wrote glosses on his father-in-law's Talmudic commentary and whose own commentary on the concluding portion of Tractate Makkot is contained in most editions of the Talmud. Another daughter, Jokhebed,[14] married Rabbi Meir ben Samuel of Ramerupt (c.1060-c.1135), one of the earliest Tosafists in the north of France. The husband of the third daughter, Belle Assez or Rachel, was one Eliezer, known also as Vasselin (Jocelyn), but that marriage ended in divorce.[15]

Jochebed and her husband, Rabbi Meir ben Samuel of Ramerupt, had four sons, all of whom became luminaries in the Rabbinic world: Rabbi Samuel ben Meir (RaSHBaM; c. 1085-1174), Rabbi Jacob ben Meir Tam (c.1100-1171), Rabbi Isaac (RIBaM), and Solomon.

Rabbi Samuel ben Meir, the eldest of the four, earned his livelihood from sheep-farming and viticulture.[16] The author of commentaries on the Bible and the Talmud, a grammatical work (*Sefer Dayekot*) and numerous responsa,[17] he sat at the feet of his maternal grandfather, with whom he frequently discussed the latter's methods of interpretation.[18]

Samuel was greatly respected by his younger brother, Rabbi Jacob ben Meir, who became known as Rabbenu Tam[19] and who is generally regarded as the leader of the French Tosafists. Addressing his elder brother in one of his responsa, Jacob praises Samuel metaphorically as "being adorned with a garment of beauty and splendor, wearing a crown of glory, having trodden above the depths and reached into the mighty waters to retrieve a scattering of sapphires."[20] Although he was opposed to emendations of the Talmudic text suggested by Rabbi Samuel, Rabbenu Tam concedes that they were products of his elder brother's "greatness of heart and depth of intellect."[21]

Rabbi Samuel ben Meir was a very pious man, so humble in his piety that he always walked about with his eyes cast down.[22] However, he was anything but a recluse; in fact, he was no stranger to the scholarly world of the Gentiles. He knew Latin[23] and engaged in discussions with members of the Christian clergy.[24] After Rashi's death Rabbi Samuel assumed the spiritual leadership of his grandfather's community.[25] Samuel had a daughter named Marona, who personally supervised the milking of her father's cows to make sure that non-Jewish farmhands would not render the milk unfit for Jews by adding to it milk of dubious origin.[26]

Rabbi Jacob ben Meir Tam was apparently one of the younger of the four sons of Rabbi Meir ben Samuel[27] and also the greatest of the brothers.[28] A dynamic, impulsive person, he had acquired considerable wealth from moneylending, viticulture and trading in wine.[29] He had both Jewish and Gentile servants who attended to his household chores and prepared the parchment he used for his writings.[30] He seems to have been frequently involved in public affairs,[31] including matters connected with the French royal court.[32] He was seriously wounded during the Second Crusade but miraculously recovered, an experience which is echoed in many of his responsa.[33] Rabbenu Tam was held in high regard by the great rabbinic scholars of his day. In the middle of the 12th century he presided over a rabbinical synod which was held in Troyes and attended by hundreds of noted rabbis, including Rabbi Eliezer ben Nathan of Mayence (RABaN; c.1090-1170). The rabbinical rulings adopted at this synod were considered binding on the Jews of all the countries represented.[34] Queries were sent to Rabbenu Tam by rabbis from as far away as Bari, Italy,[35] and all the rabbis who directed their questions to him addressed him with great humility and respect. They would refer to Ramerupt, the city where Rabbenu Tam resided, as *Ramah* ("The High Place"), recalling Ramah, where the prophet Samuel worshipped.[36] Rabbenu Tam himself was accorded the title "Enlightener of his generation, head of the people,"[37] and his house of study was reverently described as "The Tent of Meeting" (after the Biblical Sanctuary) and "the Dwelling Place of Torah."[38] Isaac bar Sheshet of Spain (1326-1408) said of him that "since the completion of the Talmud there has not been so sharp a mind who is completely familiar with the Talmud. Himself as solid as Sinai, he uproots mountains which he grinds against one another with the profundity of his intellect."[39]

Rabbi Isaac (RIBaM) died at a relatively early age while his father was still living. Rabbi Jacob ben Meir Tam mentions the death of this brother in one of his responsa addressed to Rabbi Eliezer ben Nathan of Mayence: "I cry out in bitterness and, owing to incessant prayer, I have no strength left, my happiness is gone because the Holy Ark, crown of my head, my brother Rabbi Isaac, was requested to take his place in the Academy on High a month ago."[40] Nothing is known about Rabbi Isaac's personal life. His writings are included in some of the comments by the Tosafists. Apparently he also participated in the formulation of rabbinic decisions handed down by his father and brothers.[41]

Very little, too, is known of the personal life of Solomon ben Meir. He is mentioned briefly in the Tosafists' comments on Tractate Pesahim[42] in connection with the question of whether or not a cup of wine was required for reciting the Grace after Meals when a person ate alone. We find a reference to this grandson of Rashi also in the *Mahzor Vitry*,[43] among the laws pertaining to mourning, where there is mention of Rabbenu Jacob Tam sending his brother Solomon to fetch a certain Joseph to the synagogue. It is assumed that this brother Solomon was born after the death of his grandfather and was named for him.[44] Solomon was particularly interested in the study of Hebrew grammar and was called "the father of the grammarians."[45] Rashi's commentary on Tractate Hullin 116b[46] contains a reference to the "Arguments of Solomon ben Meir." This is obviously an interpolation inserted into the Rashi text long after Rashi's death; however, it indicates that Solomon was the author of a compendium on Jewish law.

Thus, Rashi's illustrious progeny became the disseminators of Rabbinic learning throughout western Europe. They were instrumental in the shifting of the center of Jewish scholarship from the shores of North Africa to the European continent. The *Tosafot* — the critical glosses on the Talmud found in all editions in the outer margin of each folio opposite Rashi's commentary — were begun by members of this family, whose love of Torah was no doubt inspired in large measure by their renowned ancestor.

Rashi's Teachers

Though Rashi was born in France, he spent his student years in Germany and — aside from his native Troyes — his life and impact were closely bound up with the German cities of Worms and Mayence.

Jews first came to Europe from the Near East, in some cases voluntarily, but on occasion also under duress, in the wake of the Roman conquerors. Some were brought to Germany as captive slave laborers by the Roman legions; others followed the Roman victors as soldiers, merchants and even physicians.[47] In the course of the centuries, liberated Jewish slaves and other Jews chose to settle in the Rhenish areas. By the 10th century we find a Jewish community in the city of Mayence. In fact, the well-known legend of the martyred Rabbi Amnon of Mayence, whose *Unetaneh Tokef* is one of the most moving prayers in the High Holiday service, suggests that the city of Mayence may have had a Jewish community as far back as the 9th century.[48] A document supporting this assumption is a query sent by Archbishop Frederick, who occupied the see of Mayence from 937 to 954, to Pope Leo VII asking whether it would be better to baptize the Jews by force or to expel them from the city. The pope replied that Frederick should not cease preaching the Gospels to the Jews, but that if they continued to resist conversion they should be expelled because Christians should have no traffic with the enemies of the Lord.[49] Also (in the year 937), a priest by the name of Gerard transmitted to this archbishop some data concerning the Jews.[50]

It seems that the Jewish community of Mayence began to flourish with the arrival of the Kalonymus family from Lucca (southern Italy) sometime during the 9th century.[51] This family produced a number of famous scholars who lived in Mayence and then branched out to the cities of Worms and Speyer.[52] Judah ben Meir HaKohen, a French Talmudist (active ca. 1000) variously known as Leontin, León and Léonte, was the teacher of Rabbenu Gershom ben Judah.[53] Rabbenu Gershom speaks of his mentor Leontin with the greatest admiration. He considered him the outstanding scholar of his generation and regarded his rulings as permanently binding on all Jews. In fact, he said he would rather rely on Leontin than on the decisions handed down by the Geonim.[54] Together with Leontin, Rabbenu Gershom founded in Mayence a Talmudical academy which produced the luminaries who became the teachers of Rashi: one of these, Jacob ben Yakar (d. 1064), together with Rabbi Eliezer HaLevi of Worms (called Eliezer the Great; d. 1070), took charge of the Mayence academy after the death of Rabbenu Gershom.[55] Jacob ben Yakar had a profound influence on Rashi. It appears that the complimentary expressions "my wise old teacher"[56] or simply "my teacher"[57] in Rashi's Talmudic commentaries refer to him. Rashi declares that all his own "understanding, reasoning and wisdom came from his [i.e., Jacob's] mouth."[58] According to Rashi's grandson Rabbi Samuel ben Meir (RaSHBaM), Rashi also referred to Jacob ben Yakar as "my teacher of Talmud and Bible."[59].

It was at Rabbenu Gershom's academy that Rashi first gained access to a definitive, accurate text of the Talmud. Rabbenu Gershom had not only written commentaries on the Talmud but also had tried to ascertain the correct reading for the text itself. Over the generations, many errors had crept into the manuscript texts and the more the copyists attempted to correct these on their own initiative, the more the inaccuracies were compounded.[60] Rabbenu Gershom therefore wrote out in his own hand whole tractates of the Talmud in order to provide his disciples with an accurate text. Rashi leaned heavily on Rabbenu Gershom's text; however, he felt compelled to deviate from it whenever, in his judgment, other versions seemed to him more logical or more nearly correct.[61]

Another one of Rashi's teachers was Rabbi Isaac ben Judah of Mayence, who had also sat at the feet of Rabbenu Gershom. Rashi was in frequent contact with this teacher[62] even after his return to Troyes. In one of his queries Rashi refers to Rabbi Isaac as "my teacher in righteousness"[63] while the latter, in an introductory statement to one of his responsa, pays a most flowery tribute to his disciple:

> My very gifted colleague, endowed with the upper and nether founts which supply explanations and expositions; my friend and companion!
>
> May the Almighty bestow upon him days of pleasure and cause him to blossom to become a glorious stock; thus, too, may it be the will of the Almighty, even as my own soul desires it, eager as it is to hear of his peace of mind.[64]

In the same responsum Rabbi Isaac asks Rashi to be kind enough to pray that God might have mercy upon him, Rabbi Isaac.[65]

After the death of Rabbi Jacob ben Yakar in 1064[66] Rashi left Mayence and entered the academy in Worms; this academy was under the direction of Rabbi Isaac ben Eliezer HaLevi of Worms,[67] who is frequently quoted in Rashi's writings.[68] In one letter, Rashi addresses this scholar as "Prince of the Capital, right-hand Pillar and Luminary of Israel"[69] Rabbi Isaac's reply, in turn, ended with the following complimentary close: "I am well aware of your piety, geninue wisdom and good intentions beyond any doubt... and I always seek your perfect and abundant peace."[70] In another responsum Rabbi Isaac addresses Rashi as "My dearest, most respected friend! May Israel be blessed with many more like you."[71]

The relatively insignificant number of responsa addressed to Rashi by Rabbi Jacob ben Yakar justifies the assumption that Rashi had studied at Rabbi Jacob's academy and thus was able to consult with him personally, remaining under Rabbi Jacob ben Yakar's guidance until the latter's death in 1064, a date documented in an inscription unearthed in 1922 on an ancient wall in Mayence which reads, "Tombstone of Rabbi Jacob ben Yakar, who passed into the Garden of Eden in the year 4824 [1063/64]."[72]

NOTES

1. S. M. Chones, *Toledot HaPosskim*, p. 6. See also Abraham Berliner, *Raschi: Der Kommentar den Salomo B. Isaak ueber den Pentateuch*, p. VIII, Note 7; V. Aptowitzer, *Introductio ad Sefer Rabiah*, p. 403, Note 4. *Siddur Raschi*, ed. Yakov Freiman, Berlin, 1911, LVIII, par. 12 and *Sefer HaOrah*, ed. Salomon Buber, Lemberg, 1905, Introduction, p. 60, par. 23.

2. *Sefer Yuhasin HaShalem*, ed. Zvi Philipovsky, London-Edinburgh, 1857, p. 217b. The Warsaw edition, printed by the Levin-Epstein Brothers, contains a statement (p. 147) that "He died in the year 4865, and the days of Rashi were 76 years." Leopold Zunz, in his *Literaturgeschichte der synagogalen Literatur*, Beilage I, p. 626, quotes from a list of *Seliha* authors: "Rashi was a man of great integrity and dwelt in exile in Germany for seven years.... And he died at the age of 75 in the years 865... in the fifth millennium [after Creation]..."

3. Jehiel ben Solomon Heilprin, *Seder HaDoroth*, I, Warsaw, 1886, p. 197a: "He was born in the year that Rabbi Hai died."

4. *Ibid.*, p. 217: "Rabbenu Hai, son of Rav Sherira... died in the year 4791."

5. *Ibid.*, p. 194b: "I noted in one treatise that it was the year 4788."

6. Heinrich Graetz, *Geschichte der Juden*, Leipzig, 1870, Vol. V, p. 364.

7. Commentary on Shabbat 85a: "I found support [for this opinion] on the basis of [a statement by] Rabbi Simon the Elder, my mother's brother."

8. S. M. Chones, *op. cit.*, p. 207: "Rabbi Simon the Great or the Elder, son of Rabbi Isaac and uncle of Rashi."

9. Commentary on Avodah Zarah 75a: "The words of my honored father, of blessed memory."

10. Leopold Zunz, *Toledot Rashi*, Hebrew translation by Samson Bloch, Warsaw, 1862, Note 1: "In the Di Rossi Library in Parma there is a manuscript copy of Rashi's commentary on the Pentateuch dating from the year 65 of the sixth millennium [after Creation; i.e. 1305], at the conclusion of which there is the following statement: The great teacher, our Master Solomon, may the memory of the righteous be a blessing, son of the holy one, Rabbi Isaac of blessed memory, the Frenchman..."

11. Y.L. HaKohen (Fischman) Maimon, *op. cit.*, p. 8.

12. Jehiel ben Solomon Heilprin, *op. cit.*, II, p. 201a: "I, the author, Jehiel, have in my possession a family tree stating that my mother's father is a descendant of Rabbi Johanan the Sandal-maker, and the genealogy is traced through Rashi, the Luminary of the Exile, and to the Gaon Solomon Luria and my aforementioned grandfather..." See also Chones, *op. cit.*, p. 6; Hayim Joseph David Azulai, *Shem HaGedolim*, republished Jerusalem, 1954, p. 76.

13. V. Aptowitzer, *op. cit.*, p. 399. [Seeking to identify the wife of one certain Eliezer], "And this would be correct if we adhere to the text, 'Miriam,

daughter of the daughter of Rashi,' and even more so if Zunz is correct in his assumption that Rashi had a *daughter* named Miriam..." See also *Teshuvot Maimoniyot*, belonging to *Hilkhot Maakhalot Assurot*, par. 5. "This is how it was done at the home of Miriam, daughter of the daughter of our teacher Solomon... [The reading should be] the daughter of our teacher Solomon, not the daughter of his daughter." E. E. Urbach, *Ba'alei HaTosafot*, Jerusalem, 1955, p. 36. See also Solomon Zeitlin, "Rashi", in *American Jewish Year Book, 5700*, New York, 1939, p. 115ff.

14. S. M. Chones, *op. cit.*, p. 288a: "Rabbenu Tam, grandson of Rashi, of blessed memory; [he was] the son of Mistress Jokhebed, daughter of Rashi." E. E. Urbach, *op. cit.*, p. 38: "Rabbenu Meir ben Samuel, who married the pious Jokhebed, daughter of Solomon, may the memory of the righteous be a blessing." See also Solomon Zeitlin, *op. cit.*, p. 216.

15. Quoted in *Sefer HaYashar leRabbenu Tam*, section on Responsa, annotated by Shraga Feish Rosenthal, Berlin, 5658 (1897-98), p. 44: "When our kinsman Rabbi Eliezer divorced our aunt, Mistress Rachel — his name was Vasselin and her name was Belle Assez. However, they wrote 'Eliezer' and 'Rachel,' which were their Hebrew names."

16. E. E. Urbach, *op. cit.*, p. 43.

17. Shimon bar Zemah, *Sefer HaTashbetz*, Lemberg, 1891, III, par. 246: "The RaSHBaM of blessed memory is our teacher Samuel son of Rabbi Meir of Ramerupt, who was from the city of Ramerupt and was the author of a commentary on the Talmud." Chones, *op. cit.*, p. 543b relates that Samuel compiled a commentary on the entire Talmud while Rashi was still living. However, Rashi was highly displeased with the lengthy explanations given by Samuel and he burned the commentary before Samuel's eyes. According to another source, Rashi did not burn the work but merely gave instructions that it should not be studied. Only Samuel's commentaries on most of Tractate Bava Bathra and on the closing chapter of Tractate Pesahim have survived. See also E. E. Urbach, *op. cit.*, pp. 45-47.

18. Regarding Genesis 37:2 ("These are the generations of Jacob..."): "Also Rabbi Solomon, my mother's father, Enlightener of the Eyes of the Exile, who wrote commentaries on the Pentateuch, the Prophets and the Holy Writings, gave particular attention to explaining the straightforward, literal meaning of the verse. I, Samuel ben Meir, engaged him in debate, and he admitted to me that if he had had more time, he would have written additional commentaries in accordance with the new realities that come to light each day." (See also Chapter V this volume, p. 120.)

19. Rabbi Jacob ben Meir's by-name "Jacob Tam" is an allusion to Genesis 25:27, where the patriarch Jacob is characterized as a "simple man [the Hebrew term used, *tam*, can mean either "a simple man" or "a man of integrity"], a sitter in tents." According to Rashi, the "tents" were the tents of Shem and Ever, who maintained schools for the study of the Torah (Genesis

Rabbah 63). In his commentary on Genesis 25:22 ("and the children [Jacob and Esau] struggled together within [the womb of Rebekah]") Rashi explains that the twins struggled with one another in their mother's womb whenever she passed the tents of Shem and Eber or places of idol worship. When she walked past the schools of Torah Jacob would struggle to emerge, and when she walked past heathen altars Esau fought to come out.

20. *Sefer HaYashar*, Part II, p. 31.

21. *Sefer HaYashar*, Zhitomir, 1869. Introduction by Rabbenu Tam: "And although Rabbenu Gershom, Light of the Exile, cursed all those who corrupt the Talmud[ic text]... people did not refrain from corrupting [it]... yet it is impossible for any God-fearing person to do so, for even my grandfather, Rabbi Solomon [i.e., Rashi], may the memory of the righteous be a blessing, whenever he did make emendations, he inserted his emendations only in his commentary, not in the text. However, those who drank of his waters [of wisdom; i.e., his disciples] emended [the text] in accordance with his explanations.... May the Almighty forgive our teacher, my brother Samuel, for where our master Solomon made one emendation, he made twenty, and not only this, but he even made deletions from the text. But I know well that he did it [only] out of his greatness of heart and depth of intellect."

22. In one instance, this pious habit nearly caused Rabbi Samuel to transgress a prohibition based on Biblical law (Deut. 22:10), relating to forbidden combinations of animal species. He almost climbed aboard a wagon drawn by a horse and a mule as related in *Hagahot Mordekhai* on Tractate Eruvin, par. 528:

"He was very pious, so much so that he would not lift up his eyes. As a result, it happened one day that he almost climbed into a wagon drawn by a horse and a mule and did not notice this. But a miracle came to pass, for by chance his brother Rabbenu Tam was there and reprimanded him, saying to him, 'Do not be overpious; rather, lift your eyes and see the horse and wagon coming toward you.' He stepped aside and did not climb into the wagon."

23. RaSHBaM rejects the Latin translation, which renders both the prohibition לא תרצח ("Thou shalt not murder") in the Sixth Commandment (Exodus 20:13) and the verb אמית ("I shall kill," Deut. 32:39) by a form of the same expression, *occidere*, when in fact the verb אמית refers to killing in general, while the verb תרצח in the Sixth Commandment refers only to murder. See his commentary on Exodus 20:13.

24. D. Rosin, *R. Samuel ben Meir als Schrifterklaerer*, Breslau, 1880, p. 77 ff.

25. Solomon ben Jehiel Luria, *Sefer She'elot u-teshuvot RaSHaL*, 1768, p. 146, par. 29: "Rashi, the Light of Israel, died and Rabbi Samuel ben Meir reigned after him."

26. V. Aptowitzer, *Introductio ad Sefer Rabiah*, p. 410. There was always the suspicion that non-Jewish farmhands might add milk from non-kosher animals (e.g., pigs or horses) to the cows' milk.

27. *Sefer HaYashar*, Part II, p. 71: "And I, Jacob, the younger of the brothers, am writing [this] with tears."

28. Shimon bar Zemah, *Sefer HaTashbetz*, III, p. 38b, par. 246: "There were three brothers and he [RaSHBaM] was the eldest. After him came Rabbenu Jacob, called Rabbenu Tam, who was greater in Torah than all the others and was the author of the *Sefer HaYashar*."

Isaac bar Sheshet, *She'elot u-teshuvot RIBaSH*, p. 240a, par. 394: "...Rabbenu Tam is different because he is of great strength and is like them, perhaps even greater than they, with regard to acumen and expertise, as can be seen from his original interpretations of the Talmud. Indeed, all the sages in Israel nowadays are like garlic skins and poppy seed [i.e., not worth a penny] as compared even to the least of his disciples."

It seems that there were four brothers, of whom Rabbenu Tam was one of the younger and the greatest. Eliezer ben Nathan (in *Even HaEzer*, II, p. 297a, ed. New York, Grossman's Publishing House) talks of the four "tributaries" that emanate from one single "source"; i.e., Rabbi Meir. This is an allusion to the river with the four heads that went forth from the Garden of Eden (Genesis 2:10-14). Rabbenu Tam is likened to the fourth of these tributaries, the Euphrates, which was the greatest of all the four. See also *Sefer HaYashar*, II, pp. 69-70, Note 4.

29. *Seder HaDoroth*, p. 208b: "And it appears from many references in [*Hagahot*] *Mordekhai* that he engaged in moneylending." S. M. Chones, *op. cit.*, 288b: "And Rabbenu Tam did not make his livelihood as a scholar of the Law, but sustained himself from his business; he was [also] occupied with the needs of the community, world affairs and matters of business." E. E. Urbach, *op. cit.*, p. 57: "Rabbenu Tam earned his livelihood from moneylending and viticulture, which he viewed as two [legitimate] means of sustenance for the Jews of his generation."

30. Urbach, *ibid.*,: "He employed Jewish and non-Jewish servants in his home... and they helped him in his household chores and in his establishment, and even in the preparation of the parchment for the holy books he wrote."

31. *Sefer HaYashar*, Part II, 34, p. 59. In this responsum Rabbenu Tam apologizes for his brevity, explaining that he had to be brief because of the pressure of public affairs: "Had the heavy yoke not burdened me — until the emergency shall pass and this ruler of mine is gone — I would have gone into greater detail and been clearer in my language. However, those who keep disturbing me pursue me. But perhaps they will soon disappear and I will have a more stable life and [be able to] arrange my time [i.e., the time I set aside for the study of the Torah] with the help of the Rock of my fathers, for life and for peace."

32. *Ibid.*, 15, p. 26: "Because the couriers had to hurry back and whenever they come to me I am very busy. The work for others devolves upon me, and so does the work for the king."

33. *Ibid.*, 68, p. 157 (written in rhyme form): "They troubled me greatly/ They stirred me up like a locust [cf. Psalms 109:23]/As one shakes out a cloth [cf. Nehemiah 5:13]/And thus the wicked people came upon me.../and nothing remained except for my book and my body/The light of my eyes, too, is no longer with me... But even for this I will give thanks unto Thee [i.e., to God]."

Ibid. 72, p. 168: "Had our dwelling places not been disturbed by the hordes I would have gone into greater detail as my respect for you would have required. I wish I could do so. [Please] do not regard me as conceited, but rather as walking in humility/For they are like a cedar against a thorn./May my gift be acceptable to you like pleasant scent...and peace."

34. S. Auerbach, *Die rheinischen Rabbinerversammlungen im 13. Jahrhundert* (Dissertation), Wuerzburg, 1931, p. 13.

35. *Mahzor Vitry*, ed. S. Hurwitz, p. 51: "...even though in his reply to the noble R. Samuel of Bari he had said that this was permissible...."

Zedekiah ben Abraham HaRofe, *Shibbolei haLeket haShalem*, ed. S. Buber, par. 9, p. 5: "...even though in his reply to R. Samuel of Bari he had said that this was permissible..."

36. *Sefer HaYashar*, Part II, p. 63: "And I chose to inquire at Ramah, the place where the Divine Presence dwells...."

37. *Ibid.*, p. 26: "Enlightener of his generation, head of the people, *HaRav Yaakov.*"

38. *Ibid.*, p. 65: "They chose to go to the Tent of Meeting, the abode of justice, the dwelling place of Torah, where the flocks are watered and from where a spring of fresh water bursts forth and flows down to guide them onto the right path, to save the oppressed from his oppressor and to rescue the prey from his teeth and to punish the oppressor. Justice to all, to be as eyes to the blind and legs to the lame, so that there shall be no one forsaken or without a guide or leader."

39. Isaac bar Sheshet, *op. cit.*, par. 394a, p. 240a.

40. Eliezer ben Nathan, *op. cit.*, p. 297b.

41. See also *Sefer HaYashar*, Part II, p. 71; Eliezer ben Nathan, *op. cit.*, 297a. For R. Isaac's contribution to the Tosafot to various Talmudic tractates see E. E. Urbach, *Ba'alei HaTosafot*, p. 53.

42. Pesahim 105a: "Our teacher Solomon, son of our teacher Meir, says that one must drink [a cup of wine] even if one [has eaten] alone..."

43. *Mahzor Vitry*, p. 243: "And after the afternoon service had been recited at the synagogue on Friday, R. Solomon, brother of our teacher (the latter was praying), was sitting there. Then his brother, our teacher Jacob, asked him, 'Fetch my son Joseph to the synagogue....' When he arrived at the synagogue, R. Solomon went before the Ark and recited the *Barekhu* [opening of the evening service]."

44. E. E. Urbach, *Ba'alei HaTosafot*, p. 54. See also Note 122 *ad loc.*

45. Abraham Berliner, "Beitraege zur Geschichte der Raschi-Commentare," Hebrew translation in *Sefer Rashi*, Jerusalem, 1955, p. 141.

46. "... I found this in the Arguments of our teacher Solomon, son of Rabbi Meir."

47. Adolf Kober, *Aus der Geschichte der Juden im Rheinland*, XX, Cologne, Rheinischer Verein fuer Denkmalpflege und Heimatschutz, Heft 1, p. 11.

48. Rabbi Amnon, a wealthy and respected man, was frequently urged by the Archbishop of Mayence to convert to Christianity. Finally, Rabbi Amnon requested three days' grace to consider the question. When at the end of three days Amnon failed to report to him,the archbishop had him arrested. Rabbi Amnon then pronounced his own sentence; he said that his tongue should be cut out for even having made such a request of the archbishop. The archbishop ordered Amnon's hands and feet cut off instead. On Rosh HaShanah Amnon, with his amputated limbs beside him, was carried into his synagogue on a stretcher. As the reader was about to begin the *Kedushah*, Amnon signaled him to stop and recited the *Unetaneh Tokef* prayer which he had composed. After he had completed the prayer, he died. Three days later, according to legend, he appeared in a dream to Rabbi Kalonymus, taught him the prayer and requested him to disseminate it among the Jews.

However, Julius Aronius (in *Regesten zur Geschichte der Juden*, Hildesheim, Georg Olms Verlag; New York, 1970, No. 146, p. 62) voices doubts about the credibility of the Amnon legend. He claims that the style of the legend closely resembles that of a legend of Christian origin which is set in Regensburg and in which a man named Emmeram (probably a corruption of Amram) suffered a martyr's fate similiar to that of Rabbi Amnon.

49. Julius Aronius, *op. cit.*, No. 125, p. 54: *De Judaeis autem... utrum melius sit eos sacrae subiugare religioni an de civitatibus expellere, hoc vobis praeceptum mandamus, ut fidem... cum omni sagacitate... illis praedicare non desistatis. Si autem credere noluerint de civitatibus vestris... illos expellite, quia non debemus cum inimicis dei societatem habere* ("However, as to the Jews... whether it is better to subjugate them to the [holy] faith or to expel them from your cities, we [herewith] instruct you not to cease preaching the faith to them with all [your] cunning. However, if they refuse to believe, expel them from your cities because we must not have any social intercourse with the enemies of God.")

50. *Monumenta Moguntina*, ed. Philippus Jaffe, p. 338, No. 15: "Gerhard the priest wrote to Frederick, Archbishop of Mayence, concerning the Jews..."

51. The exact date of the family's arrival in Germany is not known. For the members of this illustrious family see Julius Aronius, *op. cit.*, No. 70, pp. 25-26; No. 136, p. 58; No. 170, p. 71; Julius Aronius, "Karl der Grosse und Kalonymus von Lucca," in Ludwig Geiger's *Zeitschrift fuer die Geschichte der Juden in Deutschland*, II, pp. 82-87. Also Salomon Judah Loeb Rapoport, *Sefer Toledot Gedolei Yisrael*,Warsaw, 1904, pp. 41-46.

52. V. Aptowitzer, *Introductio ad sefer Rabiah*, pp. 391-94.

53. S. M. Chones, *op. cit.*, pp. 207-10; Hayyim Joseph David Azulai, *Shem HaGedolim*, No. 13, p. 17; V. Aptowitzer, *op. cit.*, pp. 330-35; Hayyim Michael, *Or HaHayyim*, Jerusalem, Mossad HaRav Kook, 1965, No. 677, p. 307: "Rabbenu Gershom, Enlightener of the Eyes of the Exile, said he had received this from his teacher Leontin."

54. S. M. Chones, *op. cit.*, p. 207: "Rabbenu Gershom, Light of the Exile, said concerning Rabbi Leontin that he would rather rely on him than on the rulings of the Geonim because he [Leontin] is an expert in his generation and his words will not be altered."

55. V. Aptowitzer, *op. cit.*, p. 356. "After the death of Rabbenu Gershom, Light of the Exile, he [Jacob ben Yakar] and Rabbi Eliezer the Great together headed the Academy of Mayence."

56. See commentaries on Gittin 82a, Shabbat 80b and Eruvin 6a.

57. See commentaries on Sukkah 35b, Betzah 24b and Hullin 46b.

58. I. Elfenbein, *Teshuvot Rashi*, New York, 1943, p. 57.

59. Commentary on Pesahim 111a: "... from the mouth of my teacher of Talmud and Bible, who heard it from the mouth of his teacher."

60. *Sefer HaYashar*, Part II. Introduction by Rabbenu Tam: "For I saw that those who turn to the emender of books drink bad waters... and even though Rabbenu Gershom, Light of the Exile, cursed all those who would corrupt the text, saying that such and such will happen to them, they did not refrain from corrupting [the text nor did they confine this] to oral traditions."

61. *Ibid.*, S. M. Chones, *op.cit.*, p. 210: "And so Rabbenu Gershom sought to preserve [the accurate] text and wrote out in his own hand the text which had been handed down." However, Solomon Zeitlin, *op. cit.*, p. 128, states that Rashi deviated from the text when "internal evidence" required it.

62. Commentary on Avodah Zarah 69b, Tosafot: "But Rabbenu Isaac ben Judah sent a reply to Rashi, saying that their casks, which were made of clay, required only one seal..."

63. Commentary on Yoma 16b: "And the excess between the ramp to the wall and to the small columns was explained to me by my teacher in righteousness, Rabbenu Isaac bar Judah of blessed memory..." I. Elfenbein, *op. cit.*, p. 147: "I inquired of my teacher in righteousness..." Solomon ben Jehiel Luria, *op. cit.*, 29, p. 14b: "And Rabbi Isaac bar Judah, who is called 'my teacher in righteousness.'"

64. *Hofes Matmonim sive Anecdota Rabbinica Continentia*, ed. Berl Goldberg, Berlin, 1844, No. 14, p. 11.

65. *Ibid.*: "... that in his kindness and goodness he may beg for mercy [on my behalf]..."

66. See Note 72.

67. On the assumption that Rashi began his studies in Worms and went to Mayence only afterwards, see V. Aptowitzer, *op. cit.*, p. 356 and 397, 2.

68. Leopold Zunz, *op. cit.*, p. 19. See also Zunz, *Literaturgeschichte der synagogalen Poesie*, Hildesheim, Georg Olms Verlag, 1966, p. 155, Note 4.

69. I. Elfenbein, *op. cit.*, p. 57.

70. *Ibid.*, p. 67.

71. *Hofes Matmonim...* No. 13, p. 10.

72. V. Aptowitzer, *op. cit.*, p. 356: "In the year 1922 an ancient wall was discovered in Mayence. Among the stones there was one bearing the following inscription: Tombstone of Rabbi Jacob ben Yakar, who passed into the Garden of Eden in the year 4824."

CHAPTER TWO

The Man

The achievements of great men are reflections of their personalities. The reactions of men to the environment and the circumstances in which they live, and the manner in which they express these reactions, mirror their own innermost beings and convey their character and temperament to posterity. Thus, too, disparities in character and personality may, to some degree, explain the differences in the interpretations offered by various Bible exegetes for the same text or idea. The character and personality of the commentator will also determine his selection of one particular explanation from many other possible ones. One case in point: Verse 6 of I Samuel, Chapter 1, where we are told concerning Hannah's childlessness, "And her rival [Penina] vexed her greatly, to make her fret because the Lord had closed up her womb." R. David ben Joseph Kimhi (1160-1235) comments on the phrase *to make her fret:* "So that she should become jealous and her heart should ache." Rashi quotes the Sages who interpret the phrase to mean, "So that [Hannah] should pray and she [Penina] did it for the sake of Heaven." Hannah vows (I Samuel 1:11) that if she will have a son, "no razor shall come upon his head." Levi ben Gershon (Gersonides; 1288-1344) comments: "And no open razor shall come upon his head to shave off his hair because he shall be a Nazirite and holy unto the Lord." Rashi writes: "The Targum Jonathan [renders this to mean] that he will not be subject to human authority."[1] This is a play on words: מורה (razor) and מרות (authority).

Rashi drew his interpretations of the Biblical text predominantly from the wealth of Midrashic and Talmudic material which had accumulated over hundreds, if not thousands, of years during which the Bible and its concepts had molded the character of the Jewish people. Of this vast body of material Rashi selected that with which he personally felt able to identify best.[2] By introducing this material into his commentary in the form of slight, seemingly insignificant emendations of the original text, Rashi left the mark of his own personality upon the comments he wished to set down for future generations. Thus, to Genesis 6:9 ("These are the generations of Noah") he notes, "The true progeny of the righteous are their good deeds," an idea he derives from Midrash Tanhumah, "Man's progeny are his good deeds." Commenting on Tractate Shabbat 129a where it is stated that one should sell his household goods, if necessary, in order to have sufficient money to buy shoes so one does not have to go barefoot, Rashi, recalling a statement in Yevamot 63b according to which "nobody is more abominable before God than one who goes naked into the market place," writes, "No one is so despicable as he who goes into the market barefooted." (This may be interpreted as reflecting changes in concepts of personal modesty from the Talmudic era to Rashi's day.)[3]

If it is correct that "the style is the man" then it may be said in the case of Rashi that his commentaries are true reflections of his personality. The Torah which Rashi taught to others was the same Torah that he followed in his own personal life.

Despite his great intellectual and scholarly attainments and the esteem in which he was held by his teachers as well as by his disciples, Rashi remained a most humble man. In one of his letters to the Jews of Chalon-sur-Saône in Burgundy he states that he is not qualified to set aside an excommunication imposed by another Rabbinic authority: "Far be it from me to assume the title and appoint myself an accepted *Bet Din* [court of religious law]. Were I living in your midst I would have joined you in this nullification, but who am I to make myself part of another place, I being rather poor [in wisdom] and young in years?"[4] In a ruling attributed to him regarding a question of inheritance Rashi again pleads incompetence, insisting that he is not really worthy of being consulted; he says he expresses his opinion only to the extent "that it was shown [to him] by Heaven;"[5] i.e., to the extent that it seemed to him self-evident. His commentaries were inspired primarily by his search for the truth. He was never ashamed to admit that he had been in error. When, on one occasion, his misinterpretation of a Talmudic passage[6] led him to hand down a ruling which he later realized had been in error, he readily retracted it, explaining, "I have made an error"[7] and he thanked his colleagues for having drawn his attention to it.[8] With the same candor he admitted that he had been mistaken in his interpretation of a verse in the Book of Ezekiel, an error he subsequently corrected after reviewing the verse with one of his closest disciples, Shemaiah of Troyes.[9] When he had difficulty understanding a verse or an idea he did not hesitate to say so.[10]

Rashi had the greatest respect for his teachers and considered it his duty to transmit their teachings and interpretations to his own disciples in keeping with the spirit and intent of Jewish tradition. His own complete reliance on the teachings of his masters imprinted the seal of legitimacy, as it were, upon his own disquisitions. His rulings contain frequent references to his teachers; e.g., "according to what I have received from my teachers."[11] In another instance he states, by way of an apology, as it were, "I was not privileged to consult my teacher, but now, after his death, I have heard..."[12] Elsewhere he says, "Thus I received it from my old teacher Jacob ben Yakar and I am inclined [toward his view]."[13] As we have already seen, he frequently admits to a feeling of intellectual dependence on his master Jacob ben Yakar.[14]

Yet, Rashi did not hesitate to express disagreement with

the views of his teachers when they seemed to contravene his own sense of intellectual integrity. Thus, he sharply dissents from a halakhic prohibition handed down by Isaac ben Eliezer HaLevi of Worms:

> Ever since I have come to understand the Talmudic passage involved, my heart has sided with those who permitted [the act under discussion]. I built up argument upon argument before my teacher but he rejected them all, though he really could not produce any proof in support of his opinion. I, on the other hand, had many reasons for my leniency and have substantiated [them]. However, he did not accept these [reasons] and [so] I continued arguing before him...[15] and will continue doing so until he will agree with me, just as happened in another case where he came to agree with me in the end."[16]

One well-known halakhic controversy between Rashi and his teachers concerned the *kosher* status of a lamb whose lungs had not been properly examined for disease.[17] Despite his wholehearted admiration for his teachers Rashi vents his sense of outrage at the decision handed down by his masters in this matter:

> I do not seek to contest your great learning and scholarship but this is Torah and it is incumbent upon me to understand it.... If you had merely wanted to curb the brashness of the butcher [in question]... I would have agreed with you, but if this injunction is to be based on *halakha* with proper substantiations I shall contest it to the utmost [literally, "I shall eat my own flesh with my teeth"] and adduce proofs and reasons for leniency...[18]

He also wrote on this matter to his son-in-law, Rabbi Meir ben Samuel of Ramerupt [then in Worms]:

> I, your loved one, herewith inform you that I have not retracted [my opinion] and shall not retract [it]. The words of my teachers are not acceptable to me. They replied in a superficial manner [literally, "they rendered lip service"]. Nevertheless, I am communicating my words only to a few people.... I base my own words on the great authority of Rabbi Jacob ben Yakar. They have not based their ruling on tradition, not even on Talmudic arguments, but solely on their personal judgment. If they will [be able to] reply to me in a

convincing manner, I shall retract [my opinion] but it is difficult for
me to cause financial loss to my people. For a variety of reasons it is
clear and proper that one should be lenient in this matter.[19]

With this sincere, selfless, almost agonizing quest for the
truth Rashi demonstrates his own integrity and his courage to
confront even his most revered teachers on the battlefield of
Torah. Especially noteworthy here is his concern about the
material loss that he might cause a fellow Jew by an ill-
considered ruling.

In his insistence on truth and integrity Rashi was never
motivated by thoughts of petty triumphs. When he attended
preparations for the wedding of the daughter of one of his
teachers, Rashi noted that the hindquarters of a deer which
was being readied for the feast had been "porged" (deveined) as
required by the dietary laws but that only the muscle, and not
the fat, had been removed from the thigh of the carcass:

> My teacher was busy with other matters and [so] he did not
> notice the omission. I was hesitant about how I should react. If I
> corrected the oversight, I would be [improperly] assuming authority
> in the presence of my teacher. If, however, I did not correct it, a
> transgression [of the Law] would be committed. I therefore pre-
> sented the matter in the form of an inquiry and I asked my teacher,
> "Is the fat of the thigh muscle of a non-domesticated animal forbid-
> den [as food] or not?" He replied, "Certainly it is forbidden"... and
> he immediately gave instructions to "porge" the thigh of the deer
> just as is required with regard to [the hindquarters of] a domesti-
> cated animal.[20]

At the same time Rashi prized peace and harmony above all
else. "If there is no peace, there is nothing; peace outweighs
everything,"[21] he notes in his commentary on Leviticus 26:6.
Discord is detestable but peace is great, he states in his commentary on Genesis 11:9, the account of the Tower of Babel.[22]
In one decision concerning a partnership dispute Rashi advises
the litigants, "Take heed to pursue peace.... peace will save you
from your enemy and Satan will not be able to exercise dominion over you... and may He Whose Name and blessing is peace
bring peace unto you."[23]

In his love for his fellow men, Rashi insisted on leniency and careful consideration before condemning the conduct of another. "If you see an act committed that can be interpreted as emanating from either good or evil intentions, try to view it as having been well-intentioned."[24] Love generates love, while hatred only breeds more hatred.[25] At times Rashi's feelings of compassion superseded even generally accepted religious strictures (though never, of course, in contravention of clear-cut *halakha*). Thus we find Rashi, out of respect for a bereaved family, reciting the *tzidduk ha-din* (the prayer recited at funerals to signify the mourners' acceptance of the Divine judgment) and the Mourners' Kaddish at a funeral held on one of the intermediate days of a Jewish festival, notwithstanding the frowns of those who felt that such expressions of mourning were not appropriate for a semi-holiday. After the funeral, he went to the house of the mourners to offer his condolences even though this, too, was not considered in keeping with the joyous spirit of the religious festival.[26] Rashi did not have much patience with those who were quick to issue prohibitions instead of making an effort to exercise leniency wherever possible. "The authority of those who prohibit [arbitrarily] means little, for anyone can hand down a prohibition even in matters that are permissible," he notes.[27]

As we have already seen, Rashi was concerned about the material loss which a negative ruling might inflict upon a fellow Jew; he insisted that this factor be given the utmost consideration in any halakhic decision. "It should not be an unimportant matter in your eyes to cause financial loss to a [fellow] Jew, because the Torah has compassion upon him."[28] He appreciated the economic problems of his co-religionists in a Gentile world, notably those in the area where he lived and where the Jews made a living primarily from viticulture and the wine trade. The prohibition against wine handled by a Gentile because of the possibility that part of the wine might be used for idolatrous purposes imposed considerable hardship on the Jewish wine merchants. Rashi alleviated this problem somewhat by venturing the opinion that people actually were not longer familiar with the intricacies of idol worship;[29] thus he implied that the situation with regard to wine handled by a Christian was not the same as if the wine had been touched by a heathen.

Rashi seems to have inclined toward leniency under certain circumstances also with regard to laws prohibiting the offering and accepting of interest on loans, a prohibition which in the Diaspora had the effect of impeding smooth commercial relations between Jews and Gentiles. In one case he went so far as to assert that it would be "pious folly" for a Jew to refuse interest on a loan he had made to a Gentile.[30] But despite Rashi's understanding for the exigencies of coexistence with the Gentile environment, one cannot ignore a certain ambivalence on his part in this respect. As Rashi saw it, dealing with Gentiles was not a matter of the Jews' being eager to do so but was dictated by necessity and apprehension. "In the *golah* [Diaspora] we cannot keep from having dealings with [the Gentiles] because we live among them and derive our subsistence from them," he writes in a commentary on a passage in Tractate Avodah Zarah. "Furthermore, we live in fear [of them]."[31] For his own part, he decided not to enter into any business relations with Gentiles that might make it necessary for him at some point to require the Gentile partner to take an oath, for it is considered forbidden under Biblical law for a Jew to encourage a Gentile to take an oath in the name of an alien deity.[32] He strongly condemned the custom of some of his co-religionists to give Purim gifts to Gentile servants who escorted Jewish children on the latters' visits from house to house to collect Purim goodies.[33]

Rashi's warnings against fraternization with Gentiles were not motivated by any prejudice on his part against non-Jews — hatred was an emotion of which he was utterly incapable — but solely by his love for his own people and his resulting fear that too close relations with Gentiles might lead to assimilation.[34]

His loyalty to his people also explains Rashi's personal meticulous observance of religious law and custom. "If they [i.e., the Jewish people] are not prophets themselves, they are still sons of prophets; their customs, which they learned from their fathers, are Torah and nothing must be added to, or diminished from, them."[35] At times he went against his own better judgment in order not to tamper with accepted custom and tried to find an authoritative justification for his decision. Thus, he justified the retention of a grammatically incorrect combination generally in vogue in Hebrew liturgy by citing certain unique Biblical passages that showed similar inconsistencies.[36] Rashi tended to uphold time-honored custom even over explicit law, knowing that customs which had stood the test of time and had gained universal acceptance would not be likely to yield to a law which, though of equally long standing, might be known to only a very few. In his love for his people he tended to apply the dictum that it was better that a Jew should infringe upon a legal provision because he did not know the law than that he should know the law and trangress it deliberately.[37] However, he qualified this statement carefully in order to avoid any misapplication of his words.[38] Rashi's respect for time-honored custom was, without doubt, inspired by his fervent desire that the Jewish people should remain united, not only within their own generation but also with the generations that had gone before them. To him, such cohesion was the main ingredient of peace without which, in his view, nothing else could long endure.[39]

His love for his people influenced also his attitude toward individuals who had defected from Judaism no matter whether they had done so due to active Gentile coercion or whether they had been driven to this step by their own fears. He declared that it was forbidden to insult or humiliate apostates who had turned away from Judaism only out of "fear of the sword" and had hurried back into the fold as soon as they had seen an opportunity to do so.[40] He severely rebuked one litigant in a court case who, seeking to blacken his opponent's name, had pointed out that the latter had been baptized and lived as a Christian for some time before returning to Judaism. On that occasion Rashi quoted Rabbenu Gershom's edict that it is forbidden to remind a repentant sinner of his past weakness.[41] Likewise, Rashi refused to read a transgressor out of the Jewish community; in this, he followed the Talmudic adage that even though a Jew has sinned, he is still a part of the people of Israel[42] with all the rights, privileges and duties of a Jew.

Rashi insisted on the inalienable right of his people to the Land of Israel. At the very outset of his commentary on the Pentateuch he set forth the Divinely-ordained right of the Jews to their land. He refutes the argument that the Jew is homeless; every Jew, he says, has a share in the Land of Israel, while the Gentiles who conquered the Land had no legitimate claim to it because land could not be stolen from its rightful owners:

> *In the beginning God created the heaven and the earth.* He [God] declared to His people the strength of His works in order that He might give them the heritage of the nations. For if the peoples of the world say to Israel, "You are robbers because you took by force the land of the seven nations of Canaan," Israel may answer them, "All the earth belongs to the Holy One, blessed be He. He created it and gave it to whom He pleased. When He willed it He gave it to them and when He willed it He took it from them and gave it to us."[43]

The Land of Israel belonged to the people of Israel even if, at the moment, the Jews did not have political sovereignty over it:

> There is not one [person] among the Jewish people who has no soil in the Land of Israel. The Gentiles may have seized it and captured it but they have no permanent right to it. We have an established law that land can never be stolen and can never be taken by violence... and the Land of Israel is in our possession forever, even if we do not have [political] sovereignty over it.[44]

Jerusalem, Rashi exults in his commentary on Zechariah 14:10, will extend to the ends of the earth.[45]

The principal idea and, indeed, philosophy of life that pervades all of Rashi's teachings no less than his personal conduct is his own deep piety, the love and fear of God which, in his view, superseded even the study of Torah that was considered paramount in Jewish life. *"The beginning of knowledge is the fear of the Lord:* This [tenet] must be accepted before all else," Rashi notes in his commentary on Proverbs 1:7. "Before you set out to acquire knowledge, learn first to fear your Creator, and *that* should motivate you to acquire knowledge."[46] Where fear of God is lacking, Rashi comments in the same passage, there can be only contempt for both knowledge and ethics.[47] Indeed, if a man's intellect is allowed to control his potentialities without restraint from a higher authority above human limitations, it is likely to destroy his fellow men and ultimately to prove his own undoing as well. The fear of Heaven is the best guarantee of ethical behavior. If they are not aware of their Creator, even great men are in danger of acquiring the mentality of beasts, Rashi notes to the story of the evil city of Nineveh in the Book of Jonah.[48] Moral behavior, though it may benefit society, is not an automatic outgrowth of social coexistence. An individual may seek to justify his own unethical conduct by insisting that he had acted only with the best intentions. The sole safeguard against such excuses which can never be proven conclusively true or false is the fear of Heaven. Scripture states, "But thou shalt fear thy God" Who knows all the secret thoughts of man. Similarly, in regard to any action where it is given only to the heart of him who performs it to know the motive which prompts him and where others have no insight into his true motivations, Scripture commands, "But thou shalt fear thy God."[49]

In Rashi's view the fear of Heaven is inseparably linked with the love of Torah. The study of the Torah must be pursued in a spirit of self-dedication and, if need be, even amidst toil and hunger. He himself recalls that he sat at the feet of his teachers even though he lacked "bread and adequate clothing — and [had] a millstone around his neck [i.e., he already bore the responsibilities of married life]."[50] He who loves Torah, Rashi declares, will never be able to get enough of it.[51] One who does not feel a deep yearning for the Torah will not appreciate even the most plausible statements in the text, while one who has such a yearning will savor even vexing questions posed by the text as pure delight.[52] Rashi used the most lyrical, indeed romantic metaphors to describe the Torah and its disciples: "Like the forest which is ever verdant, so are the words of Torah," he notes in his commentary on Song of

Songs 5:16.[53] "Its [i.e., the Torah's] words are like the doves which have a graceful gait," he adds.[54] He likens the student of the Bible to a budding vine, the Mishnah scholar to the vine blossom, and the Talmudic savant to the seed-filled pomegranate because those steeped in the Talmud are so full of wisdom which they are also well qualified to disseminate.[55] Scholars are as tender and pleasant as roses,[56] and just as doves look expectantly toward their dovecotes for sustenance, so does the Almighty look toward the houses of study,[57] which are the sources of nourishment for the people of Israel.[58]

In addition to devotion and love for the subject matter, however, Rashi demands a high standard of proficiency for the study of Torah. "Review it and delve into the depths [of the Torah] so that you will not have to be hesitant about answering questions."[59] His attitude toward piety and study was basically a restatement of an ideal hallowed by age-old tradition. Until the dawn of the modern era the study of Bible and Talmud with Rashi's commentaries was considered not only the duty of every Jew but also one of the most exquisite spiritual pleasures to be enjoyed by the People of the Book — sometimes by choice but at times also due to the hostility of the Gentile world which excluded Jews from partaking of the fruits of human intelligence (and which thereby deprived itself as well of the rich potential of Jewish contributions). Rashi accompanied the Jew in his studies throughout the lights and shadows of his tragic history. Like a mentor's guiding hand, Rashi's commentaries molded the character of the Jew from early childhood on through his formative years and until the last conscious stirrings of his intellectual life. No wonder, therefore, that ethics, morality and Godliness were household concepts in the life of the Jew, drawing a sharp line of demarcation between him and the alien environment in which he lived.

Commentaries by their very nature and definition direct the reader's attention to the text they seek to explain rather than to themselves. In almost every case they lose their independent standing as literary creations in their own right and become a mere appendix to the text which they serve. As a result, important data which the commentaries may mention only in passing and which have only indirect relevance to the text are often overlooked. Yet some of this "incidental" information may be of great significance to many disciplines other than to which the text central to the commentary refers. The work of a commentator who lives in times and under conditions quite different from those that produced his text reflects the milieu, the customs and the life of his own era. And since his purpose is to convey the meaning of his text, as he sees it, to his contemporaries he must address them in the idiom of their own day, not in that of the text with which he is working. As a consequence, the discerning student and sensitive researcher, in reading a commentary, may unearth information of incalculable value for the historian and the social scientist which may yield new perspectives not merely on the text which the commentary was intended to explain, but also on the period during which the commentator lived and worked.

A great many biographical and ancillary works have been written about Rashi and his commentaries. Most of the texts in the latter category seek to shed new light on Rashi's commentaries as such, and perhaps also to find deeper meanings for the Biblical and Talmudic passages to which Rashi's writings refer. But very few, if indeed any, of these authors treat Rashi's commentaries as documentary or source material for the political, social and economic conditions that prevailed in Rashi's day.

Rashi's contributions to the study of the history and development of the French language have been expertly acknowledged by Darmesteter and Blondheim. A more specific and thorough analysis of Rashi's commentaries was made by M. Paul Klein in his thesis which was submitted at the École Nationale of Chartres in 1949 and which deals specifically and exhaustively with the terms used by Rashi in his commentaries with reference to housing. It is unfortunate that until relatively recent times Jewish historiography concerned itself primarily with great individuals; only very few historians gave attention to how the average Jew lived, dressed and worked. Unlike the Jews of Spanish Africa, who developed a rich Responsa literature reflecting all the phenomena and problems of their daily lives, medieval Franco-German Jewry developed a literary heritage which centered on theory — on the legal intricacies of the "sea of the Talmud" rather than on the practical application of Rabbinic law to everyday life. It takes a profound understanding of the Talmud to glean from these works any data capable of shedding some light upon the daily lives and activities of the Jews in medieval France and Germany. It is perhaps for this reason that the Rabbinic literature of medieval Spanish Jewry has attracted the attention of modern scholars to a greater extent than have the Rabbinic works of medieval France and Germany, even though in fact the latter bear a veritable treasure trove of important historical and sociological data within a seemingly insignificant word, phrase or analogy.

The vast literature compiled by interpreters of the Bible and the Talmud, the "bearers of the appurtenances" and the authors of the Talmudic novellae of the Middle Ages, embrace a mass of material that is invaluable for a reconstruction of the daily life of the ordinary folk of the medieval period, their customs, mores, occupations and aspirations. It is from this perspective that the present study has set out to consider Rashi, the man, the scholar and the world in which he lived.

NOTES

1. Another example:

I Samuel 1:17: [Eli says to Hannah], "May the God of Israel grant thy petition."

Rashi: "The word שלתך [thy petition] is written here without an *aleph* after the *shin* [where an *aleph* would properly belong]. This is intended to signify that the petition to be granted is for offspring since [elsewhere in Scripture] the word שליתה is used to denote the afterbirth." Cf. Deuteronomy 28:57: "... and against her afterbirth which emerges..."

Kimhi: 1) "The *aleph* is missing and the accent mark is on the *shin* because the word is identical with שאלתך [thy petition]. Eli said this to [Hannah] either in the form of a prayer [May the God of Israel grant thy petition] or in the form of a prophecy [The God of Israel will grant thy petition]."

2) "שלתך is written here [without an *aleph*], for he said to her, 'The son whom thou wilt bear will derive much gain [from שלל, "gain" or "booty"] from the Torah.'"

2. Rashi on Gittin 33a: "I explain it in this manner in every passage, based

on my own intuitive understanding. However, I have received from my teachers...."

On Gittin 65b: "I have heard this [explanation] but to me the opposite seems true."

On Menahot 4a: "There are also other ways of explaining this, but this [explanation] is the principal one..."

On Menahot 9b: "Another explanation has it that... but these explanations are not clear to me."

On Haggigah 15a: "This is how it appears to me, but my teachers explain..."

On Esther 1:7, Esther 2:5,9; Lamentations 1:15; I Samuel 1:11: "Our Rabbis offer another explanation..." Rashi does not specify these "other" explanations because he does not consider them to be of particular significance. Nevertheless, he wants to inform his readers that such explanations do exist and may be consulted if desired.

3. Other cases in point:

On Genesis 25:17: "... and [Ishmael] expired and died..."

Bava Bathra 16b: "Wherever Scripture uses the term 'expire' in connection with a word denoting death, it refers to the death of a righteous person."

Rashi: The term גויעה [expire] is used by Scriptures only with reference to righteous men."

Genesis 29:11: "And Jacob kissed Rachel and raised his voice and wept."

Rashi [Free translation]: "Jacob wept because he had been pursued by Esau's son Eliphaz, who had been ordered by his father to kill Jacob. Jacob therefore suggested to Eliphaz that he [Eliphaz] carry out his father's orders by taking all of Jacob's possessions since a 'poor man may be accounted as one who is dead.'" (According to Nedarim 64b, four classes of people are listed who may be accounted as dead; these include the blind and the poor).

Exodus 4:19: "And the Lord said to Moses in Midian, 'Go return to Egypt because all the men who sought thy life are dead.'"

Rashi comments that Dathan and Abiram, who were Moses' enemies, were still alive at the time. How, then, could the text state that all those who sought Moses' life had died? The explanation Rashi offers is that Dathan and Abiram "had come down [in the world] because they had lost all their possessions and a poor man may be regarded as dead."

Avot 4:4: "Whoever profanes the Name of God secretly is punished publicly, whether the profanation was committed on purpose or unintentionally."

Rashi (based on Kiddushin 40a: It is more acceptable for a human being to transgress in secret and not desecrate the Name of God in public.) "The profanation of the Name of God is an offense [even] more serious than idolatry."

4. I. Elfenbein, *op. cit.*, p. 88; Joel HaKohen Miller (ed.), *Teshuvot Hakhmei Tsorfat veLothir*, Vienna, 1881, p. 13. Rashi uses the expression מניני הצעיר to denote "young in years." He explains that the word *minyan*, literally, "number," can also mean "years." See Mishnah Eduyot I,5 as well as Avot 5,7 (Tosefot Yomtov *ad locum*). Rashi's choice of this interpretation demonstrates his personal humility. The Mishnah states that the decision of a court of religious law can be set aside only by an authority which is greater in wisdom and in "numbers " [i.e., of disciples]. Rashi was well aware that he was superior to the religious authorities of Chalon-sur-Saône when it came to numbers of disciples. He therefore pointed out the one respect in which he might be "inferior" to the religious elders of the town: his relative youth.

5. I. Elfenbein, *op. cit.*, No. 242, p. 282; J. Miller, *op. cit.*, No. 13, p. 7a: "And I express my opinion to them to the extent that it was shown to me by Heaven."

6. Sukkah 43b: "The procession around the *bimah* with the *lulav* on Sukkot is obligatory on all the days of the festival."

7. I. Elfenbein, *op. cit.*, par. 121, p. 149; *Mahzor Vitry*, ed. S. Hurwitz (Berlin, 1893), par. 182, p. 444: "I have been in error here... I therefore retract [my statement]."

8. *Ibid.*: "My thanks to my colleague [lit., "my brother"] from whose arguments I have learned..."

9. Abraham Geiger, *Melo Hofnayim*, Berlin, 1840, par. 10, p. 36: "I have been in error in this explanation... and now I am reviewing it with our colleague [lit., "our brother"] Shemaiah."

10. See Rashi on Genesis 28:5, 35:13; Exodus 15:1, 22:28; Leviticus 13:4, 27:3; Deuteronomy 33:24; II Samuel 17:20; Tractates Betzah 25b, Yoma 85a, Niddah 67a and many more.

11. I. Elfenbein, *op. cit.*, par. 242, p. 284; J. Miller, *op. cit.*, par. 13, p. 7b: "As my heart understands it and according to what I have received from my teachers."

12. *Ibid.*, par. 104, p. 133.

13. *Ibid.*, par. 355, p. 355.

14. See Note 58 to Chapter I.

15. I. Elfenbein, *op. cit.*, par. 103, p. 130; J. Miller, *op. cit.*, par. 11, pp. 5-6.

16. *Ibid.*, par. 103, p. 132; J. Miller, *ibid.*, p. 6.

17. I. Elfenbein, *op. cit.*, par. 60, p. 58. A. Berliner's introduction to *Mahzor Vitry*, p. 174. *Beth Talmud II* (Vienna, 1882), ed. I.H. Weiss, p. 296.

18. *Ibid.*

19. *Ibid.*, par. 59, p. 57.

20. *Ibid.*, par. 28, p. 20; *Hofes Matmonim...* par. 14, p. 11.

21. Rashi on Leviticus 26:6 ("And I will give you peace in the land...") "From this we know that peace outweighs all else."

22. Rashi on Genesis 11:9 ("Therefore its name was called Babel because there the Lord confused the language of all the earth"): "This shows how hateful is dissension and how great is peace."

23. I. Elfenbein, *op. cit.*, par. 71, p. 89; J. Miller, *op. cit.*, par. 23, p. 13.

24. Rashi on Leviticus 19:15; Shevuot 30a.

25. Rashi on Yevamot 117a: "If a man loves another, that one will love him in return, while if a man hates another, that one will hate him in return."

26. I. Elfenbein, *op. cit.*, par. 180, p. 209. *Mahzor Vitry*, p. 244: One day someone died during the intermediate days of a festival... And at the funeral there were some who declared that one must not recite the *tzidduk ha-din*, nor the [Mourners'] Kaddish on account of the holiday... But our teacher [Rashi] rose and recited the *tzidduk ha-din* and then the Kaddish, saying that this was not a eulogy which would have constituted a violation of the [spirit of the] festival but simply an acknowledgment and acceptance of the Divine judgment. And when he returned [from the funeral] he went to the house of the mourner to comfort him... it was difficult [for him] to sit [there] in silence... and so he began to speak and said words of comfort to the mourner."

27. On Betzah 2b: "It is good of him to let us know the authority of him who is permissive [in this respect] and upon whose opinion he relies. But the authority of those who prohibit [arbitrarily] means little, for anyone can hand down a prohibition even in matters that are permissible."

28. I. Elfenbein, *op. cit.*, par. 155, p. 178.

29. *Ibid.*, par. 327, p. 337: "Gentiles nowadays are not familiar with [the intricacies of] idol worship and they are therefore to be considered like infants one day old whose touch does not render the wine *nesekh* [forbidden to Jews]."
Ibid., par. 155, p. 179: "However, we have neither heard, nor have we seen, nor have our eyes beheld any one of them splashing wine for purposes of idol worship."

30. *Ibid.*, par. 229, p. 255; *Sefer HaOrah* II, par. 123, p. 218: The question was as follows: If a Jew takes a loan from a Gentile and gives him a collateral for it, and the Gentile, in turn, takes a loan from another Jew and turns over the collateral to the latter, is the second Jew permitted to accept interest even though the money comes from another Jew, and Jews are not allowed to accept interest for loans involving other Jews? Rashi asserts that a Jew who would refuse to accept the interest from a Gentile under such circumstances would be letter-pious but foolish. However, he suggests that a Jew should make every effort to avoid such situations.

31. Avodah Zarah 11b.

32. *Sefer HaOrah* II, par. 153, p. 228. We are told here that on one occasion

Rashi had made a loan to a Gentile and found himself in a position where the Gentile insisted that he owed Rashi nothing. Rashi thereupon asked the Gentile to swear a solemn oath that he, Rashi, had no claim upon him. He accompanied the Gentile to a non-Jewish house of worship so that the Gentile might take his oath. But Rashi hoped that at the last moment the Gentile might decide not to take the oath. For in fact the Sages say it is forbidden for a Jew to enter into any business relationship with a Gentile, lest the Jew find himself compelled at some point to extract an oath from the Gentile. Verse 13 of Chapter 23 in the Book of Exodus, "and make no mention of the name of other gods, neither let it be heard out of thy mouth," is interpreted to mean that a Jew is forbidden to ask a non-Jew to swear by the name of his deity. This means, Rashi notes, that "you shall make no business partnership with a non-Jew through which it could happen that he will take an oath by the name of his deity, because then you will have brought it about that it [i.e., the name of the deity] has been mentioned at your initiative." From that time on, we are told, Rashi refused to enter into any business relationships with Gentiles.

33. *Mahzor Vitry*, p. 211; see also I. Elfenbein, par. 131, p. 158; *Siddur Rashi*, p. 168: "We saw people who were in the habit of giving Purim gifts to [Gentile] servants and maids in Jewish homes. This was very displeasing to our teacher [Rashi] because it looked as if [the employer was fulfilling] the commandment to give gifts to the poor [on Purim] when, in fact, the commandment was applicable only in the case of the Jewish poor, not to poor Gentiles...."

34. Rashi on Exodus 23:13: ("And in all things that I have said to you take heed and make no mention of the name of other gods): "You shall make no business partnership with a non-Jew through which it could happen that he will take an oath by the name of his deity..." (see Note 32 above).

Rashi on Sanhedrin 26b: "One who receives charity from non-Jews is as if he had desecrated the Name of the Lord for the sake of financial gain."

35. I. Elfenbein, *op. cit.*, par. 258, p. 301.

36. *Sefer HaPardes*, p. 97: "[With reference to the benediction *ha-melekh ha-mishpat* (The King of Justice)], this is grammatically wrong [because in the definite construct case only the second noun, in this case *ha-mishpat*, should be prefaced by a definite article]... I, too, have had difficulty with this, and my heart tells me that in the course of time the readers have become accustomed to this [ungrammatical] reading. However, one should not change time-honored custom and we can cite in our support many Scriptural verses with the same structure." See also *Hofes Matmonim*... 4, p. 2; *Siddur Rashi*, 140, p. 66; *Mahzor Vitry*, par. 313, p. 345.

37. *Sefer HaOrah* II, par. 103, p. 212: "...better that Jews should [transgress the law] unintentionally than [that they should do so] deliberately."

38. *Sefer HaPardes*, p. 97. *Hofes Matmonim*.... par. 7, p. 6.

39. Rashi on Leviticus 26:6: "If there is no peace, there is nothing." See also Note 21.

40. I. Elfenbein, *op. cit.*, par. 168, pp. 188-89: "Far be it from me to insult them by not drinking their wine... and especially if they had [converted] out of fear of the sword but later retracted [and returned to Judaism] as soon as they could do so." See also *Sefer HaPardes*, p. 99.

41. J. Miller (ed.) *op. cit.*, par. 21, p. 11: "If someone is a repentant sinner one should not say to him, 'Remember your past deeds,' and if someone is a son of converts [to Judaism] one should not tell him 'Remember the deeds of your fathers.'"

42. *Sefer HaOrah* II, par. 130, p. 220: "A transgressor, even though he has sinned, is still an Israelite; that is, he still retains his sanctity [as a Jew]."

43. Rashi on Genesis 1:1.

44. I. Elfenbein, *op. cit.*, par. 255, p. 299. See also *Sefer haOrah* II, par. 155, p. 229.

45. Rashi on Zechariah 14:10: ("And all the land shall be turned as the Arabah, from Geba to Rimmon south of Jerusalem"): "Jerusalem shall extend to the ends of the earth."

46. Rashi on Proverbs 1:7: ("The fear of the Lord is the beginning of knowledge, but the foolish despise wisdom and discipline").

47. *Ibid.*, "Fools who do not fear the Lord despise knowledge and ethics."

48. Rashi on Jonah 4:11: ("... and should I not have pity upon Nineveh, where there are more than six-score thousand persons who cannot discern between their right hand and their left hand, and also much cattle?"): "Even great men will acquire the mentality of beasts if they do not recognize their Creator."

49. Rashi on Leviticus 19:14, 32: "Because in this case it is not given to human beings to know whether the intention of this man was for the advantage or the disadvantage of the person whom he advised and he might thus be able to evade responsibility by saying, 'I meant it for the best.' Scripture therefore states concerning him, 'But thou shalt fear thy God,' Who is cognizant of thy secret thoughts. Similarly, in any action where it is given only to the heart of him who performs it to know the motive that has prompted him and where others have no insight into it, Scripture states, 'But thou shalt fear thy God.'"

50. *Hofes Matmonim...* par. 1, p. 2.

51. Rashi on Ecclesiastes 5:9: ("He who loves silver shall not be satisfied with silver"): "He who loves Torah will never be able to get his fill of it."

52. Rashi on Proverbs 27:7: ("The full soul loathes a honeycomb but to the hungry soul every bitter thing is sweet"): "One who does not have a passionate desire for the words of Torah... not even reasonable explanations

will appeal to him... but as for him who has a passionate desire for them, even questions which he learns with bitterness and toil are sweet to him."

53. Rashi on Song of Songs 5:15: ("He looks like the Lebanon, of special excellence as the cedars"): "He who delves into things Divine discovers [therein] flowers and fresh branches like the forest which blooms. Thus are the words of the Torah. Whoever meditates in them always finds something new there."

54. *Ibid.*

55. *Ibid. 7:13:* ("Let us get up early to the vineyards to see whether the vine has budded...."): "The budding vine — those are the students of the Bible; the Mishnah scholar is like a vine blossom... pomegranates... those steeped in the Talmud are like them because they are so full of wisdom and are qualified to disseminate it."

56. Rashi on Psalms 45:1: ("For the Leader, upon Shoshanim [Roses]"): "Scholars... are as tender as roses..."

57. Rashi on Song of Songs 5:12: ("His eyes are like doves, beside the brooks of water"): "Like the doves whose eyes look toward their dovecotes, so are His eyes upon the synagogues and the houses of study"

58. Rashi on Song of Songs 8:10: ("I am a wall and my breasts are like its towers..."): "These are the synagogues and the houses of study which nourish Israel with words of Torah."

59. Rashi on Kiddushin 30a.

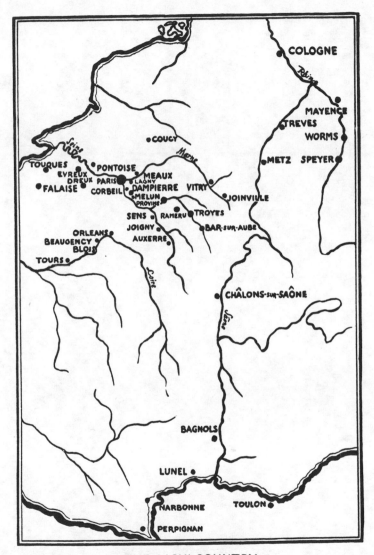

THE RASHI COUNTRY

Part II

RASHI'S TIMES

CHAPTER THREE

Horizon

It was Rashi's good fortune to live in Germany and France at a time when social, political and economic conditions in both countries were relatively stable and hence the Jews in that part of Europe also enjoyed comparative tranquility and prosperity.

Rashi himself cites a statement by Rabbenu Gershom to the effect that the Jewish merchants of Mayence in his day regularly visited the fairs in Cologne and conducted various financial transactions.[1] Christians, among them Anno, Archbishop of Cologne (r. 1056-1075), borrowed money from Jews.[2] On January 18, 1074, Emperor Henry IV (1050-1106) exempted the Jews and other citizens of Worms from paying tolls in recognition of their loyalty to him on the eve of the "investiture controversy."* The names and the sheer number of other cities mentioned in this privilege issued by the emperor bear

---

*Conflict between the emperor and Pope Gregory VII (Hildebrand) when the latter forbade the lay investiture of Church officials.

witness to the great variety of commercial enterprises in which the Jews of Worms were engaged during this period.[3]

In Speyer, Bishop Ruediger (1084) regarded the Jews as an important factor in the affluence and prestige of his city. The Jews of Speyer were free to engage in commerce anywhere in the city, including the harbor area. In addition, they owned buildings, real estate, orchards and vineyards. Ruediger even granted them the right to set up their own judicial system; the leader of the community, the *archisynagogus*, was authorized to hand down decisions in litigations between Jews.[4] Jews were permitted to employ Christian servants and wet nurses. They were allowed to sell to Christians any meat which, after ritual slaughter, was found forbidden to Jews under the Jewish dietary laws.[5] Jews also had permission to defend themselves against physical attack and to fortify their quarter of the city which was surrounded by a protective wall. Their cemetery had been deeded to them in perpetuity from Church property.[6]

However, the Jews of Speyer apparently did not feel that the privileges granted them by Bishop Ruediger in September, 1084 were sufficient to ensure their security. We know that a deputation from Speyer's Jewish community, composed of the halakhic authority Judah ben Kalonymus, the liturgical poet David ben Meshullam and one Moses ben Jekuthiel, called on Henry IV in Speyer and requested him to place their community under his personal protection. The emperor complied with this request; in the year 1090 he enacted a decree that no one was to molest the Jews or to take possession of any courtyard, house, garden, vineyard, landed property, slaves, or any other movables or immovables owned by Jews. Jews were to be permitted to do business wherever they pleased. Under this decree it was forbidden to baptize Jewish children by force. If a Jewish adult expressed the wish to embrace Christianity, a three-day waiting period had to be observed in order to give the would-be convert a chance to reconsider his act before taking the final step. Jews were permitted to have Christians work for them, except on Sundays and Christian holidays. Disputes between Jews and Christians, the decree further stipulated, were to be resolved in accordance with the laws of both parties; disputes involving Jews only were to be settled under the terms of Jewish law. The decree also specified that Jews were free to sell wine, herbs and medicines to their Christian neighbors.[7]

In the year 1090 Henry IV extended to the Jewish community of Worms privileges which were substantially the same as those conferred upon the Jews of Speyer.[8] Actually, the privileges granted to the Jews by this emperor were merely confirmations of earlier rights which had been in effect ever since the rule of the Carolingians, particularly the reign of Louis the Pious (814-840).[9]

It seems that the Jews of Mayence in particular lived in peace and security during Rashi's day. When Archbiship Bardo of Mayence died in 1051, the Jews were grief-stricken; they prostrated themselves before his casket and placed ashes on their heads as a sign of mourning.[10]

Troyes: The City as Rashi Knew It

Rashi spent his student years at the Talmudical academy of Mayence and at the academy of Worms 25 miles to the south. The date when he returned to his birthplace, Troyes, is not known. But we do know that Rashi continued his studies for some time after his marriage although his economic situation was rather precarious. He himself relates — as we have already noted — that he continued to sit at the feet of his teachers even when he lacked bread and decent clothing and after he had assumed the responsibilities of marriage.[11]

Eventually, however, Rashi returned to Troyes in order to disseminate the learning he had acquired from his great masters. On at least one occasion he expressed regret that — apparently due to personal circumstances which he does not explain — he had not been able to visit his teachers in more than 25 years.[12] He missed the personal contact with them, because the responsa correspondence that passed between them and him very rarely went beyond the limits of arid legal queries and rulings.

It was probably in Troyes that Rashi compiled his commentaries on the Pentateuch, the other books of the Bible and the

Talmud. It was there, too, that the foundations for *Sefer HaOrah*, *Sefer HaPardes* and *Mahzor Vitry*, all products of the school of Rashi, were laid. In the course of time the Jews came to view Troyes as one of the principal abodes of Jewish learning; eventually, the city acquired fame as the seat of the French school of Bible exegetes and Talmudic commentators.

In Rashi's day Troyes, located approximately 90 miles southeast of Paris, was important as the meeting point of two main routes which led to Italy and the Near East. The famous fairs of Troyes, which were held twice each year,[13] attracted merchants from many lands who turned the city into a cosmopolitan center, exposing its populations, Jewish and Gentile alike, to the customs and manners of many nations. The city's Jewish quarter, known as the Broce-aux-Juifs (or La Juiverie), was adjacent to the Abbey of Saint Loup, a community of Augustine canons. Also near the Jewish quarter was the Cathedral of St. Peter, which housed a school devoted to the seven arts and elementary theology. It was at this institution that the famous Peter Comestor, whose *Historia Scholastica* (one of the most widely-disseminated textbooks in the Middle Ages) quotes many of the interpretations suggested and used by Rashi, served as dean in the middle years of the 12th century.[14]

During the 11th and 12th centuries Troyes had a relatively large number of Jews who lived a rather peaceful life under the rule of Thibault I, Count of Champagne. Their skills and interests in economic and communal affairs contributed substantially to the city's development and prosperity. During that period we find among the Jews of Troyes bankers and all kinds of affluent artisans.[15] The Jews of Troyes lived in harmony with their Christian neighbors;[16] they hired Christian laborers under contract,[17] had their horses shod in workshops owned by Christians and their clothes laundered and repaired by Christian tailors.[18] Jews borrowed money from Christians[19] and the Christians in turn supplied the Jews with fresh fodder for their cattle on Jewish holidays when Jews were not permitted to perform the chores entailed in fodder-getting.[20] (The Christians in the city were familiar with the religious laws and customs of the Jews.).[21] Jews owned vineyards and fields and lived in spacious homes.[22] Except, of course, for the practices and strictures of their day-to-day religious observances, the everyday life of the Jews was not so very different from that of their Christian neighbors. They spoke — or at least understood — the same language, wore similar attire and enjoyed much the same niceties of life.

A Meeting Ground Between Christians and Jews: The Bible

It was only natural that the business and social contacts between Christians and Jews should lead to exchanges of ideas and cultural aspirations. It is noteworthy that Christian Bible exegesis had its beginnings toward the middle of the 11th century. The contacts between Jews and Christians of necessity led to a strong awareness of the religious differences that separated the Jew from his Christian neighbor. This awareness in turn engendered a desire to resolve mutual doubts and suspicions. Situations of this kind frequently trigger aggressive moods. In civilized societies such moods are generally vented by the use of the word, while societies of lesser culture frequently cater to these impulses by resorting to the sword. In the middle of the 11th century, the period during which Rashi began his activities, the enthusiasm of scholars and laymen alike was kindled by disputations and verbal polemics.[23] (Only toward the end of the century — and of Rashi's life — did verbal polemics degenerate into verbal and physical persecution of the Jews.)

The meeting ground for the disputations that took place between Christians and Jews during that period was the Bible. Though the Old Testament was accepted by both religions as the supreme canon of human ideals and conduct, divergences in its interpretations by Jews and Christians made for profound disagreements between the two faiths.

The Biblical interpretations upon which Christians built their religious doctrines were based on the text of the Vulgate and the commentaries of St. Jerome, neither of which were consistently faithful to the Hebrew original. Furthermore, in the Christian view the need for arriving at the straightforward meaning of the Biblical text was overshadowed by the "hidden" propositions which the Christians so eagerly accepted. Already Origen (c.185-c.253), the Greek father of the Early Church, made a clear distinction between the letter and the spirit of the Word: "When the Word was shown to man through the law-giver and the prophet, it was not without suitable vesture... but the spiritual sense within is recognized as divinity."[24]

The more this patristic distinction between "letter" and "spirit" was encouraged, the more was the "letter" relegated to the position of an amorphous shell which served only to accommodate and protect a variety of "spirits," as it were. Spiritual expositions were motivated by pious meditation or religious dogma, for which the literal text merely supplied convenient points of departure. To cite one instance, the four rivers which emanated from the Garden of Eden (see Genesis 2:10-14) were interpreted by the Church as symbolizing four distinct "senses" of Scripture: the "literal" sense; the "allegorical" sense, which revealed tenets of faith; the "moral" sense, which was intended to guide the deeds of men; and finally the "mystical" sense (anagoge), which dealt with the world to come.

A text becomes in need of interpretation when it can no longer be read and understood without effort, when certain words, turns of phrase and expressions begin to pose difficulties to the reader. The further away we are from its time of origin the less likely are we to grasp fully the true intent of the text. The difficulty is compounded if the original language of the literary creation is no longer widely known and we are compelled to turn to translations so that we lose the imponderables which only the original can truly reproduce.

As long as Hebrew was the everyday language of the Jewish people living in their own land, no detailed explanations of the Biblical texts were needed. But after the destruction of the Jewish state in the first century of the Common Era, when Hebrew gradually ceased to be widely understood among Jews, it became a matter of urgent necessity to translate the Biblical text into the languages which the Jews, now increasingly scattered throughout the Ancient World, employed in their daily lives. Before long, commentaries were offered by scholars to preserve whatever they considered to be the true meaning of the original Hebrew text. The most outstanding among the early medieval commentaries on the Bible was that of Saadia Gaon (882-941), whose main objective was to refute the doctrines and allegories of the Karaites.

The Jews of medieval France received many of their Bible interpretations directly from the Holy Land. This bond still existed in the days of Rashi. As Rashi himself put it in his commentary on a passage in Tractate Berakhot, he would encounter "readers who came from the Land of Israel"[25] and who had apparently brought with them Midrashic (allegorical) interpretations[26] of Biblical passages on which they expanded and which they preached to various audiences. The best-known disseminator of Midrashic interpretations during Rashi's day was Rabbi Moshe HaDarshan (Moses the Preacher) of Narbonne. It seems that his interpretations enjoyed wide popularity. He is frequently cited by Rashi himself,[27] who accepts some of his views and rejects others.[28]

Rashi's grandson Rabbi Samuel ben Meir (RaSHBaM), too, stated — with an overtone of disapproval — that "the older commentators who, by reason of their piety, were inclined to preach sermons (derashot), which they regarded as the most important objective, were not accustomed to delve into the depths of the literal meaning of the Biblical text."[29]

The many beautiful Midrashic explanations that have come down to us are, of course, firmly rooted in the "letter," the literal text, of the Bible. Their purpose, however, was to graft a particularly edifying idea onto a Biblical concept or verse by associating that concept with words of simliar meaning or sound.[30]

In some instances Biblical words or passages were given completely divergent connotations by associating them with an identical or similar Hebrew word root. One interesting example of this practice is noted in Rashi's commentary on Verse 26 of the first chapter in Genesis. The text reads, "And God said, 'Let us make man in our image... and let them have dominion over the fish of the sea.'" The Hebrew word employed in the text for "let them have dominion" is וירדו, which also could be rendered as "let them descend." Rashi explains: "The expression וירדו may imply dominion as well as descending. [This means that] if [man] is worthy, he is dominant over the beast and cattle; if he is not worthy, he will sink even lower than they, and the beasts will rule over him."

In the course of the steady accumulation of interpretative material hallowed by time and tradition, the link of the interpretations with their original literal basis became so tenuous and obscure that, to the layman's non-discriminating eye, there seemed to be no relationship at all between the two.

At a time when Christians contended that "the words of our teacher Moses are nothing but allegories; i.e. enigmatic words and metaphors, and divorced the word completely from its meaning,"[31] it could hardly be expected that the Christians' own allegorical interpretations of Scripture would readily defer to a Jewish refutation which, in essence, would itself be based on allegory or mysticism. In order to gain credibility, therefore, the views of the Jewish commentators would have to submit to the touchstone of the original literal text.

Indeed, it was the problems arising from the "closed" original Hebrew text of the Bible that led many Christian scholars in the 11th and 12th centuries to study the Hebrew language intensively and to establish close contacts with Jews, who were the only well-informed source on the subject. Thus, Peter Abelard (1079-1142) advises the *virgines Paracletenses*, the students housed in the Paraclete, the monastery he had built near Troyes, to learn Hebrew so that they might be in a position to gain an insight into the original text of Scripture.[32] The Benedictine hagiographer Sigebert of Gembloux (c.1030-1112), teaching in Metz (ca. 1050-60), accepted Hebrew interpretations of the Biblical text.[33] The abbot Sigon of St. Florent de Saumur (d. 1070) was familiar with the Old Testament in the original Hebrew and with the New Testament; he knew how to read and write Hebrew as well as Greek.[34] In the centuries that followed, the idea that a knowledge of Hebrew was indispensable to Christian exegetes became increasingly accepted in Christian circles.

It was perhaps under the impact of these circumstances that Rashi directed Jewish Bible exegesis into new channels. It

seemed that the two methods of interpretation, the allegorical
(derash) and the literal (peshat), had come to a parting of the ways.
The Jewish de-emphasis of allegory in favor of the literal
method may have been abetted also by the cosmopolitan character of the city of Troyes, where the exchanges between the
local populace and merchants from far-away lands may well
have encouraged exchanges of religious ideas as well, resulting
in a few cases of Jewish apostasy. Nevertheless, Rashi did not
regard the two methods of interpretation as mutually exclu-
sive. On the one hand, he quoted the words of the Prophet
Jeremiah (23:29): "Is not My word like fire? says the Lord, and
like a hammer that breaks the rock into pieces?" implying that
just as a hammer can break a rock into many splinters, so, too,
the word of the Torah is amenable to a variety of interpretations.[35] On the other hand, he subscribed unconditionally to
his own dictum, written in his Introduction to his commentary
on the Song of Songs, that a verse must not be distorted to
surrender its literal meaning and plain sense.[36] Rashi held that
neither method of interpretation by itself was adequate. A
satisfactory commentary required a synthesis of both. These
two self-imposed guidelines left room for allegorical explanations that did not do violence to the literal meaning of the text.
Accordingly, Rashi selected from the many nuances found in
Midrashic literature the ones that in his view were most faithful to the text and at the same time satisfied the moral and
educational objective he sought to attain.[37] Always sensitively
attuned to the literal text, he made careful distinctions
between the use of a word in its context,[38] on the one hand,
and the literal meaning on the same word when detached from
its specific context,[39] on the other. Rashi coined his own technical expressions.[40]

His primary aim, through it all, was to produce a commentary that would explain the Biblical text in the clearest, most
lucid manner possible.[41] In many instances he rejected interpretations from great Talmudic sages simply because, in his
opinion, they neither corresponded to the intent of the text
nor fitted into the flow of the context.[42] But whenever he
found himself at a loss to discover any meaning in the literal

text he readily conceded that the verse would have to be interpreted in a non-literal meaning.[43]

NOTES

1. *Sefer HaPardes,* ed. H.L.Ehrenreich, Budapest, 1924, p. 73: "Rabbi Solomon [i.e., Rashi] said in the name of Rabbenu Gershom that it is not permitted to conduct oneself as they do in this kingdom, to bring to the fairs in Cologne a silver *zakuk* [coin] of 12 ounces and then, in Mayence and Worms, to receive 13 ounces in return."

2. Julius Aronius, *op. cit.,* No. 164, p. 68; R. Hoeniger, "Zur Geschichte der Juden Deutschlands im fruehen Mittelalter," in *Zeitschrift fuer die Geschichte der Juden in Deutschland,* Vol. I, p. 96, 97.

3. Sara Fischmann, "Heinrichs IV Verhalten zu den Juden zur Zeit des ersten Kreuzzuges," *ibid.,* Vol. III, No. 1, p. 51, Note 50.

4. Julius Aronius, *op. cit.* No. 168, pp. 69-71: *"Deinde sicut tribunus urbis inter cives, ita archisynagogus suus omnem iudicet querimoniam, que contigerit inter eos vel adversus eos."* ("Just as the mayor among his constituents, so the archisynagogus shall act as arbitrator in disputes among or against them.")

5. *Ibid.* "*Nutrices quoque et conducticios servientes ex nostris licite habeant. Carnes mactatas, quas viderint sibi illicitas secundum legis sue sanctionem, licite vendant christianis, licite emant eas christiani."* ("They shall be permitted to have [Gentile] wet nurses and hired servants. They shall be permitted to sell to Christians that slaughtered meat which is forbidden to them according to their law, and the [Christians] shall be permitted to buy it [from them].")

6. *Ibid.* "*Dedi insuper eis de praedio ecclesie locum sepulture sub hereditaria condicione."* ("Furthermore, they shall obtain from the [landed] estates of the Church a burial place in perpetuity".)

7. Julius Aronius, *op. cit.,* No. 170, pp. 72, 73:
"Nullus eos inquietare... neque de rebus eorum, quas... possident in areis, in casis, in ortis, in vineis, in agris... auffere quidquam audeat... intra ambitum regni nostri libere et pacifice discurrere, negocium et mercinomium suum exercere.

"Nullus filios aut filias eorum invitos baptizare presumat. Si aliqui eorum sponte baptizari velint, triduo reserventur ut integre cognoscatur, si vere christiane religionis causa aut aliqua illata iniuria legem suam abnegent.

"Liceat etiam christianos homines ad opera sua facienda conducere, exceptis diebus festis et dominicis.

"Quod si christianus contra Iudeum vel Iudeus contra christianum litem... habuerit, uterque prout res est secundum legem suam iusticiam faciat.

"Quod si Iudei litem inter se... habuerint... a suis paribus et non aliis... iudicentur.

"Habeant preterea licenciam, vinum suum et pigmenta et antidota vendere christianis."
("No one shall molest them... nor shall anyone dare to remove anything

from their possessions in courtyards, houses, gardens, vineyards, fields...
they shall be permitted to move about freely and in peace within the empire,
and to engage in trade and commerce.

"No one shall baptize their sons or daughters by force. Those among
them who wish to undergo baptism out of their own free will shall be given
three days in which to come to a clear understanding as to whether they
[wish to] forsake their religion for the sake of [accepting] Christianity or
whether they [only wish to] do so because of some illicit injury done them.

"They shall be permitted to hire Christians for their work, except on
Sundays and [Christian] holy days.

"Disputes between a Christian and a Jew, or between a Jew and a Christian... shall be decided in accordance with their respective laws.

"Disputes among Jews... shall be decided by their peers and no others.

"They shall have permission to sell their wine, herbs and medicines to
Christians.")

8. For the difference in the privileges, see Julius Aronius, *op. cit.*, No. 171,
p. 75.

9. Heinrich Graetz, *Geschichte der Juden*, Magdeburg, 1860; ed. Institut zur
Foerderung der Israelitischen Literatur, Vol. V, p. 246.

10. *Monumenta Moguntina*, ed. Philippus Jaffe, Berlin, 1866, p. 562: *"Iudei
etiam — quibus nulla bona curae sunt — ei obviam facti, ut venerandi viri feretrum
viderunt, terrae consternati, caput pulvere consperserunt et dixerunt: Heu, heu pie pater; heu
pie pater; uddebantque: Si christiani anima unquam requiem meruit, merito tua requiescere
potuit."* ("Even the Jews... when they beheld the coffin of this venerable man,
prostrated themselves, placed ashes upon their heads and said, 'Woe! Woe! O
pious father! Woe, O pious father!' and they added, 'If the soul of a Christian
ever deserved peace, surely yours deserves to rest in peace.'"

11. See Chapter 2, Note 50.

12. *Hofes Matmonim*... p. 2: "Ever since I have returned here I have had no
time to visit them... these twenty-five years."

13. F. Bourquelot, *Études sur les foires de Champagne*, Vol. V, in Series
Memoires presentés par divers savants a l'Académie des Inscriptions et
Belles-Lettres, p. 72; M. Crubellier, *Histoire de la Champagne*, Toulouse, 1975, p.
108.

14. Esra Shereshevsky, "Hebrew Traditions in Peter Comestor," in *Jewish
Quarterly Review*, LIX (July, 1969), pp. 268-89.

15. Théophile Boutiot, *Histoire de la ville de Troyes et la Champagne méridionale*,
Troyes, 1870, Vol. I, p. 249.

16. *Sefer HaOrah*, ed. S. Buber, II, 41: "A question was addressed to the
teacher [i.e., Rashi] concerning a Jew and a non-Jew who owned an oven in
partnership..."

17. *Ibid.*, p. 53: "With regard to your question whether one may hire a

Christian for the festival to carry wooden beams and lumber for purposes of construction..."

18. *Ibid.,* p. 54: "With regard to your question whether one may have horseshoes repaired with nails of iron... one may say... it may be done on the intermediate days [of a festival] by a Christian artisan... but giving clothes to Christian artisans for laundering or repairing... is a contractual arrangement [which is] forbidden [on festivals]..."

19. J. Miller, *op. cit.,* par. 86: "With regard to your question, Reuben, who owed one *litra* [a sum of money] to a non-Jew..."

20. *Sefer HaOrah,* II, par. 56: "Regarding your question whether one may go on a festival to a Gentile whom one knows well and take from him some bundles of grass, or hay, or sheaves, [as fodder] for his cattle..." This question is mentioned also in Elfenbein, *op. cit.,* p. 127, No. 102. The problem was whether it would be a violation of the laws of festival observance if a Jew were to ask a Gentile acquaintance to give him some fodder with which to feed his cattle on the holiday, promising the Gentile that he would return an equal amount of fodder to him after the holiday. The fact that this transaction entailed a promise on the part of the Jew to "repay" the Gentile after the holiday made it resemble a "sale" of sorts, which could be construed as a violation of the festival.

21. *Sefer HaOrah,* II, par. 112: "[An incident] involving a Gentile who made the [unintentional] mistake of removing the stopper from a barrel [of wine] because he was not familiar with things Jewish..." This statement seems to imply that, as a rule, Gentiles in the area where Rashi lived *were* familiar with Jewish customs. In any event, Rashi in this case ruled that the wine left in the barrel after the Gentile had removed the stopper was not forbidden to Jews.

22. J. Miller, *op. cit.,* par. 13. "Furthermore, they testified... that [the deceased] had left her two vineyards and four houses as her property for life..." Par. 91: "Reuben gave his vineyards as a collateral for ten dinars to Shimon, and then he died. It is not known under what conditions [he gave the vineyards as collateral]. His widow subsequently married Levi [i.e., a third party] and she was helped to collect half of Reuben's property [which was hers under the provisions of] her marriage contract [with Reuben] and the other half was left to Reuben's children."

23. I. Baer, "Rashi and the Historical Reality of His Time," *Tarbiz,* Vol. X (1950), p. 221.

24. Quoted in *Patrologia Latina,* CIV, 615.

25. Berakhot 62a.

26. In his commentary on Genesis 47:2 Rashi states, "This is the version of Genesis Rabbah, which is an *aggadah* [roughly: legend] from the Land of Israel."

27. E.g., on Numbers 7:19: "But I have found the following in the work of

Rabbi Moses the Preacher," and on Numbers 26:24: "I have found in the work of Rabbi Moses the Preacher why this was so."

28. E.g., on Numbers 26:24.

29. RaShBaM on Genesis 37:2.

30. Rashi on Deuteronomy 3:23: ("And I besought the Lord at the time..."): "All forms of the verb חנן [of which the Scriptural text used a form to denote 'I besought'] signify an *ex gratia* gift. Although the righteous might cite their good deeds as their claim to a reward, they solicit [the favor] of the Omnipresent only as an *ex gratia* gift."

31. Joseph Bekhor Shor (Numbers 12:7).

32. *Patrologia Latina*, CLXXVIII, 325: "*... ut eas origine sua melius cognosceret ac verius diiudicare posset...* ("To know them in their original, so as to be able to decide more intelligently....")

33. *Patrologia Latina*, CL, 641: "*Nec solummodo christianis, sed et Judaeis in eadem urbe commanentibus erat carissimus, pro eo quod Hebraicam veritatem et caeteris editionibus secernere erat peritus, et in his quae secundum Hebraicam veritatem dicebant, judeorum erat consentiens assertionibus*" ("He was most dear not only to the Christians but also to the Jews who lived in the same city because he was experienced in differentiating between the [true Hebrew text] and other editions, and he agreed with what was claimed to be in accordance with the [true Hebrew text].")

34. B. Altaner, "Zur Kenntnis des Hebraeischen im Mittelalter," in *Biblische Zeitschrift* (Freiburg), XXI (1933), p. 290, par. 3.

35. Rashi on Genesis 33:20; see also on Tractate Shabbat 88b, Sanhedrin 34a: "It may be said that the words of the Torah may be given many different interpretations just as a hammer splits a rock into many different pieces."

36. Rashi's Introduction to his commentary on the Song of Songs; see also Rashi on Genesis 33:20: "I, however, make it my purpose to give the straightforward meaning of Scripture."

37. Rashi on Genesis 3:8: "I am only concerned with the straightforward meaning of Scripture and with such aggadic material as explains the words of Scripture in a way that fits in with them."

38. פשוטו של מקרא: The meaning of the Scriptural word or passage within the context in which it occurs.

39. משמעו של מקרא: Precedes the understanding of the context but is concerned primarily with the understanding of the words as such.

40. a. Rashi on Leviticus 25:14: פשוטו כמשמעו, ("In this instance the literal meaning and the sense of the text are the same."

b. On I Samuel 20:14: ואינו זז ממשמעו ("The literal meaning cannot be changed.")

c. On Deuteronomy 22:26: לפי פשוטו זהו משמעו ("Here the literal meaning must be adjusted [to the sense within the given context.]").

41. Rashi on Genesis 6:3: "But this is the [straightforward] meaning of the text in transparent clarity."

42. Rashi on Lamentations 1:1; see also on Genesis 3:8, Exodus 33:13: "There are many Midrashic explanations... but I am concerned only with the straightforward meaning of Scripture."

43. Rashi on Genesis 1:1; see also on Genesis 25:22: "This verse calls for a Midrashic interpretation."

Page from Rashi's Commentary on the Pentateuch, Reggio 1475.
(The first printed Hebrew book.)

Part III

THE SCHOLAR

CHAPTER FOUR

Rashi's Interpretative Techniques

In his attempt to elucidate the ideas which the Scriptural text seeks to convey, Rashi utilized various Hebrew grammatical rules and interpretative techniques which had already evolved by his time. However, he was highly innovative in his use of linguistic and grammatical devices for his interpretation of the original texts, and this led him to the formulation of concepts radically different from those accepted in the Latin and Greek translations of the Bible that had preceded him by many centuries.

1. Rashi's Use of Prepositions

As a rule, words in an isolated state cannot convey ideas. The coherent expression of ideas requires the arrangement of groups of words into logical thought or sentence formations. Such formations as a rule require the help of prepositions or conjunctions which give the words their proper setting and the whole sentence its real meaning.

The small, seemingly insignificant particles such as את, אף, גם,

כי, which are used so frequently in the Hebrew language, offer endless possibilities. Likewise, the single consonants ב, ה, כ, ל, מ, for which the Hebrew language has devised an infinite variety of uses as prefixes, can best be compared to the cement which is spread between the bricks of a building in order to stabilize the edifice as a whole.

In most modern languages a subordinate clause with a qualifying connotation is introduced by a conjunction other than that which precedes a clause expressing causality, and a preposition signifying direction is not the same as one employed to denote time or place. In the case of ancient languages, however — Greek, Latin and particularly Hebrew — which by the time of Rashi had long fallen into disuse as daily vernaculars, many conjunctions and prepositions seem identical, so that it is left to the reader or listener to sense their meaning in the context of the sentence in which they appear. Thus, the Greek prepositions *hos* and *hoti* have innumerable meanings, and the Latin *qui* and *cum* can be interpreted in a vast variety of connotations. It is in the ability to interpret these particles correctly and logically that the language virtuoso and sensitive master of text reveals himself.

In the case of ordinary literature, this skill may be of secondary importance, but it assumes paramount significance when the texts to which it is applied are Biblical passages which have become the basis of religious and ethical doctrines, philosophies of life and, indeed, in many instances, of life itself. Interpretations of the Scriptural text which have caused upheavals in the history of mankind, which have led some men and women to the stake and others to the highest honors life can afford, frequently hinge on the meaning one attaches to these seemingly unimportant auxiliary particles that weave key words into a fabric of concrete ideas. It is in this special area that Rashi, particularly in his Bible commentary, demonstrates his originality.[1]

Though by no means all translators or grammarians agree with Rashi's concepts and formulations, the fact remains that the fine nuances in which he understood the prepositions and conjunctions in the original text of the Bible gave new meaning to complex Biblical passages. He did not, as translators usually do, limit each Hebrew particle to one specific connotation but gave them idiomatic interpretations.

For instance, the preposition אל, usually rendered as "to," is frequently interpreted by Rashi as if it were על, meaning "into," "about," or "because of." This differentiation becomes significant, for example, in Rashi's interpretation of Genesis 37:35, where Jacob mourns his son Joseph, saying, "I will go down to the grave אל בני." As opposed to other translations, which render אל בני as "*to* my son,"[2] Rashi interprets it as if it were על בני, "*because of* my son." Rashi seems to empathize with Jacob's refusal to be comforted. The father may have felt instinctively that his son might still be alive somewhere. Nevertheless Joseph was obviously lost to Jacob, and while one may eventually be comforted after the loss of a loved one in death, one does not accept consolation for the loss of someone who may still be alive (Genesis Rabbah 84). Jacob found the pain of separation from his beloved son so difficult to bear that he felt he would go down into the grave not *to* his son (who might not be in a grave at all) but *because of* his son, who, though perhaps still alive, was now so far beyond the reach of his father's affection. Rashi supports this interpretation by citing many other Biblical passages to which he has applied the same interpretative device.[3] In his commentary on Numbers 14:14, Rashi interprets אל יושבי הארץ הזאת not as "they [i.e., the Egyptians] will say *to* the inhabitants of this land [i.e., of Canaan]" but as if the preposition אל were equivalent to על; i.e., "they [i.e., the Egyptians] will say *about* [or *concerning*] the inhabitants of this land [i.e., of Canaan]."[4] Moses' plea is that a demonstration of God's wrath aroused by Israel's cowardly refusal to enter the land of Canaan would be interpreted by the Egyptians as a sign of weakness and frustration on the part of the God of Israel. If God were to pour out His anger upon Israel, the Egyptians would assume that unlike Egypt, which had only one king, the Canaanite tribes, with their 31 kings and petty rulers, had proven too formidable for the God of Israel, and that therefore God had permitted Israel to be destroyed. Accordingly, Rashi explains that if God did indeed allow Israel to be annihilated, the Egyptians would express these assumptions not *to* the inhabitants of Canaan, but proclaim them to the world *concerning* the Canaanites. In a similar vein, Rashi in his commentary on Tractate Berakhot 31b considers the particle אל in the reply of Samuel's mother Hannah to the priest Eli as if it were על. Instead of interpreting Hannah's statement "I prayed אל הנער הזה" literally as "I prayed *to* this child" (which would be absurd), her words are to be construed as if she had said על הנער הזה, "I prayed *for,* or *because of,* this child."[5] However, Rashi refrains from citing this interpretation in his commentary on the pertinent verse in the First Book of Samuel. Another conception of the preposition אל suggested by Rashi is that of בשביל ("for the sake of")[6] and עם ("with"). Anxious as ever to leave his reader with an edifying thought, he interprets Lamentations 3:41, "Let us lift our hearts upon our hands to God in the heavens" to mean, "If we lift our hands to heaven then let us lift our hearts along *with* them."[7] Similarly, he comments on Tractate Ta'anit 16a: "Along *with* our hands, we must lift up our hearts to heaven; i.e., in order that we may correct our shortcomings."[8]

The most varied and controversial rendering suggested by Rashi pertains to the particle את, which precedes the object of a sentence. While contemporary Hebrew authors tend to omit this particle for the objective case, Rashi frequently inserts it in order to avoid basic misunderstandings, as in his commentary on Job 30:15: כרוח רעה את נדיבתי: תרדף כרוח נדיבתי "It [i.e. בלהה, the terror] pursues my honor [i.e., my respectability] like an evil spirit."[9]

In many instances Rashi renders את as if it were עם ("with") and thus he diverges considerably from the various translations of the Bible. For example, he interprets Genesis 4:1 — Eve's pronouncement at the birth of her son Cain — קניתי איש את ה' as if את were עם; i.e., as "I have acquired a man *with* [the help of] the Lord." This is an allusion to the Talmudic statement that there are three partners in the creation of every newborn infant: the father, the mother and God.[10] The Septuagint rendering is, "I have acquired a man *through* the Lord;"[11] the Vulgate offers the same translation.[12] Luther in his German translation disregards the preposition את altogether; he translates Eve's statement as, "I have the man, the Lord."[13] The Authorized English (King James) Version reads, "I have gotten a man *from* the Lord." By substituting עם for את, Rashi resolves two other difficult passages in the Book of Genesis; one in 20:16,[14] the other in 49:25.[15] (In the case of the latter passage, most translations disregard the preposition את. In every instance where Rashi follows this device he succeeds in putting his interpretation across without doing violence to the original Hebrew text.)[16]

In other instances Rashi renders את not as "with" but as if it were מן ("from"). Thus in Genesis 6:13, where God announces His decision to destroy mankind והנני משחיתם את הארץ, Rashi comments that את הארץ really means מן הארץ; i.e., God does not say that He will destroy mankind "[together] *with* the earth" but that He will destroy mankind "*from* the earth." Rashi supports this reasoning by citing his interpretation of two other Biblical passages: בצאתי את העיר (Exodus 9:29) is tantamount to בצאתי מן העיר ("When I go forth *from* [not *with*] the city") and חלה את רגליו (I Kings 15:23) is tantamount to חלה מן רגליו ("He suffered *from* his feet"). In the case of the latter verse Rashi conceives of the accusative with the preposition את in the same manner as the accusative in Latin, which frequently has a connotation of "in relation to" or "as to." It is interesting to note the Greek, Latin and German translations of the same verses, which are completely divergent from Rashi's interpretation, with Luther, for instance, rendering Genesis 6:13 as "I will destroy them *with* the earth."[17]

The preposition ב receives a variety of interpretations in Rashi's commentary. He frequently introduces it in order to make the original text more intelligible. Thus, in the case of Genesis 35:7, where Jacob builds an altar to God "and called the place El-Beth-El," Rashi explains אל בית אל by adding the preposition ב in the connotation of "in"; i.e., אל בבית אל, that "אל" (God) is *in* Beth-El." The Septuagint, Vulgate and Luther simply disregard the first אל.[18]

Rashi points out that the Biblical text frequently omits the preposition ב when in fact it should occur as a prefix to a noun,

and he cites several examples to prove his contention; e.g.,
Genesis 45:16: והקול נשמע בית פרעה means נשמע בבית פרעה והקול נשמע בית פרעה ("and
the report of this was heard *in* the house of Pharaoh").[19] In
Micah 1:9[20] Rashi adds the particle ב to מכותיה ("her wounds") to
eliminate the problem of the seemingly ungrammatical use of
an adjective in the singular with a noun in the plural — a
difficulty which was apparently glossed over by both Septuagint and Vulgate.[21] In the case of Psalm 73:21, too, neither
Septuagint nor Vulgate pays attention to the grammatical
inconsistency in וכליותי אשתונן. Both consider כליותי ("my reins") as
the subject of אשתונן ("I was pricked").[22] But this is impossible
since כליותי is a plural noun, while אשתונן is a verb in the first
person singular. Hence Rashi, "While I have sharpened my
thoughts *in* my reins" (ובכליותי). Rashi empathizes with the Psalm-
ist's sense of outrage at the success of the wicked. (The
"reins" or "kidneys" were considered the seat of the human
emotions or passions, while the heart was viewed as the seat of
the intellect; cf. Jeremiah 17:10, "I, the Lord, search the heart, I
try the reins"). He eliminates yet another grammatical difficulty in Daniel 9:25, by adding ב to רחוב, thus implying that
ונבנתה ברחובות, not just the *streets* (רחובותיה) of Jerusalem will be built
again, but Jerusalem will be rebuilt ברחובותיה ("*with* all [her] broad
places"). This difficulty, too, seems to have been ignored in all
the translations, which regard ונבנתה as the *verbum finitum* to
רחוב.[23] In this case Rashi establishes the gender of the word רחוב.

In several instances Rashi substitutes בשביל for the particle ב,
thereby giving the particle a causal connotation. Thus, in the
case of Genesis 6:3 לא ידון רוחי באדם he adds the explanation that
באדם means בשביל האדם ("*because of* man"); the spirit of God shall
not be vexed because of, or on account of, man. The Septuagint[24] and Vulgate,[25] on the other hand, render this verse as
saying that the spirit of God shall *not remain in* man. The King
James Version is in agreement with these two translations.[26]
Luther's interpretation deviates completely from the original
text; his translation is, "Man no longer wants My spirit to be
punished."[27] The differences between Rashi and the Bible
translations in the interpretation of Psalm 142:8 כי יכתירו צדיקים
are noteworthy. Here, again, Rashi interprets כי in the sense of

בשבילי; i.e., David, a most humble individual, declares that "the righteous will crown Him [i.e., the Lord] *because of* me." David hopes that his deliverance will strengthen the righteous in their faith and motivate them to come closer to God. The Septuagint[28] and the Vulgate,[29] on the other hand, translate the verse as "the righteous shall expect me," while Luther translates it as "the righteous will gather around me."[30] Perhaps Rashi was aware of the Christological implications of these three translations: the idea that the righteous are waiting for, or rallying around, the suffering son of the Davidian dynasty, who will come as the Messiah to redeem the world.

Another common preposition which lends itself to a variety of connotations is ל. Like the Latin accusative of direction, which is used primarily in connection with places, Rashi frequently inserts the particle ל to signify direction or relationships.[31] Rashi adds ל to the noun ארץ ("land") in Isaiah 9:18 (usually translated as, "through the wrath of the Lord of Hosts is the land burned up"), explaining that, in view of the masculine form of the verb in the sentence, the subject of the sentence cannot be ארץ, which is feminine, but must be the masculine עשן ("smoke") from the preceding verse (Verse 17). Rashi's conception, based on grammatical considerations, gives Verse 18 a much less fearsome connotation than does the conventional translation. The land is not literally burned up through God's wrath; it is merely "the smoke [caused by God's wrath] that has settled לארץ [*over* the land]."[32] In Ezekiel 32:20 the combination חרב נתנה (lit. "the sword is given") is noted by Rashi as unacceptable. He therefore adds ל to חרב, making the phrase read לחרב נתנה ("She [i.e., Egypt] is given [or delivered] *to* the sword").[33] Again based on grammatical considerations Rashi, in the case of Numbers 34:17, interprets לכם (*to* you") as if it were בשבילכם ("*for* you"), for if one were to accept the Septuagint and Vulgate renderings the verb of the sentence should be in the causative *hiph'il*, not in the simple *kal* inflection, which it takes here.[34]

Rashi insists on accounting for every word in the original Biblical text. Thus, Numbers 17:5 ends with the word לו.[35] On the face of it, this word appears misplaced, and indeed most translators either ignore it as superfluous or else regard it as belonging with the verb דבר ("spoke") and therefore as equivalent in meaning to אליו ("*to* him").[36] Rashi, however, explains that לו is equivalent to עליו ("*about* him" or "*concerning* him"), so that the verse ends with the phrase "just as the Lord spoke to Moses *concerning him* [i.e., Aaron]."

2. Conjunctions

The particle ו is interpreted by Rashi in a great variety of meanings, much as the Greek *kai* and the Latin *et*, too, may be given any number of connotations other than "and." In some instances Rashi conceives of ו as a conditional particle ("if");[37] in other cases he takes it to denote purpose ("in order that").[38] Thus, unlike all the translations of Proverbs 7:15, which consider the ו in ואמצאך[39] as a conversive particle and hence render the verse as "To seek Thy face *and* I have found Thee,"[40] Rashi interprets ו in this instance as denoting purpose; i.e., "To seek Thy face *in order to* find Thee."[41]

In other instances Rashi has the particle ו denote choices or alternatives, as if it were או ("or"). In his commentary on Exodus 12:5 (concerning the Paschal sacrifice) he employs this interpretation to point out that the term שה (which is usually rendered as "sheep") may be a collective noun referring either to כבשים ("sheep") or עזים ("goats").[42] In other words, the Passover sacrifice requires not both a sheep *and* a goat, but *either* a sheep *or* a goat. Rashi notes that שה in this instance occurs in the singular;[43] the Septuagint disregards this and translates the phrase as if שה were in the plural; i.e., "from the sheep *and* the goats."[44] On the other hand, in the case of Exodus 21:15, where we are told of the death penalty to be meted out to a child who strikes his father or his mother, both the Septuagint and the Vulgate correctly render ו not as "and" but as "or" ("and he who smites his father *or* his mother").[45]

In view of the differences between the legal concepts of גר ("stranger" or "alien") and תושב ("settler"), Rashi interprets the expression גר ותושב in Leviticus 25:35 (lit. "as a stranger *and* a settler [shall he live with thee]") to mean גר או תושב ("whether he be a stranger *or* a settler [he shall live with thee]"). This fine distinction, too, escaped the attention of the Greek and Latin translations.[46]

In his commentaries on the Talmud, too, Rashi differentiates between the use of the particle ו as "and," on the one hand, and "or," on the other, to forestall any possible misunderstanding of fine legal points.[47] In this connection, too, note Mishnah Eruvin I:2, where the schools of Shammai and Hillel discuss detailed technical aspects of Sabbath observance.[48]

Sometimes Rashi construes ו as explaining or identifying the word immediately preceding, in the sense of the Latin id est.[49] He himself on occasion uses the particle ו in this connotation. For instance, he obviously knew that Avtzan and Boaz are identical: hence, if he says עתניאל ואבצן ובועז[50] he must mean עתניאל ואבצן שהוא בועז; i.e., not "Othniel and Avtzan and Boaz" but "Othniel and Avtzan, that is, Boaz" (as corrected by Solomon ben Yehiel Luria).

In other instances Rashi understands the use of the particle ו as a conjunction introducing a temporal clause. Thus, in Genesis 32:32 ("the sun rose on [or "for"] him... and he limped..."), the account of the injury to Jacob's thigh resulting from his struggle with the angel, there is no cause-and-effect relationship between the shining of the sun and Jacob's limping. Rashi cites the Midrashic explanation implying that the sun rose "for the sake of Jacob," namely, for the purpose of healing him, but he does this only in order to justify the Hebrew לו ("on him" or "for him")."[51] The shining of the sun was not the cause of Jacob's limp. Rashi explains the verse to mean that when the sun began to shine it became apparent that Jacob was limping.[52] The sunrise and Jacob's development of a limp happened independently of one another.

The conjunction כי is fairly common in the Hebrew language. Like the Latin quod and quia or the Greek hoti it has many different connotations and hence is also interpreted by Rashi in a variety of ways. As early a source as the Talmud cites Rabbi Shimon ben Lakish as saying that the conjunction כי is used in four different connotations: "If," "perhaps," "but" or "because."[53] One of Rashi's responsa includes a rather lengthy discourse dealing with the various possible connotations of כי.[54]

Accordingly, too, Rashi interprets the כי in Exodus 34:9 not as
because or *for* but as if it were אם ("if"). Moses asks God to forgive
Israel not *because* it is a stiff-necked people but *[even] if* it is a
stiff-necked people.[55] It was without doubt his love for his
people that induced Rashi to mitigate the harshness implicit in
the causal interpretation given to כי in all the translations.[56]

Rashi's interpretation of the statement כי קרבן ה' לא הקריב
("because he did not bring the [Passover] offering of the Lord"
— Numbers 9:13)[57] is most interesting. He insists that in this
case כי is not causal; i.e., it is not intended to introduce the
reason why the soul of an individual who failed to bring the
Passover offering should be "cut off from his people." Rather,
כי in this verse marks the beginning of a new thought.[58] The
text accordingly means, "But the man who is [ritually] pure
and is not on a journey, and [yet he] fails to bring the Passover
offering, that soul shall be cut off from his people. If — [*not*
"because"] — he did not bring the offering of the Lord in its
appointed season, that man shall bear his sin." This construction of the verse would justify the interpretation according to
which "its appointed season" in this case refers to *Pessah Sheni*,
the "Second" or "Lesser" Passover, on Iyar 14, which comes
exactly one month after the true Passover and on which those
who were unavoidably prevented from bringing the Passover
offering on the true Passover have an opportunity to make up
for their omission.

Elsewhere, Rashi interprets כי in the sense of possibility —
as tantamount to פן or שמא ("lest" or "perhaps"). According to
Rashi's commentary on Exodus 20:22 the use of hewn stones
in the construction of the altar is forbidden not *because* (or *if*) an
iron cutting tool is used in the operation (an iron tool has
connotations of war and destruction) but *lest* the stones be
defiled by having been hewn with an iron cutting tool.[59] Rashi
applies a simliar interpretation of כי in the case of Exodus 23:5,
where we are told to help even the donkey of our enemy if we
see the animal about to collapse under its burden. He rejects
out of hand the idea that a human being should have to be told
how to behave in such a situation. "*If [*כי*] thou seest the donkey of him
who hates thee*: Is it *possible* that thou couldst see the donkey and

refrain from helping him?"[60] Again, in connection with Deuteronomy 7:17, "If [כי] thou wilt say in thy heart, 'These nations are more than I'....: Is it *possible* that thou wilt say in thy heart that, 'Because of their multitude I will be unable to expel them?' Do not say such a thing!"[61]

Apart from these more common interpretations, Rashi in several instances accords to כי connotations which make the Pentateuchal passage appear in an interesting new light. In his commentary on Exodus 15:19 (referring to the disaster that overtook Pharaoh and his hosts at the Red Sea) he construes כי as denoting not *"for"* ("*for* the horses of Pharaoh went in with his chariots and with his horsemen into the sea") but as a concept of time, as if it were כאשר ("when"); i.e. "*When* the horses of Pharaoh went in....."). Verse 20 then follows quite logically: "[It was then that] Miriam, the prophetess... took a timbrel [and led the women in a hymn of thanksgiving]."[62] Similarly, Rashi interprets Deuteronomy 32:3 כי שם ה' אקרא not as "*for* I will proclaim the Name of the Lord; ascribe ye greatness to our God" but in the sense of "*when* I will proclaim the Name of the Lord [you will join in giving Him praise]."[63]

In his interpretation of Isaiah 57:16 Rashi appears to take issue with the Christian theologians when he stresses כאשר רוח האדם שהוא מלפני שניתן בו מאתי יעטף יודה ויכנע על מעלו: The Lord declares that "I shall not be wroth forever when [for once] the spirit of man — which was given by Me — will surrender and admit its iniquity; likewise the souls which I have made." In other words, once the spirit of man surrenders and admits that it has sinned, God will relent from His wrath. This is in notable opposition to the Septuagint and Vulgate interpretations, both of which read, "As the spirit comes forth from My face."[64] In his explanation of Ecclesiastes 8:6 (usually rendered as "for everything there is a time and judgment, *for* the evil of man is great upon him"), Rashi says, "*For the evil of man is great upon him:* This means, '*When* the evil of man is great upon him.'" He thus establishes a logical connection between evil and its punishment: *When* (or once) the measure of evil has overflowed, the time of "judgment" will have come.[65] The Greek and Latin translations indicate no logical link between the two concepts.

More rarely, Rashi sees כי in a comparative connotation in the sense of "just as,"[66] or a concessive one, in the sense of "although" or "nevertheless."[67].

3. Verbs

Rashi's acquaintance with the rules governing the Hebrew verb stems from writings of the 10th-century philologists Menahem Ibn Saruk and Dunash Ibn Labrat of Spain. The former was the author of *Mahberet Menahem*, a dictionary of the Hebrew language; the latter, a poet, wrote an exhaustive criticism of the dictionary.

However, it would be erroneous to assume that Rashi followed these two contemporaries without reservations. Some of the Hebrew verbs (פ״י, פ״נ, ל״ה, פ״א, ל״א)* which Ibn Saruk and Ibn Labrat regard as bi-literal (having a root composed of two letters only) are classed by Rashi as tri-literal (having a three-letter root).[68] Rashi disagreed with these two philologists also with regard to the formation of verbal nouns.[69] The correct and sensitive understanding of the tenses is a most intricate aspect of Hebrew grammar, rather divergent from the rigid, systematic categorization that prevails in European languages. Rashi's sense for the Biblical text helped him gain the correct understanding of the functions inherent in the Hebrew verb tenses. "It frequently happens in simultaneous action," he observes, "that it is expressed in some instances in a past tense form and in other instances in the form of the future tense. In either case, however, the connotation is one of simultaneity."[70] Or, "the idea of frequentative action is expressed randomly by the future tense or by the past tense because any action that occurs continually has already occurred in the past and will occur again in the future."[71]

4. The Role of Accents in Rashi's Commentary

A printed or written text can rarely — if ever — be under-

---

*First root letter, *yod*; first root letter, *nun*; third root letter, *he*; first root letter, *aleph*, and third root letter, *aleph*.

stood in the exact manner and sense originally intended by its author. In the case of translations from the original language into another it must be expected that much of the meaning of the original will be lost, since each language has not only specific words expressing its own highly individual concepts but also carries with it imponderables which cannot be adequately reproduced in any other language. But this is true even of written texts in which no translation is involved; the author's words set down on paper can hardly be expected to convey the full meaning intended by the author, complete with all the personal moods and sensibilities which influenced his work.

It is for this reason that almost every literate language has evolved its own system of punctuation and accentuation. The Greek system of accents (*acutus, gravis* and *circumflexus*) aids us primarily in the correct pronunciation and accentuation of individual words. The accent marks of the Hebrew language, however, may do more than that; they frequently indicate the actual meaning of words and verb forms which are, in many instances, derived from similar roots. In fact, the Hebrew accent marks are referred to as טעמים, literally, "meanings." In the Hebrew language, a slight change of accents on words with identical spelling indicates that the words, though spelled in the same way, do not have the same root and hence do not have the same meaning. Accents can connect or separate word groups and inject a variety of nuances into the text.

In the case of the Hebrew Bible, the transmitters of the text, always mindful of the fact that they were dealing with a book sacred to all mankind, exercised painstaking care to preserve the traditional text in as accurate a form as possible in order to avoid misinterpretations and to adhere as closely as possible to what they considered to have been the true intent of the transmitted text. For this reason the Hebrew Bible has been "protected" from misconstruction by an elaborate system of accents and diacritical marks whose purpose far transcends that of mere phonetic devices. The accent system used in the written text of the Hebrew Bible performs an ambitious task: it attempts to reproduce the fine vocal intonations and stresses used by the savants of antiquity to convey their interpretation of the text as they recited it before vast audiences. In his *Kuzari* Judah HaLevi writes:

> And in this remnant that was left in our Divinely-created language there are very fine and profound matters ingrained for the purpose of understanding and replacing those movements which operate in face-to-face encounters. These are the *te'amim* [accents] with the aid of which the Bible is to be read — where to pause and where to continue, question and answer, subject and predicate, where to read fast and where to slow down, where in tones implying a command and where in tones implying a request. Whole books could be written on this subject.[72]

Further on, Judah adds, "The creator of this fine science possessed secrets not known to us, though perhaps we have discovered some of them [since]."[73]

The accents פיסוק הטעמים are already mentioned in the Talmud. In Nedarim 37b and Megillah 3a the statement in Nehemiah 8:8 ויבינו במקרא ("and [they] caused them to understand the reading [of the Law]") is explained to mean that the teachers of the Law mentioned in the text taught the people how to separate the words of the text into sentences with the help of the accents.[74]

The accent marks do not appear in the Torah scrolls kept in the Ark and used for the Pentateuchal readings at public religious services, but they are inserted in the *humashim*, the printed editions of the Pentateuch.

Undoubtedly טעמים in some form were already known early in the history of the Jewish people, for the Levites who chanted the Psalms and other sacred texts in the Temple in Jerusalem had to know when to raise or lower their voices and when to vary their intonation. The מנצח ("conductor" or "songmaster") certainly knew how to signal stresses and stops. However, it seems that at least until the Tannaitic period the טעמים had been transmitted by oral means only, not in the form of universally accepted written marks, because we find R. Hisda expressing uncertainty about a halakhic ruling which hinged on the accentuation for the word עולות ("burnt offerings") in Exodus 24:5.[75] Isi ben Judah alludes to five Biblical verses where the lack of accent marks leads to ambiguous interpretations.[76] In the course of time, it became increasingly difficult to read the Biblical text properly without accent marks, and we may safely assume that by the end of the fifth century C.E. the טעמים had evolved into a system of marks introduced into the written text.

Rashi paid strict attention to the accents.[77] "Had I not seen the accent...." he admits in his commentary on Ezekiel 1:11, "I would not have known how to explain [this passage] but the *zakef gadol* mark teaches us that the[se] two words ["their faces" and "the wings"] are to be separated from one another."[78] Also, he seems to object to a wrong accentuation which led Jonathan ben Uziel to mistranslate another passage in the Book of Ezekiel.[79]

In his painstaking care to adhere strictly to the transmitted Biblical text, Rashi in numerous passages diverges from the many interpretations which seem either to have ignored the accents or else failed to understand them. Noting the disjunctive *tippha* under the word אחי (in Genesis 10:21), Rashi is inclined to consider Japhet to be older than his brother Shem,[80] not vice versa. As a matter of fact, Sanhedrin 69b, too, states that Japhet was the eldest of Noah's sons.[81]

The dove which Noah sent from the Ark returned with an olive leaf which it had plucked with its mouth (Genesis 8:11).[82] This interpretation (as distinct from the rendering "... in her mouth an olive leaf freshly plucked") accords with the disjunctive *tippha* under the word זית ("olive") and the conjunctive accent which links טרף ("plucked") with בפיה ("in her mouth"). Rashi construes טרף as a verb and enters into a lengthy discourse demonstrating that יונה ("dove"), though usually in the feminine gender, is masculine in this particular passage.[83]

The accent mark on the penultima in פחז כמים ("unstable as water") (Genesis 49:4) leads Rashi to the conclusion that the word פחז is a segholate noun denoting instability rather than a verb implying an act of having acted recklessly. For if פחז had been intended as a verb, the accent would have been placed on the ultima and on its vowels *kamatz patah*.[84] The Septuagint translates פחז as a verb form; i.e., "thou hast run riot,"[85] without having any grounds for adding the pronoun "thou." The Vulgate, in a similar vein, renders פחז as "thou hast broken out,"[86] while Luther conceives of פחז as a verb in the past tense,[87] the very thing Rashi sought to forestall.

In explaining a difficult passage in the Book of Habakkuk (3:9) ("sworn are the rods of the word") Rashi states that the accent on the penultima in אמר proves that it is a segholate noun, not a verb, as understood by the Greek and Latin translations.[88] Accordingly, he explains the passage as follows: "Thy [i.e., God's] might is obvious; the oath which Thou hast sworn to the [twelve] tribes is a word for eternity."[89]

In his comment on Job 14:9 Rashi emphasizes that נטע ("plant")[90] is a segholate noun, since it has the accent on the penultima. Without this accent the word could be erroneously interpreted by the reader as a verb in the perfect tense. Rashi points out the pausal position of the noun as affecting the *seghol* to be changed into *kamatz*. Nevertheless, both the Septuagint and Vulgate wrongly translate נטע as if it were a verb,[91] and, oddly enough, as one in the passive mood.[92]

In Proverbs 17:10 ("A rebuke enters deeper into a man of understanding than a hundred lashes administered to a fool") Rashi insists that תחת is a noun[93] ("fear" or "embarrassment") because its accent on the penultima excludes the possibility that it might be a verb form[94] as construed by all the translations. Thus, "The embarrassment of a rebuke enters deeper into a man of understanding," etc. It is indeed puzzling how these translations accommodate the preposition ב preceding מבין, which is to be dependent on the root נחת. Rashi's insistence upon the correctness of his interpretation is accentuated by the fact that he reiterates his view in his comment on Berakhot 7a.[95] The Septuagint appears to have noticed the problem of the preposition ב and translates the passage as if the text were לב מבין ("the heart of a man of understanding").[96]

In the case of Job 34:16 Rashi diverges completely from all other interpretations; he bases his interpretation on the accentuation of the word בינה; he interprets it as an imperative ("understanding this") rather than as a noun ("[if thou hast] understanding").[97]

Similarly, in the case of Proverbs 23:7 ("as one who has reckoned within himself, so is he...") Rashi emphasizes that the word שער[98] is a verb and not a noun, because the accent is on the final syllable. In his interpretation of שער as a verb he cites the passage in Jeremiah 29:17 ("I will... make them [i.e., the people of Jerusalem] like vile figs that cannot be eaten") which he, on the same grammatical basis, interprets to imply that "the heart of a miser is full of vileness even though he encourages thee to eat."[99] It is interesting to note that in his commentary on Sotah 38b Rashi cites the interpretation of Menahem Ibn Saruk,[100] who associates שער with the noun שיעור ("measuring"). Indeed, the Septuagint wrongly interprets the word as if its first letter were not a *shin* (ש) but a *sin* (ש) and hence it translates the word as "hair"(!)[101] Luther renders it as "demon,"[102] while the Vulgate combines the latter interpretation with the one suggested by Ibn Saruk.[103]

In many instances Rashi seeks to demonstrate that the accents determine the tenses of verbs — the most important components of a sentence. In the Hebrew language the accent frequently indicates the tense of a verb, particularly in verb forms with identical spellings. Rashi pays meticulous attention to these forms, which occur mostly in the ע"ו* and ע"ע** verbs, where the accent very often determines whether the verb is to be understood as a present or as a past form. Thus in his comment on Genesis 18:20 Rashi emphasizes that because of its accentuation the adjective רבה implies a past, not a present, form of "to be great;" i.e., "the cry of Sodom and Gomorrah *was* great," not "*is* great."[104] With regard to Genesis 15:17 he points out that the smoking of the furnace seen by Abraham occurred after the sun had set, not — as implied by most translations — "at the time of the sunset."[105] In Genesis 42:21 the verb באה is in the past tense ("...*has* this distress *come* to us").[106] In Genesis 46:26,27, where we are given the number of the descendants of Jacob and Joseph, respectively, who migrated from Canaan to Egypt, the differentiation between the present tense with

---

*Second root letter *vav*.
**Second and third root letters identical.

the accent on the ultima in Verse 26, on the one hand, and the past tense with the accent on the penultima in Verse 27, on the other, serves to resolve the seeming contradiction between the figures "threescore and six" (Verse 26) and "threescore and ten" (Verse 27). The present tense signifies the number of individuals who actually left Canaan with Jacob, while the past tense indicates the number of those who, as we might put it today, "hailed" from Canaan, which would include Joseph and his Egyptian-born progeny.[107] In the case of Isaiah 26:11 neither the Septuagint nor the Vulgate seems to have noticed that רמה[108] expresses a past, not a present form; i.e., "Lord, Thy hand *was* lifted up," not "...*is* lifted up." In Deuteronomy 33:23 the verb ירשה[109] is interpreted by Rashi as an imperative (i.e., "*possess thou* [the sea]") because of the accent above the *resh* (ר). In support of his interpretation he cites several examples of the "lengthened" form of the imperative.[110] The Septuagint and the Vulgate, on the other hand, apparently construe ירשה as a future form of a root רשה ("will possess").[111]

Yet another purpose served by the accents is to separate or connect two adjacent words; this device has a decisive effect on the meaning of the passage involved. Rashi acknowledges the importance of this function of the accents when he notes, in his comment on Ezekiel 1:11, that if he had not seen the disjunctive *zakef gadol* on the word ופניהם, he would not have known how to explain the prophet's description of the creatures he beheld in his vision. "The account," he says, "taught me to isolate the word ופניהם[112], and the verse is to be explained as follows: *And they had faces:* and their wings were separated above their faces and covered them... "The same applies to Verse 18: "*As for their backs:* they have height and inspire fear." The word גביהם ("their backs") is to be separated from the word that follows.[113] Neither the translation in the Septuagint, nor that in the Vulgate, both of which connect the words ופניהם and כנפיהם, seems logical.[114]

It is interesting to note how, in his comment on Deuteronomy 11:30, Rashi interprets אחרי as an adverb of place and not as a preposition, because of its disjunctive accent. He further proves his point by citing the *dagesh* in the next word, דרך, which should have begun with a *dalet raphe* if אחרי had been intended as a preposition to which דרך should be linked.[115] Hence, the meaning of the passage is, *"Beyond* the Jordan, westward, through the wilderness...." None of the translations took notice of this interpretation, which is based on the correct grammatical construction of the original text.[116]

Also in Deuteronomy, Rashi explains what seems to be an inconsistency of the expressions ספר התורה הזה ("...in this book of the Law" — Deuteronomy 29:20) and ספר התורה הזאת ("...in the book of this Law" — Deuteronomy 28:61). In his explanation, he cites the accents which connect, or separate, respectively, the word תורה and the demonstrative pronoun that follows it.[117]

At times it appears — if one may suggest this — that Rashi makes use of accents as a mnemonic device of sorts whenever he wants to commend a particular law or concept to the reader's special attention. Thus, in the case of Joshua 7:15 ("And it shall be that he who is taken with the devoted thing shall be burned with fire, he and all that he has"), he points to the disjunctive *zakef* over באש ("with fire"), which differentiates between the destruction of the possessions of Achan, son of Carmi, and the punishment to be meted out to Achan himself according to Verse 25 ("And all Israel stoned him [i.e., Achan] with stones, and they burned them [i.e., his possessions] with fire, and stoned them with stones").[118] According to Rashi's explanation, the destruction by fire applies to Achan's possessions only. His personal punishment will not be death by fire but execution by stoning. Apparently, Rashi alludes to the question raised by Rabina (Sanhedrin 44a), who was puzzled by the Biblical text which, on the face of it, seems to imply that the punishments of burning and stoning were applicable both to Achan and his possessions.[119] Rashi's interpretation of Isaiah 45:1 כה אמר ה' למשיחו לכורש... ("Thus says the Lord to His anointed, to Cyrus, whose right hand I have held"),[120] which echoes that of R. Nahman in Megillah 12a, is intended to stress that Cyrus, King of Persia, was not to be equated with the "anointed" of the Davidian dynasty. Rashi substantiates R. Nahman's interpretation by pointing to an unusual phenomenon: In this passage there is a *zarka*, which in every other instance is followed by a *seghol,* but which in this instance is followed by a *ma'arikh (merkha)* for the explicit purpose of separating the word למשיחו ("to His anointed") from כורש ("Cyrus").[121]

5. *Rearrangements of Word Order in the Biblical Text (מקרא מסורס)*

"Let Scripture be explained in its literal sense, so that each statement will fit into its proper context,"[122] Rashi urges in a commentary on a passage in the Book of Exodus. It appears that at times his desire to fit each statement "into its proper context" induced Rashi in his interpretations of the Biblical text to rearrange the word order of a verse if in his opinion the original word order made the verse difficult to understand or subject to misinterpretation. As a master of style, intimately acquainted with the spirit of the Hebrew language, Rashi sensed at once when the components of a sentence were not in proper order from the point of view of syntax or logic. In rearranging words within a Biblical verse, Rashi cited in his support Canon 31 of the 32 canons set down by Rabbi Eliezer ben Rabbi Jose HaG'lili for the interpretation of Scripture. ("Rabbi Eliezer, the son of Rabbi Jose HaG'lili, says, 'The Torah is to be interpreted in accordance with 32 canons.'").[123] Canon 31 states:

> "Early in the text but late in the substance." How is this to be understood? One case in point: [The verse] *"And the lamp of God was not yet gone out, and Samuel lay down to sleep in the Sanctuary of the Lord"* [I Samuel 3:3]. It is not permissible to sit down in the Sanctuary. Certainly, therefore, one is also not permitted to lie down there. For the only ones permitted to sit down even in the court of the Temple are kings of the Davidian dynasty, as it is written: *"And King David went in and sat before the Lord"* [II Samuel 7:18]. What, then, could be the meaning of [the statement that] *"Samuel lay down"?* The position of this phrase is too "early in the text;" the text should read, *"And the lamp of God was not yet gone out in the Sanctuary of the Lord, and Samuel lay down to sleep."*[124]

Oddly, Rashi has an entirely different conception of what Samuel did. He follows Targum Jonathan, suggesting that "Samuel lay down in his place in the section reserved for the Levites who guarded the Sanctuary. This is [also the understanding of] Targum Jonathan, which reads, 'And Samuel lay down in the Levites' section.'"[125]

Although the case in point cited by Rabbi Eliezer ben Rabbi Jose HaG'lili entails an obvious rearrangement of the text, the term סרס (lit., "disarrangement") does not appear in his canons. We first encounter this term in Bava Bathra 119b, where it is suggested by Rabbi Ishmael, who was perturbed by the disrespectful context in which the name of Moses seems to appear in Numbers 27:2, the story of the daughters of Zelophehad. According to the text, the daughters of Zelophehad, claiming their inheritance, went first to Moses, then to the High Priest Eleazar, then to the leaders and finally to the people. Rabbi Ishmael says that this makes it appear as if the women had refused to abide by Moses' ruling in their case and had appealed his decision before the high priest and the leaders, all of whom ranked below Moses. Since the women could not possibly have acted in this manner, Rabbi Ishmael suggests a "rearrangement" of the verse in such a manner as to accord Moses his proper place as the final authority.[126].

It will become apparent, however, that the suggested textual rearrangements are not a *sine qua non* for the understanding of the Biblical text since, for every explanation based on such a rearrangement, we will find, on the spot, an opposing view which offers an explanation that does not require a "rearrangement" of the original text.[127] Nevertheless, Rashi uses the "rearrangement" method for making changes in a text which otherwise could not be understood or would be in danger of being misinterpreted. It is interesting to note that many of the textual "rearrangements" suggested by Rashi in his interpretations were actually incorporated into some of the Bible translations that were produced after Rashi's death.

Genesis 41:57 states that at the time of the famine וכל הארץ באו מצרימה לשבר אל־יוסף (literally, "all countries came to Egypt to buy corn *to* Joseph"). Rashi transposes the words לשבר ("to buy corn") and אל־יוסף ("to Joseph") because he could find no precedent in the Biblical text that would have justified his interpreting the particle אל ("to") as if it were מן ("from"). Accordingly, he interprets the passage as follows: *And all countries came to*

Egypt to buy corn to Joseph: They came to Egypt, to Joseph, to buy corn...." The Septuagint translates the verse as if the original text had read מן יוסף ("from Joseph"). The Vulgate evades the issue by simply omitting the reference to Joseph: "All the provinces came to Egypt in order to buy corn..."[128] Only the King James Version takes notice of the textual problem and renders the passage as, "All the countries came into Egypt to Joseph for to buy corn."

A literal reading of Numbers 19:7 ("...and afterwards he may come into the camp and the priest shall be unclean until the evening") would make it appear as if a priest who had been impure may return to the camp after having bathed and washed his garments, even though in fact he remains impure until that evening. Rashi rearranges the word order of this passage to read, "....he shall be unclean until the evening and afterwards he may come into the camp," thus resolving what would appear to be a contradiction in the text. None of the translations takes note of this obvious contradiction, much less attempts to resolve it.[129] The King James Version reads, "....he shall come into the camp and shall be unclean until the even." Only the translation of the Pentateuch published by the Jewish Publication Society of America in 1962 and the Jerusalem Bible seem to indicate awareness of the problem. They use the conjunctions "but" (i.e., "he may reenter the camp *but* shall be unclean until evening") and "though" (i.e., "He may reenter the camp *though* he shall be unclean..."), respectively.

In I Samuel 2:29 Eli and his sons are rebuked for enriching themselves from the offerings made by the people of Israel. However, the word לעמי[130] presents a difficulty in the proper understanding of the text. It cannot mean "to My people." Rashi eliminates the problem by rearranging the verse so that לעמי is transferred from the end to the middle of the verse so that it can be rendered as "in public." The verse then reads, "Thou honorest thy sons more than Me *in public* by fattening thyself from every gift of Israel..."[131] None of the translations resolves this difficulty, with the result that לעמי is mistranslated[132] as "My people [i.e., Israel]."

In II Samuel 3:27 we are told that Joab took Abner aside into the midst of the gate to speak with him. This sentence ends with the word בשלי,[133] the meaning of which in this particular context is somewhat obscure. The Septuagint renders it as *en paralogismo* ("deceitfully"); the Vulgate as *in dolo* ("in fraud," "in deceit"). Both renderings link it with "to speak with him" (Septuagint:... *lalesai pros auton;* Vulgate:... *ut loqueretur ei*). But neither of these two adverbs properly describes the manner in which Joab spoke with Abner. Rashi interprets בשלי as בשגגה ("inadvertently"). He transposes the word בשלי from the end of the verse to its logical place; i.e., after ויטהו יואב ("And Joab took him aside"), and he has the verse say that Joab inadvertently took Abner into the gate to speak with him.[134] Apart from offering this logical interpretation, Rashi seems to accept Menahem Ibn Saruk's explanation of the root של as being equivalent to שגגה[135], as opposed to more recent linguists who connect the word בשלי with שלו ("quietly").[136]

In the original Hebrew, the first part of Isaiah 66:16 ("For by fire will [the Lord] contend [נשפט], and by His sword with all flesh") seems to lack a subject. Rashi, however, maintains that נשפט, though a passive form, can be construed as an active form implying mutuality; namely, the act of being both "contender" and "judge","[137] a dual capacity describing the Lord. The Septuagint,[138] probably not aware that the verb נשפט can be used as a deponent in this case (i.e., "will [the Lord] judge [or contend]..."), arbitrarily supplies as a subject "the earth" ("for in the fire of the Lord the whole earth is judged"), for which there is no justification in the original text. The Vulgate obscures the meaning of the verse even more by adding the preposition *ad* ("to") before the noun *carnem* ("flesh"), lit. "and in His sword to all flesh."[139] Only the King James Version, which follows the rearrangement suggested by Rashi,[140] comes closest to a meaningful translation: "For by fire and by His sword will the Lord plead with all flesh."

In its Hebrew original, Jeremiah's simile of the potter's work (18:4: "And whensoever the vessel that he made of the clay was spoiled in the hands of the potter, he made it again another vessel, as seemed good to the potter to make it")[141] can bear out the simultaneity of God's word and action ("At one

instant I may speak concerning a nation..." — 18:7,9)[142] only if
the verse is rearranged as explained by Rashi: "...which he
makes of clay broken in the hand of the potter while it is still
moist."[143] Here again, both the King James Version and Luther
follow Rashi's interpretation. (*King James:* "And the vessel that
he made of clay was marred in the hand of the potter." *Luther:*
"And the pot... was spoiled while in his hands.")[144]

A superficial reading of Jeremiah 24:5 would make it appear
as if God meant to say He had sent Judah into Babylonian exile
for a good purpose ("So will I regard the captivity of Judah
whom I have sent out of this place into the land of the Chaldeans for good").[145] This concept seems to be supported also by
the Septuagint ("Just as [I recognize] these good fig trees, so
shall I again recognize the uprooted of Judah, whom I have sent
away from this place to the land of the Chaldeans for good")
and the Vulgate ("Just as [I recognize] these good figs, so shall I
recognize the transplants of Judah, whom I have sent out from
that place into the land of the Chaldeans for good")[146]. In order
to correct this misconception Rashi links the word לטובה ("for
good") with אכיר ("will I regard" or "will I recognize"). In this
manner the intent of the verse becomes clearer. God does not
consider it "a good thing" that the people of Judah were sent
out of their land into exile; rather, He declares that He will give
credit, as it were, to the people of Israel for their exile.[147]

The Hebrew text of Hosea, Chapter 8, Verse 2, is most
ambiguous.[148] Many translations reflect this predicament,
without, however, attempting to resolve it. (*Septuagint:* "To Me
they cry out: O God, we know Thee!" *Vulgate:* "They will
invoke Me: My God, we know thee, Israel." *Luther:* "Then they
will cry unto Me: Thou art my God. We know thee, Israel").[149]
Rashi's transposition of the words "Israel" and "God" so as to
make the verse read: "Israel shall cry out to Me: My God, we
know Thee!"[150] clarifies the meaning of this verse. Here again,
only the King James Version ("Israel shall cry out unto Me: My
God, we know Thee!") concurs with Rashi's interpretation.

The original text of Psalm 17:7 הפלה חסדיך מושיע חוסים ממתקוממים
בימינך cannot be understood without re-positioning the word
בימינך ("thy right hand" plus the preposition ב). The preposition

ב belongs either to חוסים or to מושיע but not to ממתקוממים. The Septuagint clarifies nothing by its verbatim rendering ("Saving those who trust in Thee from those who oppose Thy right hand").[151] The Vulgate attempts to overcome the difficulty by attaching the second part of Verse 7b to Verse 8a: "Saving those who trust in Thee. From those who oppose Thy right hand protect me like the apple of the eye."[152] Luther: "Show Thy wondrous goodness, O Thou Savior of those who trust in Thee, to those who rise up against Thy right hand."[153] Rashi removed the problem by rearranging the word order of the text, thus, "To save with Thy right hand those who put their trust in Thee from those who rebel."[154] Once again, only the King James Version ("O Thou that savest by Thy right hand them which put their trust in Thee") agrees with Rashi's interpretation.

In the case of Psalm 22:30[155] Rashi is alone in his interpretation of דשני ארץ ("the fat of the land") as the object of ענוים ("the humble ones" — in Verse 27); i.e., "The humble shall eat all the fat of the land and worship."[156] All the translations consider דשני ארץ as the subject of Verse 30. (*Septuagint, Vulgate and Luther:* "All the fat [ones] of the land shall eat and bow down."[157] *King James Version:* "All they that be fat upon earth shall eat and worship"). The most recent commentaries, however, explain the verse in a manner similar to Rashi.[158] Judging by the theme of this psalm, which, according to Rashi, is the cry of Israel in exile, Rashi's interpretation of Verse 30 seems to be more appropriate to the spirit of the psalm than the version given in the standard translations.

In order to give some sense to Verse 2 of Psalm 36[159] ("The transgressions of the wicked says within my heart: There is no fear of God"), the Septuagint reads the noun לרשע ("to the wicked") as if it were a verb ("being wicked") and reads לבי ("my heart") as לבו ("his heart"), referring to פשע ("transgression"), which is not vocalized; thus, it can be read פושע ("the sinner"), i.e., "The sinner speaks of sinning within himself: There is no fear of God."[160] Rashi eliminates all the difficulties by moving בקרב לבי ("within my heart") to the beginning of the verse; thus, "It seems to me that פשע [transgression] i.e., the evil inclination, says to the wicked: There shall be no fear of God before you."[161]

In the case of Psalm 45:6[162] ("Sharp are thy arrows; nations fall before thee amidst the enemies of the king") the question arises whether בלב should be construed literally as "in the heart" or as a metaphor ("amidst"). Using his technique of rearrangement, Rashi decides in favor of the former interpretation ("Thy arrows are sharp in the heart of the king's enemies").[163] Though the metaphorical interpretation makes little sense, it is nevertheless maintained by the Septuagint ("Thy arrows are sharpened... nations fall amidst the enemies of the king") and the Vulgate ("Thy arrows are sharp; nations fall amidst the enemies of the King").[164] The King James Version, however, follows Rashi's suggestion: "Thine arrows are sharp in the heart of the king's enemies."

In his interpretation of Proverbs 12:27[165] ("But the precious substance of men is to be diligent") Rashi demonstrates how a light touch can help explain obscurely-worded statements. Also, again by means of textual rearrangement, he decides that חרוץ, which can connote either "gold" or "diligence," should be interpreted in this case in the latter sense: "The possessions of a diligent man are precious."[166] The Vulgate, however, accepts the literal interpretation, which is much less satisfactory: "The possessions of man are worth [the price of] gold."[167]

The instances of Rashi's textual rearrangements cited here are far from exhausting the subject. However, they are sufficient evidence of Rashi's profound impact on later Bible translations. They present one of the many varied methods employed by Rashi to bring the Bible closer to the heart of the ordinary reader. Rashi was too pious to tolerate wanton corruptions of the original text of the Bible; yet, his genius enabled him to penetrate deeply into the spirit of Scripture. A combination of profound religious faith and unique intellectual gifts gave Rashi the courage to attempt to solve occasional complexities in the Biblical text. Identifying himself with the spirit no less than with the letter of the Bible, and always mindful of the great overall purpose of the text, he was not concerned with petty technical details. Though at times he was puzzled by the text, he never underrated the importance of any word or words included in it. He also paid close attention to the style and syntactic peculiarities of each Biblical verse.

One of the 32 canons of Biblical interpretation enumerated by Rabbi Eliezer ben Rabbi Jose HaG'lili is the concept of the "elliptical verse."[168] Rashi maintains that the elliptical sentences in the Bible omit the subject of the verb because that subject is considered to be self-understood.[169] Similarly, some elliptical verses may be explained by the logical consequences they imply[170]

NOTES

1. E.M. Lipschuetz, *Raschi*, Tuschijah, Warsaw, 1914, p. 40.

2. *Septuagint: Pros ton hyion mou;* Vulgate: *Ad filium meum;* Luther: *Zu meinem Sohne;* King James Version: To my son.

3. E.g. I Samuel 4:21: אל הלקח ארון האלוקים :כמו על הלקח ("...*because* the Ark of God was taken").

II Samuel 21:1: אל שאול :על עון שאול ("*because* of the sin of Saul").

4. Both Septuagint and Vulgate simply ignore the אל. Luther renders it as *zu* ("to"); the King James Version, "...to the inhabitants."

Additional examples in Rashi where אל is interpreted as על:

II Samuel 3:18: אמר אל דוד :אמר על דוד ("*Said to David:* Said concerning David").

Jeremiah 11:23: אביא רעה אל אנשי ענתות :כמו על אנשי ענתות ("*I shall bring evil to the people of Anathoth:* [To be interpreted as] *because of* the people of Anathoth").

5. I Samuel 1:27: אל הנער הזה התפללתי :על הנער הזה. ([Lit.:] *To this child I have prayed:* For this child I have prayed").

6. See Rashi on I Samuel 20:34: נעצב אל דוד :בשביל דוד. ("[Lit.:] *Grieved to David:* On account of David").

And on Nehemiah 5:1: אל אחיהם היהודים :בשביל אחיהם היהודים. ("[Lit.:] *Then there arose a great cry... to their brethren the Jews:* On account of their brethren the Jews").

7. נשא לבבנו אל כפים :כשאנו נושאים את כפינו אל השמים נשא אף לבבנו עמהם.

8. עם הכפים צריך לישא לבו לשמים, כלומר שיחזור מקלקולו.

9. The Septuagint renders this verse as: *Ocheto mou he elpis hosper pneuma* (My hope has gone like the wind)."

Vulgate: *"Abtulisti quasi ventus desiderium meum* (Thou hast taken away my hope like the wind)."

Luther: *"Schrecken hat verfolgt wie der Wind meine Herrlichkeit* (Terror has pursued my glory like the wind)".

See also on Isaiah 49:13: נחם ה' עמו :את עמו, עמו ("The Lord has comforted His people").

And on Psalm 34:22: תמותת רשע רעה: תמותת את הרשע הרעה שהוא עושה. ("*Evil shall kill the wicked:* The evil that he does will kill the wicked").

The Septuagint renders this passage as: "*Thanatos hamartolon poneros* (The death of sinners is painful)."

Vulgate: *Mors peccatorum pessima* (The death of sinners is painful)."

Luther most closely follows Rashi: "*Den Gottlosen wird das Unglueck toeten* (Misfortune will kill the godless one)."

10. The allusion is to Niddah 31a: "There are three partners in the creation of every man: his father, his mother, and the Holy One, blessed be He."

11. *Ektesamen anthropon dia tou theou.*

12. *Possedi hominem per deum.*

13. *Ich habe den Mann, den Herrn.* A rather obscure rendering.

14. ואת כל ונוכחת: ועם כל באי עולם...יהיה לך פתחון פה להתוכח. ("Thou wilt be able to defend thyself against [lit., "with"] all the people of the world").

Septuagint: *Kai panta aletheuson* ("And everything will be truthful").

Vulgate: *...hoc erit tibi in velamen oculorum... et quocumque prerexeris, mementoque te deprehensam* ("This will be for thee a covering [i.e., a proof in thy favor]... and wherever thou goest... and remember that thou wert embarrassed...").

Luther: *... und allenthalben; und das war ihre Strafe* ("and under all circumstances; and this was her punishment").

King James Version: "... and before all men thou art righted."

15. ואת שדי ויברכך: ועם הקב"ה היה לבך... והוא יברכך ("*And by the Almighty Who shall bless thee:* And thy heart was with the Holy One, blessed be He... and He shall bless thee").

Septuagint: *Kai eboethese soi ho theos ho emos* ("And my God has helped thee").

Vulgate: *...et omnipotens benedicet tibi benedictionibus* ("And may the Almighty bless thee").

Luther renders ואת parallel to מאל אביך: *...und von dem Allmaechtigen bist du gesegnet* ("and from the Almighty thou art blessed").

The King James Version follows Luther: "By the Almighty...."

16. Additional examples:

a. Exodus 2:24: ....את בריתו את אברהם את יצחק ואת יעקב: עם אברהם. ([Lit.:] *His covenant, Abraham, Isaac and Jacob:* [His covenant] with Abraham...").

b. Numbers 8:26: ושרת את אחיו: ושרת עם אחיו. ([Lit.:] *And thou shalt minister their brethren:* And thou shalt minister with their brethren").

c. Isaiah 49:25: ואת יריבך: ועם מריבִיך. ([Lit.:] *Who contends thee:* Who contends with thee").

d. Jeremiah 32:11: את החתום: עם התימתו. ("With its signature").

17. Septuagint: *Kataphtheiro autous kai ten gen* ("I shall destroy them and the earth").

Vulgate: *Disperdam eos cum terra* ("I shall destroy them with the earth").

Luther: *Ich werde sie verderben mit der Erde* ("I shall destroy them with the earth").

Even more divergent interpretations:

a. Exodus 9:29: מן העיר: כצאתי את העיר ([Lit.:] *When I go forth the city:* [When I go] forth from the city").

Septuagint: *Hos an exeltho ten polin* ("When I have left the city").

Vulgate: *Cum egressus fuero de urbe* ("When I have left the city").

Luther follows Rashi most closely: *Wenn ich zur Stadt hinauskomme*. More correctly, in modern German parlance: *Wenn ich von der Stadt hinauskomme* ("When I will come out of the city").

b. Exodus 32:3 ...מנזמי: מזהב הזה: ויתפרקו כל העם את נזמי הזהב ("*And all the people broke off the golden·rings that were in their ears:* [They unloaded themselves from] the golden rings..."). פרק is a term denoting the unloading of a burden. Since this is a transitive verb, one would expect ויפרקו rather than the *hitpael* form. What Rashi means is that when they unloaded the golden rings from their ears they themselves became unburdened of their earrings; hence "they unloaded themselves" is the proper usage.

18. Septuagint: *Kai ekalese to onoma tou topou baithel*)"And he called the name of the place Beth El").

Vulgate: *...et appelavit nomen loci illius Domus Dei* ("and he called the name of that place the House of God").

Luther: *...und hiess die Staette El Bethel* ("and he called the place El Bethel").

19. Additional examples:

Deuteronomy 22:21: בבית אביה. :לזנות בית אביה ("[Lit.:] *To harlot [i.e., debauch, pollute] her father's house:* [Debauch] in her father's house"). By stressing the ב ["in"] Rashi apparently seeks to avoid the idea that she might be ruining the reputation of her parental home by polluting or debauching the home. She "ruins" only herself, not her father's house.

I Samuel 2:29: במעוני. :אשר צויתי מעון ("[Lit.:] *Which I have commanded habitation:* In My habitation").

20. Micah 1:9 כי חולה היא במכותיה. :כי אנושה מכותיה ("[Lit.:] *For her wound is hopeless:* For she is sick with her wounds").

21. Septuagint: *Hoti katekratesen he plege autes* ("Because her wound has prevailed").

Vulgate: *Quia desperata est plaga eius* ("Because her wound is hopeless").

22. Septuagint: *Kai hoi nephroi mou elloiothesan* ("And my reins have changed").

Vulgate: *Et renes mei commutati sunt* ("And my reins were changed").

Luther (reflecting Rashi's influence?): *Es sticht mich in meinen Nieren* ("It pricks me in my reins").

23. Septuagint: *Kai oikodomethesetai plateia* ("The street will be built").

Vulgate: *Et rursum aedificabitur platea* ("And the street will be rebuilt").

Luther: *So werden die Gassen wieder gebaut werden* ("Thus the streets shall be rebuilt").

24. *Ou me katameine to pneuma mou en anthropois* ("My spirit shall not remain in man").

25. *Non permanebit spiritus meus in homine* ("My spirit shall not remain in man").

26. My spirit shall not abide in man.

27. *Die Menschen wollen sich meinen Geist nicht mehr strafen lassen.*

28. *Eme hypomenousin dikaioi.*

29. *Me expectant justi.*

30. *Die Gerechten werden sich zu mir sammeln.*

Additional examples:

Daniel 10:12: באתי בשליחות זו בשביל דבריך :באתי בדבריך ("*I have come in thy words:* I have come on this errand because of thy words"). The Septuagint renders this passage literally: *Kai ego elthon en tois logois sou* ("I have come in thy words"). Vulgate: *Et ego veni propter sermones tuos* ("I have come because of thy words"). Luther: *Und ich bin gekommen um deinetwillen* ("And I have come because of thee").

Nehemiah 9:17: בשביל מרי שלהם :במרים ("*And in their rebellion:* Because of their rebellion"). Here the Septuagint reads במצרים ("in Egypt") instead of במרים ("in their rebellion").

31. E.g. Exodus 13:18: כמו לים סוף :דרך המדבר ים סוף ([*"Lit.:*] *By way of the wilderness of the Sea of Reeds:* [To be interpreted as if the text read], 'To the Sea of Reeds.'").

Septuagint: *eis* ("towards" or "into").

Vulgate: *juxta* ("along [the Sea of Reeds]").

Luther: *am Schilfmeer* ("along the Sea of Reeds").

Also Deuteronomy 29:9: ראשיכם לשבטיכם :ראשיכם שבטיכם ("*Your heads your tribes:* The heads of your tribes").

32. Septuagint: *Synkekautai he ge hole* ("The whole earth was consumed by fire").

Vulgate: *Conturbata est terra* ("The earth was thrown into confusion").

Luther: *Ist das Land verfinstert* ("has the land grown dark").

33. Vulgate: *Gladius datus est* ("The sword is given").

Luther: *Das Schwert ist schon gefasst* ("The sword has already been taken up").

34. ינחלו לכם :בשבילכם. ולא יתכן לפרש לכם זה ככל לכם שבמקרא, שאם כן היה לכתוב ינחילו לכם, ינחלו משמע שהם נוחלים.

("[These are the names of the men who] *shall take possession of the land for you:* It would not be correct to explain this לכם as one does לכם in all the other Biblical passages where it occurs, for had this been so it should have been written

ינחילו לכם [in the *hiph'il* inflection], 'They will give the possession to you.' But ינחלו [*kal* inflection] implies that they themselves are to take possession").

כאשר דבר ה' ביד משה לו: כמו עליו, על אהרון דבר אל משה. 35.
("*As the Lord said to him by the hand of Moses:* [To be interpreted as if the text read] 'concerning him.' As He [the Lord] spoke to Moses concerning Aaron").

36. Septuagint: *Katha elalese Kyrios en cheiri Moyse* ("Just as the Lord said through Moses").

Vulgate: *Loquente Dominus ad Moysen* ("As the Lord had said to Moses").

Luther: *Wie der Herr ihm geredet hatte durch Mose* ("As the Lord had spoken to him through Moses").

King James Version: "As the Lord spoke unto him."

37. Several examples:

a. Leviticus 10:19: ואכלתי חטאת: ואם אכלתי חטאת
("*And I had eaten the sin offering:* And if I had eaten the sin offering").

b. Numbers 12:14: ואביה ירק: ואם אביה ירק
("*Her father had spat:* And even if her father had spat").

c. Judges 6:13: ...ויש ה' עמנו: ואם
("*And the Lord is with us:* If the Lord is with us").

d. Ruth 2:9: וצמית והלכת: ואם תצמאי
("*Thou art thirsty, go:* And if thou art thirsty, go").

e. Malachi 1:7: ואמרתם: כלומר ואם תאמרון
("*And you say:* And if you should say").
Septuagint: *Kai eipate* ("And you said").
Vulgate:*Et dicitis* ("And you said").
Luther: *So sprecht ihr:* ("And you say").

38. Several examples:

a. Numbers 17:5: ...ולא יהיה כקרח: כדי שלא יהיה
("*And he will not fare like Korah:* In order that he may not fare like Korah").

b. Isaiah 51:14: ולא ימות לשחת: כדי שלא ימות לשחת
("*And he shall not go down dying into the pit:* In order that he may not go down dying into the pit").

c. Jeremiah 5:28: דין לו דנו דין יתום ויצליחו: למען יצליחו
"[Lit.:] *They do not plead the cause, the cause of the fatherless they might make it prosper:* In order that they might prosper").
Septuagint: (Apparently omits "in order that they might make it prosper"):
Krisin orphanou kai krisin cheras ouk ekrinosan ("They do not plead the cause of the orphan or the cause of the widow").
Vulgate: *Causam viduae non judicaverunt, causam pupilli non direxerunt et judicium pauperum non judicaverunt* ("They do not plead the cause of the widow and they do not direct the cause of the orphan").
Luther: *Dem Waisen foerdern sie die Sache nicht und gelingt ihnen* ("They do not promote the cause of the orphan and they prosper").

לשחר פניך ואמצאך 39.

40. Septuagint: *Heureka se* ("I have found Thee").
Vulgate: *Et reperi* ("And I have found Thee").
Luther: *Und habe dich gefunden* ("And I have found Thee").

41. כדי שאמצאך

42. מן הכבשים ומן העזים: או מזה או מזה ("*From the sheep and from the goats:* From either the one or the other").

43. שה תמים זכר...שיים *Sifthei Hakhamim* points to the reason why Rashi interprets the foregoing in the sense of "either-or"; namely, because it is written שה (singular), not שיים (plural).

44. *Apo ton arnon kai ton eriphon.*

45. Septuagint: *Patera e metera.*
Vulgate: *Patrem aut matrem.*

46. Septuagint: *Hos proselytou kai paroikou* ("As a stranger and a settler").
Vulgate: *Quasi advenam et peregrinum* ("As a stranger and a settler").
But Luther: *Einem Fremdling oder Gast* ("A stranger *or* a guest").

47. Three examples:
a. Yevamot 66a: שנשא אשה וקנה עבדים: או קנה... ("*One who married a wife and purchased [Canaanite] slaves:* Or purchased [Canaanite] slaves..."). The complete Talmudic text implies that all the members of a priest's household who are regarded as his personal property (wives and slaves) are entitled to partake of the *terumah* set aside for the use of the priests. This provision is applicable not only if the priest has a wife *and* slaves but also if he has only a wife *or* only slaves.
b. Shabbat 71a: קצר וטחן: קצר או טחן ("*He who harvests and grinds:*He who harvests *or* grinds"). Either harvesting *or* grinding—not just a combination or harvesting *and* grinding—is to be construed as a violation of the Sabbath.
c. Bava Kamma 111b: הגזל... והניח לפניהם... או שהניח... ("*He who steals.... and leaves [the stolen property] to his children:* Or leaves [the stolen property] to his children"). Children are under no legal obligation to make restitution for property stolen by their father and turned over to them by him. This holds true regardless of whether they had already used up the property *or* whether the father had left them the stolen property outright at the time of his death and the children are still in possession of it.

48. בית שמאי אומרים לחי וקורה ובית הלל אמרים לחי או קורה ("The School of Shammai says that a vertical pillar *and* a horizontal barrier are needed. The School of Hillel says, either a vertical pillar *or* a horizontal barrier"). This refers to the sealing off of a public highway so that objects may be carried on it on the Sabbath.

49. E.g. Leviticus 25:47: גר ותושב: גר והוא תושב ("*A stranger and a settler:* A stranger; that is, a settler").

Septuagint: *Proselytou e paroikou* ("A stranger or a settler").

Vulgate: *Advenae atque peregrini:* ("A stranger and a resident alien").

50. Sanhedrin 36a.

51. ויזרח לו לצרכו לרפאות את צלעתו: כשיצא מבאר שבע מיהרה לזרוח בשבילו
("And [the sun] rose for him [i.e.,] for the purpose of healing his lameness: When he left Beersheba the sun set before its time on his account").

52. היה צולע כשזרחה השמש ("He was lame when the sun rose").

53. Cf. Rosh HaShanah 3a, Ta'anit 9a and at the end of Gittin and Shevuot.

54. Rashi's *Responsa*, ed. I. Elfenbein, No.251.

55. "If now I have found grace in Thy sight, O Lord, let the Lord, I pray Thee, go in the midst of us, for it is a stiff-necked people, and pardon our iniquity and our sin, and take us for Thy inheritance."

56. Septuagint: *Ho laos gar skelerotrachelos esti* ("For it is a stiff-necked people").

Vulgate: *Populus enim durae cervicis est* ("For it is a stiff-necked people").

Luther: *Denn es ist ein halsstarrig Volk* ("For it is a stiff-necked people").

57. והאיש אשר הוא טהור ובדרך לא היה וחדל לעשות הפסח ונכרתה הנפש ההיא מעמיה כי קרבן ה'
לא הקריב במועדו חטאו ישא האיש ההוא.

58. ולא קאי אדלעיל מיניה לפירוש טעמא דמילתא דמילתא קמייתא כמו לשון דהא אלא מילתא אחריתא היא.
כמו כי יקרא, כי תכלה לעשר, כי תפגע.

("It does not refer to the antecedent explaining the reason for the first thing mentioned, as if to say 'because' but it is a separate thing, similar to 'When it happens to you....'")

Note to 57 and 58: Tractate Pesahim 93a cites three opinions regarding the punishment to which one is liable if one fails to bring the Paschal offering on time (the "Second Passover" is on Iyar 14):

1. *Rabbi:* One incurs [the penalty of] *kareth* [being "cut off"] on account of having failed as regards [the offering] of the "first [Passover]" and one [also] incurs *kareth* on account of [having failed to bring the offering] on the "Second Passover." (Rabbi holds that the "two Passovers" are independent of one another.)

2. *R. Nathan:* One incurs *kareth* on account of the "first [Passover]" but one does not incur it on account of the second.

3. *Hanania ben Akabia:* One does not incur *kareth* even on account of the "first [Passover]," unless he [deliberately] fails to keep the second.

All these opinions are based on Numbers 9:13. Rashi holds that Rabbi can derive his opinion only if he reads כי as indicating the beginning of a new thought.

59. כי חרבך הנפת עליה: הרי כי זה משמש בלשון פן שהוא דילמא, פן תניף חרבך
("The word *ki* is used here in the sense of *pen*, which signifies 'perhaps' [not

'because'] but *perhaps* it will happen that thou wilt lift up thy iron tool above it").

60. ‏כי תראה חמור שונאך: שמא תראה... וחדלת מעזב לו.‏

61. ‏כי תאמר בלבבך רבים הגויים האלה: שמא תאמר בלבבך מפני שהם רבים... אל תאמר כן.‏
("*If thou wilt say in thy heart, 'These nations are more than I [I will be unable to dispossess them]: Is is possible that thou wilt say in thy heart....").

62. ‏כי בא סוס פרעה... כאשר בא סוס פרעה.‏

63. Septuagint: *Hoti* ("Because [I will proclaim....]").
Vulgate: *Quia* ("Because [I will proclaim...]").
Luther: *Denn ich* ("For [I will proclaim...]").

64. Septuagint: *Pneuma gar par emou exeleusetai.*
Vulgate: *Quia spiritus a facie mea egredietur.*

65. ‏כי רעת האדם רבה עליו: כאשר רבה רעת האדם וסאתו גדושה אז באה פקודתו. ו "כי" משמש בלשון "כאשר".‏

66. Examples:
a. Isaiah 44:3:
‏כי אצק מים על צמא... אצק רוחי על זרעך: כמו שאני יוצק מים על צמא כן אצק רוחי על זרעך.‏
("*For I will pour water upon the thirsty land... I will pour out My spirit upon thy seed:* Just as I pour water for him who is thirsty so shall I pour out My spirit upon thy seed").
Septuagint: *Hoti ego doso hydor* ("As I shall give water...").
Vulgate: *Effundam enim aquas* ("For I shall pour out water...").
Luther: *Denn ich will Wasser giessen* ("For I will pour water...").
King James Version: "For I will pour water."

b. Proverbs 30:33:
‏כי מיץ חלב יוציא חמאה: כאשר תצא חמאה ע"י מיץ חלב כן יצא ריב ע"י מיץ אפים.‏
("*For the churning of milk brings forth butter:* Just as butter is brought forth when milk is churned, so contention will come forth from the discharge of the nose [i.e., from anger as signified by the organic symptom!]").
Septuagint: *Amelge gala kai estai boutyron* ("Press out milk and it will turn into butter").
Vulgate: *Qui autem* ("If one presses an udder...").

67. Genesis 48:14:
‏שכל את ידיו כי מנשה הבכור: יודע היה כי מנשה הבכור ואף על פי כן לא שת ימינו עליו.‏
("*Guided his hands deliberately, for Manasseh was the first-born:* Although he knew that Manasseh was the first-born, he did not place his right hand upon him").

68. Nehemias Kronberg, *Raschi als Exeget*, Halle a/S., 1882, p. 15. See also H. Englander, "Rashi's View of the Weak ע"ע and פ"נ Roots," in *Hebrew Union College Annual*, Vol. VII, p. 399.

69. *Ibid.*, p. 18.

70. Examples:
a. On Genesis 24:25:

וכן כל לשון הווה פעמים שהוא מדבר בלשון עבר... ופעמים בלשון עתיד.

b. Numbers 9:15: יהיה על המשכן: כמו הוה על המשכן

("[*The cloud] was on the Tabernacle:* [This should be interpreted to mean that the cloud] constantly hovered over the Tabernacle").

c. On Numbers 23:23: ד"א יאמר ליעקב אינו לשון עתיד אלא לשון הוה

"Another explanation: יאמר ליעקב does not express what is to take place in the future but what takes place in the present." Israel is not in need of diviners to predict the future for them because their present-day leaders will tell it to them כעת, when the time or the occasion requires it.

d. On II Samuel 22:7: כן דרך לשון הוה מדבר לשון עבר ולשון עתיד בפעם אחת

("This is the way with the present tense: It can connote either past or future").

71. a. On Genesis 29:3:

כי לשון הווה משתנה לדבר בלשון עתיד ובלשון עבר שכל דבר ההוה תדיר כבר היה ועתיד להיות

b. I Samuel 27:8: ויעל דוד: לשון הוה הוא, תמיד היה רגיל בכך

("*And David... went up:* This means the present tense; i.e., that he was accustomed to doing it all the time").

72. Vol. II, par. 72.

73. *Ibid.,* end of par. 80.

74. Nedarim 37b: "The [separation of words into sentences through] accents has been commanded in the Torah because Rav Ikka bar Abin said in the name of Hananel [who had said it] in the name of Rav '... they caused them to understand the reading' [Nehemiah 8:8]. This means that they were taught how to separate [the] words [of the text] into sentences by means of the accents."

Megillah 3a: "But did not Rav Ikka bar Abin say in the name of Rav Hananel and Rav that 'and they caused them to understand the reading' referred to the dividing of words into clauses by means of the accents?"

75. Haggigah 6b: "Rav Hisda sought an explanation for Exodus 24:5: 'And he sent the young men of the Children of Israel who offered burnt offerings and made peace offerings of oxen to the Lord.' Does this mean that they made burnt offerings of sheep and peace offerings of oxen, or did they use oxen for burnt offerings as well as peace offerings? How can this inconsistency be resolved? Mar Sutra replies: By the accents (the disjunctive accent separates 'burnt offerings' from 'peace offerings' or having a conjunctive accent to connect the two types of sacrifices)."

Rashi: "It depends on the accents. If it is your opinion that two kinds of animals are involved, you would have to place a disjunctive accent after 'they made burnt offerings' just as we read it nowadays. But if [it is your opinion that] it is only one kind of animal, you would have to read it with a conjunctive accent."

It seems that the problem was resolved in Zevahim 115b: "Rabbi Assi said: Use the disjunctive accent [i.e., meaning that only one animal was involved]."

76. Yoma 52a: "Isi ben Judah says: There are in the Torah five verses which are not clear because of a syntactic ambiguity. The place of the following five words is ambiguous: *Lifted up, almond-shaped, tomorrow, cursed* and *rise."*

Genesis 4:7: Can be read either as: "If thou doest well — good! but thou must bear [lift up] the sin if thou dost not do well," *or* as: "If thou doest well, there will be forgiveness [i.e. "lifting up" of face"], but if thou dost not do well, sin crouches at the door..."

Exodus 25:34: Can be read either as: "And in the Menorah were four cups made like almond blossoms, its knobs and its flowers," *or* as: "Four cups, its knobs and flowers shaped like almond blossoms."

Exodus 17:9: Can be read either as: "Go out and fight Amalek tomorrow; I shall stand on top of the hill," *or* as: "Go out and fight Amalek; tomorrow, I shall stand on top of the hill."

Genesis 49:7: Can be read either as: "And in their self-will they sought to hough an ox; cursed be their anger, for it was fierce..." *or* as: "They sought to hough a cursed ox. Their anger was fierce.." If the first reading is accepted, then the verse refers to the effort of Simeon and Levi to kill Joseph, who is referred to as a "first-born bullock (בכור שורו)" in Deuteronomy 33:17. If the second reading is accepted, then the verse refers to the anger of Simeon and Levi against Shechem, a descendant of Canaan who had been "cursed" (Genesis 9:25).

Deuteronomy 31:16: Can be read either as: "Behold, thou art about to lie with thy forefathers, and this people will rise up," *or* as: "Behold, thou art about to lie with thy forefathers, and wilt rise up [again]. This people will go astray..."

Cf. also Jerusalem Talmud, Avodah Zarah II:7; Tanhuma BeShalah 26; Mekhilta BeShalah to Exodus 17:9 and Genesis Rabbah 80:5.

In Exodus 17:9 it indeed appears to be doubtful whether the word מחר ("tomorrow") belongs with בעמלק ("with Amalek") or with אנכי נצב ("I will stand [on top of the hill]"). Our present accentuation links the word with the latter part of the verse by placing an אתנחתא under עמלק. The Septuagint, however, links מחר with עמלק; thus, "fight Amalek tomorrow.": *parataxai to Amalek aurion.*

In Exodus 25:34 משקדים ("almond-shaped") is separated from גבעים ("cups") by an אתנחתא. The Septuagint, however, connects the two thus: *Krateres ektetypomenoi karyiskous* ("almond-shaped cups").

77. In his comment on Kiddushin 71a Rashi refers to the accents as טרופ, apparently derived from the Greek *tropos* or the Latin *tropus* ("manner of chanting").

78. On Ezekiel 1:11.

79. On Ezekiel 47:19: "The word נחלה mentioned here is equivalent to 'to the river' [locative ה], but I found the translation [in Aramaic]: *ahasana* [i.e., "inheritance"]. Had it [i.e., the word נחלה] not been accentuated on the ultima here — and I have seen the word נחלה occur [elsewhere] with an accent on the penultima, and there really is no binding tradition [Mesorah] in matters of

accent—I would have said it is an error and Jonathan did not translate it so [i.e., as *ahasana*, "inheritance"], but that the *karaim* [i.e., the experts in text and accentuation; cf. Rashi Ta'anit 27b: *Rabbi Hanina Kara...*] made a mistake."

80. If this were to mean "the elder brother of Japhet," the words should have been accented אֲחִי יֶפֶת. The status constructus (אחי) is almost always accentuated with a disjunctive accent if the noun (in this case יפת) is followed by an adjective or a pronoun, thus emphasizing the unity of the latter two. Similarly, we will always see ספר תורה הזאת with a disjunctive *(tippha)* under ספר to emphasize the unity of תורה and זאת. On the other hand, if the pronoun זה refers to ספר we will see a conjunctive *(merkha)* under ספר.

Septuagint: *Adelpho Iapheth to meizoni* ("The elder brother of Japhet").
Vulgate: *Fratre Japhet majore* ("The elder brother of Japhet").
Luther: *Japhet des groesseren Bruder* ("Brother of Japhet the elder"). (It seems that Luther was deliberately ambiguous in his translation).

81. יפת הגדול שבאחיו הוא ("Japhet was the eldest among his brothers").

82. Septuagint: *Eiche phyllon elaias karphos* ("She held an olive leaf, a little twig, in her mouth").
Vulgate: *Ramum olivae virentibus foliis* ("A twig of an olive, with fresh leaves, in her mouth...").
But Luther: *Ein Oelblatt hatte sie abgebrochen und trug es in ihrem Mund* ("She had broken off an olive leaf and bore it in her mouth").

83. "I say it is a male bird."

84. פחז כמים: Jacob addresses his son Reuben, telling him that because he is no more stable than water, he will not enjoy the privileges which otherwise would have been rightfully due him.

85. *Exhybrisas hos hydor.*

86. *Effusus es sicut aqua* ("Thou hast broken out like water").

87. *Er fuhr leichtsinnig dahin, wie Wasser* ("He moved along lightheadedly, like water").

88. וטעמו למעלה שהוא שם דבר.

89. Septuagint: *Legei kyrios* [sic].
Vulgate: *Quae locutus es* ("As Thou hast said")
Luther seems to have omitted the word altogether in his version.

90. "It grows branches like a plant."

91. Septuagint: *Hosper neophyton* ("As if newly planted").
Vulgate: *Quasi cum primum plantatum est* ("As if it had been newly planted").

92. As if it were נִטָּע.

93. תחת גערה במבין.

94. "The word תחת here has the accent on the penultima; this occurs nowhere else in Scripture. Therefore I say that [here] it is a noun [denoting] 'fear' or 'embarrassment.'"

95. *"Tehat:* Accentuated on the penultima under the *tav* cannot be compared with *ve'al tehat* ["And do not be afraid" — Deuteronomy 1:21], where the accent is under the *het*. Rather, the accent is under the first *tav* to show that it is a noun. It cannot be understood as a verb in the active mood; i.e., 'thou wilt subdue man;' rather, it is the rebuke that will subdue man. This is why the accentuation was changed to show that the word is a noun."

96. Septuagint: *Syntribei apeile kardian phronimou* ("A threat crushes the heart of the wise").

Vulgate: *Plus proficit correptio apud prudentem* ("Reproach is more useful to the wise").

Luther: *Schelten schreckt mehr* (from the root חתת) *an dem Weisen* ("A scolding instills more fear into the wise").

97. *"And if you will understand this statement: Binah* is not a noun [in this instance] but an imperative form, similar to 'Understand my meditation' [Psalm 5:2]. Consequently, in each of these instances the accent is on the *bet*, while wherever else *binah* occurs, the accent is on the *nun."*

98. כי כמו שער בנפשו

99. "The word *sha'ar* is vocalized half *patah* and half *kamatz* and is accentuated on the ultima. It is therefore a verb and not a noun, for if it were a noun it would have had a *kamatz* and its accent on the penultima as is the case in every other instance where *sha'ar* occurs in the Biblical text. The answer is as follows: It is as if the one who eats has injected bitterness into the soul of the miser. The word *sha'ar* refers to the bitter figs" (Jeremiah 29:17).

100. *Mahberet Menahem,* ed. Zvi Philipowsky, 1854, p. 178.

כי כמו שער בנפשו במשלי (כג, ז) כמו שיעור.

101. *Ei tis ketapioi tricha* ("Just as one swallows a hair").

102. *Denn wie ein Gespenst ist er inwendig. Er spricht: Iss und trink* ("For inside he is like a demon. He says: Eat and drink...") Luther apparently construes שער as derived from שעיר ("ghost" or "demon").

103. *Quoniam in similitudinem arioli et conjectoris aestimat quod ignorat* ("For like a prophet and a soothsayer he makes conjectures about things he does not know").

104. "Every [other] time the word *rabbah* occurs in Scripture it has its accent under the *bet*; accordingly, it is translated as 'it is great' or 'it is growing.' In this instance, however, the accent is on the *resh*; consequently, it is translated here as 'has become great.'"

105. "*Ba'ah* with its accent on the penultima is to be interpreted as 'it [i.e., the sun] had already set.' Had the accent been on the *aleph*, it would have to be interpreted as, 'while it [i.e., the sun] was setting.' It is, however, impossible to say this, because it has already been stated, 'And it came to pass when the sun was about to set.' However, the smoking furnace appeared only after this.

Accordingly [this statement must be interpreted as saying that] the sun had already set."

Septuagint: *Epei de ho helios egenoto pros dysmas* ("When the sun came to [the point of] setting").

Vulgate: *Cum ergo occubuisset sol* ("When the sun was going down").

But Luther: *Als nun die Sonne untergegangen und finster geworden war* ("When the sun had gone down and it had grown dark").

106. *"Ba'ah elenu.* The accent is on the *bet;* therefore [the verb] is in the past tense; i.e., 'It has come.'"

107. *"All the souls that came with Jacob:* Every soul that left Canaan to go to Egypt. The word *ha-baa'h* ["coming"] in this instance is not a past tense form but a participle with a relative present sense... for this reason the accent is on the ultima, on the *aleph,* because when they left, coming from the land of Canaan, there were only 66 of them. But the second time the word occurs — 'Every soul of the house of Jacob which came into Egypt were 70' — it is a past tense form and therefore its accent is on the penultima, on the *bet.* For when they came [to Egypt], they were [indeed] 70 because they found Joseph and his two sons there, and Jokhebed was added to their number between the walls."

108. "Every [other] time the expression *yad ramah* ["lifted hand"] occurs in Scripture the accent is on the ultima, but in this instance the accent is on the penultima, meaning, 'The hand of Thy strength has been removed from Thine enemies and has become invisible.'" Rashi means, "A hand lifted so that it shall be invisible;" i.e., they do not understand that their success comes from the hand of the Lord.

Septuagint: *Hypselos sou ho brachion* ("Thy arm is exalted").

Vulgate: *Exaltetur manus tua* ("Thy hand is exalted").

Luther: *Deine Hand ist erhoehet* ("Thy hand is raised").

109. ים ודרום ירשה

110. שמעה, ידעה, סלחה, לקחה ("Hear," "know," "forgive," "take").

111. Septuagint: *Thalassan liba kleronomeseis* ("Thou wilt come into possession"). This is perhaps closest to the imperative form.

Vulgate: *Mare et meridiem possidebis* ("Thou wilt possess the sea and the south").

Luther: *Gegen Abend und Mittag wird sein Besitz sein* ("His possession shall be towards evening [i.e., the west] and towards noontide [i.e., the south]").

112. אלמלא שראיתי טעם זקף גדול נקוד על ופניהם לא הייתי יודע לפרשו, אבל הניקוד למדני להבדילם זו מזו ולהעמיד תיבת ופניהם בפני עצמה.

See also Note 78 above.

113. "This is the explanation: They have faces and their wings are separated above their faces and cover them.... Another example of this construction can be found in this portion. *And they have a back:* They have height and inspire fear. The phrase 'and they have a back' stands by itself."

114. Septuagint: *Kai hai ptegyres auton extatamenai anothen* ("And their wings were stretched out above").

Vulgate: *Facies eorum et pennae eorum extentae desuper* ("Their faces and their wings were extended above").

Luther: *Und ihre Angesichter und Fluegel waren oben her zertheilet* ("And their faces and their wings were separated above").

115. "Beyond the Jordan, westward;" i.e. further on, in a westerly direction, on the other side of the Jordan, far away. "The accent proves that [the word] *aharei* and the phrase *derekh mevo ha-shemesh* are two unconnected phrases, since they have two separate accents. The word *aharei* has a *pashta,* and *derekh* a *mashpel (yetiv);* it also has a *dagesh.* If *aharei* and *derekh* were meant to form one phrase, *aharei* would have been accentuated with a 'reversed shofar' [conjunctive accent] and *derekh* with a *pashta.* Also, it would not have a *dagesh.*"

116. Septuagint: *Opiso hodon dysmon heliou* ("Behind the way of the sunset").

Vulgate: *Qui sunt trans Jordanem post viam* ("Which are across the Jordan beyond the way...").

Luther: *Jenseits des Jordan, der Strasse nach gegen der Sonne Untergang* ("Beyond the Jordan, beyond the road toward sunset").

117. *"In this book of the Law:* But above [Deuteronomy 28:61] it is written 'in the book of this Law.' *Ha-zot* [of this] is a feminine form, which refers to 'Law' [*Torah* being a feminine noun]. *Ha-zeh* is a masculine form, which refers to 'book' [*sefer* being a masculine noun]. Owing to the division of the words into clauses by means of the accents the two phrases are seen to be two different expressions. In the portion containing the curses [28:61] the *tippha* is placed beneath *sefer* and *ha-Torah* and *ha-zot* are linked together; hence [the feminine form] *ha-zot,* referring to *Torah.* In this verse, however, the *tippha* is under *ha-Torah;* i.e., *sefer* and *ha-Torah* are linked together, hence [the masculine form] *ha-zeh,* referring to *sefer.*"

Neither the Septuagint nor the Vulgate show any differentiation between the two expressions:

Septuagint:

Deuteronomy 28:61: *En to biblio tou nomou toutou.*
Deuteronomy 29:20: *En to biblio tou nomou toutou.*

Vulgate:

Deuteronomy 28:61: *In volumine legis huius* ("In the volume of this law").
Deuteronomy 29:20: *In libro legis huius* ("In the book of this law").

118. *"Shall be burned by fire:* The tent as well as the possessions. He and all that is his, in accordance with the law mentioned further on. He and his cattle [are to be killed] by stoning. The *zakef* over the word *ba-esh* [by fire] proves that this word is separated from the word 'he.' We find this mode in a number of [Scriptural] verses where the words are separated from one another by accents. E.g. 'Beyond, toward the sunset' [Deuteronomy 11:30] where *aharei* is separated from *derekh* by means of accents. The interpretation here is as fol-

lows: Whatever is included in the *herem* [interdict] and can be burned is to be burned by fire, as explained further on [in Verse 25]."

119. "Are they to receive both punishments [i.e., burning and stoning]? Rabina said: What is fit to be burned shall be burned; what is fit for stoning shall be stoned."

120. Isaiah 45:1 and Rashi *ad loc.* "*Thus says the Lord to His anointed, to Cyrus:* The term 'anointed' is used to denote any kind of greatness... and our Rabbis said: The Holy One, blessed be He, says to the Anointed One [the Messiah], 'I complain to you about Cyrus,' as is stated in Tractate Megillah."

121. Megillah 12a and Rashi *ad loc.*: "Rav Nahman bar Rav Hisda explained: What is the meaning of the verse *Thus says the Lord to His anointed, to Cyrus, whose right hand I have held?* Was Cyrus the Messiah? But [we are told that] the Holy One, blessed be He, said to the Anointed One [the Messiah], 'I complain to you about Cyrus'... and the accents confirm this homily, as nowhere else in Scripture is there a *zarka* that is not followed by a *seghol*, but in this instance the word *lim'shiho* [to His anointed] is accentuated by a *zarka* and *le-Koresh* [to Cyrus] is accentuated by a *merkha* to separate it from the word[s] 'to His Anointed.'"

122. Rashi on Exodus 6:9.

123. ר״א בנו של ריה״ג אומר בשלשים ושתים מדות התורה נדרשת

124. ל״א: מוקדם שהוא מאוחר בענין: כיצד: (שמואל א' ג) ונר אלוקים טרם יכבה ושמואל שוכב בהיכל ה'. והלוא אין ישיבה בהיכל כ״ש שכיבה. ואפילו בעזרה אין ישיבה אלא למלכי בית דוד בלבד שנאמר (שמואל ב' ז) ויבא המלך דוד וישב לפני ח' ומה ת״ל שוכב? אלא מוקדם הוא וכן צ״ל: ונר אלוקים טרם יכבה בהיכל ה' ושמואל שוכב.

125. Kimhi follows the interpretation of Rabbi Eliezer: "*And Samuel lay down in the Sanctuary of the Lord:* The words *in the Sanctuary of the Lord* are connected with *and the light of the Sanctuary of the Lord was not yet gone out*, because the light was in the Sanctuary while Samuel was lying in his [proper] place."

It is interesting to note that of all the translations only the King James Version took notice of the problem raised by Rabbi Eliezer. Its rendering is, "And ere the lamp of God went out in the Temple of the Lord where the Ark was..."

Septuagint: *Ekatheuden en to nao kyriou* ("He slept in the Temple of the Lord").

Vulgate: *Dormiebat in templo Domini* ("He slept in the Temple of the Lord").

126. *"And they stood before Moses and before Eleazar the Priest and before the princes and all the congregation:* Is it possible that if Moses did not know what answer to give them, Eleazar should have known it, and that thereafter they 'stood before' the princes and the entire congregation? But [if you] rearrange the wording of the words [to read, 'Before Eleazar... and before Moses'] this should explain it. Thus said Rabbi Josiah."

127. "Abba Hanan said in the name of Rabbi Eliezer that all of them sat in the house of study and they stood in front of all of them." As far as Abba Hanan is concerned, there is no need for a rearrangement of this text.

128. Septuagint: *Kai pasai hai chorai elthon eis Aigypton agorazein pros Ioseph* ("...from Joseph").

Vulgate: *Omnesque provinciae venebant in Aegyptum ut emerant escas.*

129. Septuagint: *Kai lousetai to soma autou hydati, kai meta tauta eiseleusetai eis ten parembolen kai akatharsos estai ho hiereus heos esperas* ("And he shall wash his body in water and afterwards he shall come into the camp, and the priest shall be unclean until the evening").

Vulgate: *Ingredietur in castra, commaculatusque erit usque ad vesperum* ("He shall come into the camp and shall be unclean until the evening").

130. ‏ותכבד את בניך ממני להבריאכם מראשית כל מנחת ישראל לעמי.‏

131. "Rearrange [the word order to read], 'Thou honorest thy sons more than Me in public [lit., "before My people"]. '[The Lord says that] thou didst show My people that thou art more to be honored than I. How didst thou show this? By making thyself fat from the best of My offerings."

132. Septuagint: *Eneulogeisthai aparchen pases thysias Israel emprosthen mou* ("To be blessed from the best of all the sacrifices before Me"). It seems that the Greek translation read ‏לפני‏ or ‏לעיני.‏

Vulgate: *Ut comederetis primitias omnis sacrificii Israel populi mei* ("That thou eatest the best of all the sacrifices of My people Israel").

King James: "...of My people Israel." However, it adds a note, "Text and meaning uncertain."

133. "[To speak with him] quietly."

134. "Rearrange [the word order to read], 'And he inadvertently took him aside into the gate to speak with him.'"

135. "Inadvertently" or "in error."

136. *Mahberet Menahem,* ed. Zvi Philipowsky, p. 174.

137. ‏שהוא בעל דין ודיין ונופל בו לשון נשפט שאף הוא טרען טענותיו ומצא עונם‏
The form ‏נשפט‏ would be similar to the "medium" in Greek, which also has a passive form but an active (and reflexive) meaning. With the fire of Gehinnom, God contends with all flesh (‏את‏ = with). Yet another misinterpretation in the Septuagint is the connection of ‏באש‏ with ‏ה';‏ this demonstrates that accents were not yet known at the time of the Septuagint. Though the Vulgate avoids the latter error — this may prove that accents were known by the fourth century C.E. — it obscures the meaning of the verse by adding the preposition *ad* ("to") before the noun *carnem.* In his alternative suggestion, Rashi uses ‏נשפט‏ as a passive and rearranges the verse. However, the ‏את‏ remains difficult. (‏כי באש‏ ‏ה' נשפט .... את כל בשר.)‏

138. *En gar to pyri kyriou krithesetai pasa he ge.*

139. *Et in gladio suo ad omnem carnem.*

140. Rashi: "The simple sense is: For through the fire of the Lord and His sword all flesh is judged." Many [other] verses should be rearranged in a similar manner."

141. ונשחת הכלי אשר הוא עושה בחומר ביד היוצר.

142. רגע אדבר על גוי... ורגע אדבר על גוי.

143. Rashi: "This is another example of a rearranged verse."

144. Septuagint: *Kai epesen to angeion ho autos epoiei ek tou pelou en tais chersin autou* ("And the vessel fell to pieces which he himself had made of clay in his hands").

Vulgate: *Et dissipatum est vas, quod ipse faciebat e luto manibus ("And the vessel is destroyed which he himself had made of clay with his hands").*

Luther: *Und der Topf... missriet ihm unter den Haenden.*

145. כן אכיר את גלות יהודה אשר שלחתי מן המקום הזה ארץ כשדים לטובה.

146. Septuagint: *Hous exapestalka ek tou topou toutou eis gen Chaldeion eis agatha.*

Vulgate: *Sic cognoscam transmigrationem Juda quam emisi de loco isto in terram Chaldaeorum in bonum.*

147. Rashi: "This verse is to be rearranged. [The Lord says] Thus I shall recognize [i.e., credit] for the good the exile of Israel."

Note the rendering of Luther, whose interpretations indicate that he must have had knowledge — direct or indirect — of Rashi's commentaries: *Gleichwie diese Feigen gut sind also will ich mich gnaedig annehmen der Gefangenen aus Juda welche ich habe aus dieser Staette lassen ziehen in der Chaldaeer Land* ("Just as these figs are good, so I, too, will be gracious unto the prisoners from Judah whom I have caused to move from this place into the land of the Chaldeans."

148. לי יזעקו אלקי ידענוך ישראל

149. Septuagint: *Eme kekraxontai ho theos, egnokamen se.*

Vulgate: *Me invocabunt; Deus meus! cognovimus te, Israel.*

Luther: *Werden sie dann zu mir schreien: Du bist mein Gott! Wir kennen dich, Israel.*

150. Rashi: "Rearrange [the word order of this verse] and interpret it as..."

151. *Ho sozon tous elpizontas epi se ek ton anthestekoton te dexia sou.*

152. *A resistentibus dexterae tuae custodi me ut pupillam oculi.*

153. *Beweise deine wunderliche Guete, du Heiland derer, die dir vertrauen, so sich wider deine rechte Hand setzen.*

154. להושיע בימינך את החוסים ממתקוממים. Rashi: "This verse should be rearranged...."

155. אכלו וישתחוו כל דשני ארץ

156. אכלו ענוים כל דשני ארץ וישתחוו. Rashi: "This verse should be rearranged...."

157. Septuagint: *Ephagon kai prosekynesan pantes hoi piones tes ges.*

Vulgate: *Manducaverunt et adoraverunt omnes pingues terrae.*

Luther: *Alle Fetten auf Erden werden essen und anbeten.*

158. S. L. Gordon, Hartom-Cassuto.

159. נאם פשע לרשע בקרב לבי

160. Septuagint: *Phesin ho paranomos tou hamartanein en heauto.*

Vulgate: *Dixit injustus ut delinquat in semetipso* ("The sinner — in order that he may commit a sin — said within himself: There is no fear of God").

161. יש בקרב לבי שהפשע - הוא יצר הרע - אומר לרשע... Rashi: "This verse should be rearranged...."

162. חציך שנונים עמים תחתיך יפלו בלב אויבי המלך

163. חציך שנונים בלב אויבי המלך Rashi: "This verse should be rearranged..."

164. Septuagint: *Ta bele sou ekonemena, dynate, laoi hypokato sou pesountai en kardia ton echthron tou basileos.*

Vulgate: *Sagittae tuae acutae, populi sub te cadent in corda inimicorum regis.*

165. והון אדם יקר חרוץ

166. והון אדם חרוץ יקר הוא. Rashi: "This verse should be rearranged...."

167. Septuagint: *Ktema de timion aner katharos* ("The pure person is substance of great value").

Vulgate: *Et substantia hominis erit auri pretium.*

Luther: *Aber ein fleissiger Mensch wird reich* ("But a diligent man shall become wealthy").

168. Canon No. 9. "The short way." "How is this to be understood?... 'And I have gone from tent to tent and tabernacle' [I Chronicles 17:5]. It should read: 'From tabernacle to tabernacle,' but the verse is expressed in elliptical terms. When do you apply this principle? When the context makes it appear certain. In a similar vein, it is written, [II Samuel 13:39] *Va-tekhal David la-tzet.* [The text] should say, 'And the soul of David longed to go out.' However, this is an elliptical verse. And though we cannot cite proof for this case, we find an allusion [Psalm 84:3, where it is written], 'My soul yearns' [*kaletha*]." (The root כלה=longing, implies the connection with נפש=soul.)

169. Examples:

a. Genesis 29:2: *"They gave the flocks to drink:* The shepherds used to water the flocks; this is an elliptical phrase [i.e., the subject, 'the shepherds,' is omitted.]"

Septuagint: *Ek gar tou phreatos ekeinou epotizon ta poimnia* ("For from that well *they* gave the flock to drink").

Vulgate: *Nam ex illo adaquabantur pecora* ("For from that one the flock was watered").

Luther: *Denn von dem Brunnen pflegten sie die Herden zu traenken* ("For they used to give the flock to drink from that well").

b. Genesis 41:13: *"I was restored to my office:* This phrase is elliptical because it does not state explicitly who did the restoring. It is not necessary to state explicitly who did the restoring because it was obviously the person who had the power to restore, namely, Pharaoh."

Septuagint: *Kathos sunekrinen hemin houto kai sunebe, eme te apokatastathenai epi ten archen mou, ekeinon de kremasthenai* ("Even as he interpreted it to us, so it came to pass, I to be restored to my office and the other one to be hanged").

Vulgate: *Ego enim redditus sum officio meo, et ille suspensus est in cruce* ("I was reinstated and the other one was hanged upon a cross").

Luther: *Denn ich bin wieder an mein Amt gesetzt und jener ist gehenkt* ("For I was restored to my office but the other one has been executed [or hanged]").

c. Genesis 48:1: *"And he said to Joseph:* 'He' refers to one of the messengers. This is an elliptical phrase."

d. Genesis 48:2: *"And he told Jacob:* The text does not explicitly state who told it [to Jacob]. There are many such elliptical verses [in Scripture]."

e. Exodus 10:11: *"And he drove them out:* This is an elliptical verse; it does not explicitly state who it was that drove them out."

170. Examples:

a. Genesis 4:15: *"Therefore whoever slays Cain [shall be avenged sevenfold]:* [God says] I do not wish to take vengeance on Cain now, but at the end of seven generations, I will execute My vengeance upon him, in that Lamech, one of his descendants, will arise and slay him. The end of the verse, which states that 'vengeance shall be taken in the seventh generation' — which is the vengeance taken on Cain for Abel — teaches us that the first part of the verse is a threat made so that no creature might harm Cain. This is one of the verses where the construction is elliptical." Only a suggestion is given, not a full explanation. "Whoever slays Cain" expresses a threat suggesting the consequences of such an act, without explaining what the punishment will be." Tubal-Cain, a seventh-generation descendant of Cain, is, in fact, slain by Lamech. Thus Abel's death was avenged.

Septuagint: *Kai eipen... Pas ho apokteinas Kain hepta ekdikoumena paralysei* ("Whoever kills Cain will pay seven revenges [or will have seven revenges let loose upon him]."

Vulgate: *Sed omnis qui occiderit Cain, septuplum punietur* ("But whoever kills Cain will be punished sevenfold").

Luther: *Nein, sondern wer Kain totschlaegt, der soll siebenfaeltig gerochen werden* ("No, but whoever kills Cain shall be avenged sevenfold").

b. Exodus 22:22 *"If thou afflict them [i.e., the widow or the orphan] in any way:* This is an elliptical phrase. The text threatens but then breaks off and does not specify what the punishment will be. In a similar vein, 'Therefore whoever slays Cain...' [threatens but then] breaks off and does not specify his punishment. Thus it is also here: If thou afflict them — but then it breaks off to imply that in the end thou wilt get thy just deserts."

Septuagint: *Ean de kakia kakosete autous kai kraxantes kataboesosi pros me akoe eisakousomai tes boes auton* ("For if thou wilt harm them and they will complain crying to Me I shall indeed hear their cry").

Vulgate: *Si laeseritis eos, vociferabuntur ad me et ego audiam clamorem eorum* ("If thou wilt hurt them, they will cry out to Me and I shall hear their cry").

Luther: *Wirst du sie beleidigen, so werden sie zu mir schreien, und ich werde ihr Schreien hoeren* ("If thou wilt insult them, they will cry to Me and I will hear their cry").

None of the three above translations takes cognizance of the expression *ki im*, which must not be ignored. By treating the above verse as an elliptical passage, Rashi interprets it as follows: "If thou wilt hurt them, I shall certainly let thee have thy punishment. Why [is this so certain]? Because *(ki)* if *(im)* they will cry out to Me, I shall hear their cry."

c. Exodus 32:32: [Following the sin of the Children of Israel with the Golden Calf, Moses says to the Lord] *Yet now if Thou wilt bear their sin:* This is an elliptical sentence [the word "good and well" being omitted].... There are many like this in Scripture." Rashi probably wanted to avoid the suggestion that Moses was so discouraged that, regardless of whether or not the Lord forgave the sin of the Children of Israel, he did not care to survive. He therefore interprets this as an elliptical verse. Moses says to the Lord: "If Thou wilt forgive their sin — all well and good. Then do not erase me. But if Thou wilt not forgive, then erase me from the book...."

Septuagint: *Kai nyn, ei men apheis autois ten hamartian auton, aphes, ei de me, exaleipson me ek tes biblou sou hes egrapsas* ("And now, if Thou wilt forgive them their sin, let it be so; if not, erase me from the book....").

Vulgate: *Aut dimitte eis hanc noxam aut si non facis, dele me de libro tuo quem scripsisti* ("Either forgive them their sin or if Thou wilt not do it, then erase me from Thy book which Thou hast written").

Luther: *Nun vergib ihnen ihre Suende; wo nicht, so tilge mich aus deinem Buche, das du geschrieben hast* ("Now forgive them their sin; if not, then erase me from Thy book which Thou hast written").

EXTERIOR AND INTERIOR OF THE RASHI CHAPEL AT WORMS

FROM A DRAWING

CHAPTER FIVE

Rashi and Christian Interpretations of the Bible

It is generally assumed that Rashi was not unaware of the interpretations which the Church Fathers gave to Biblical texts. He reacted to many of these interpretations with vigorous opposition.[1] As a rule, he cautioned his students against entering into any discussions with "sectarians" or "instigators," but these epithets do not necessarily refer to the theologians of the Church.[2] Rashi's warnings were motivated by the fear that engaging in such debates might weaken the students' adherence to the basic tenets of Judaism. Rashi's apprehensions, expressed, among other places, in his commentaries on many passages in the Book of Proverbs,[3] suggest that he himself knew of some Jews who became renegades as a result of being exposed to "sectarian" interpretations of the Bible. Indeed, we have an interesting autobiography written ca. 1100 (i.e., during Rashi's lifetime) by the abbot Hermanus of Cologne (ca. 1107-1170 or 1198), a baptized Jew who cites divergent interpretations of

119

certain Biblical passages as factors in his conversion to Christianity.[4]

Given the close proximity in which Jews and Christians lived in Rashi's Troyes, it may well be surmised that Rashi himself engaged in discussions with members of the Christian clergy.[5] Also, his attention may have been drawn to Christian interpretations of various Biblical texts by his grandson, Rabbi Samuel ben Meir (RaSHBaM), who, as we have noted earlier, knew Latin and engaged his grandfather in discussions of the latter's interpretations of the Biblical text.[6] Perhaps Latin commentaries entered into these discussions. We will probably never know whether Rashi mastered the Latin language sufficiently to read the commentaries of St. Jerome or St. Augustine himself. But his grandson RaSHBaM knew something of the Latin Bible and its commentaries, as shown, for instance, in RaSHBaM's own Biblical commentary, where he rejects the Latin rendering of the distinct Hebrew terms for "killing" and "murder" by forms of the same Latin verb — *occidere.*[7]

Numerous statements in Rashi's commentaries on the Bible — particularly the Book of Psalms — attest to his knowledge of Latin Biblical commentaries written by early Christian theologians. However, many of his statements in this regard are of a rather general nature and do not necessarily prove that Rashi had a literal acquaintance with the Latin text. A favorite subject for discussion was the Christological interpretation of the "suffering servant," one "despised and forsaken of men, a man of pains and acquainted with disease... wounded because of our transgressions," described in the fifty-third chapter of the Book of Isaiah (Verses 3-5). In his comment on Verse 3, Rashi explains that this suffering servant is not one individual but the entire people of Israel. "It is the way of this prophet to address all of Israel as if it were one man [as in, e.g.]: 'Fear not, My servant Jacob [Isaiah 44:2].'" Similarly, he refutes Christological interpretations of Isaiah 9:5-6 ("For a child is born unto us; a son is given to us... that the government may be increased and of peace there be no end...") and Psalm 2:1-2 ("Why are the peoples in an uproar... The kings of the earth stand up, and the rulers take counsel together against the Lord and His anointed") by the rather general statement (in his commentary on Psalm 2:2): "Our Rabbis apply this passage [i.e., Verses 1-2] to Messiah, but according to the context in which it appears it would be more correct to apply it to David himself."[8] In his comment on Psalm 9 ("For the Leader; *al muth-labben*."), where the Christians construed the Hebrew phrase *al muth-labben* as "no death to the son", an allusion to the eternal life of a "son of God," and on Psalm 10 ("For the wicked boasts of his heart's desire..."— Verse 3), which the Church explains as referring to the sufferings of the Church in her war against the Antichrist, Rashi states (on Psalm 9:1), that "I say this Psalm refers to the distant future, when Israel will have grown hoary, when its righteousness will be revealed, its salvation will have drawn near, and Amalek and his descendants will be erased."

However, there are more specific explanations in Rashi's commentary which echo the challenge of several Latin commentaries and respond directly to that challenge. Particularly the Book of Psalms lends itself to various homiletical interpretations and hence it is not surprising that the Christian theologians should have sought constantly to use the Book of Psalms as an anchor for their own ideas and doctrines.

A most striking example of a direct response by Rashi to one Christian commentator seems to occur in his comment on Psalm 98:8 ("Let the rivers clap their hands..."). Jerome (347-419 C.E.) challenges the Jews to explain this particular passage:

> *Let the rivers clap their hands.* Let us ask the Jews who interpret the Biblical text according to its letter: Do rivers have hands? Do rivers have voices? Do rivers have feet? Do rivers have a stomach? Someone may say: Nothing is written [there] about a stomach, about feet. But I say unto thee: If we asssume the existence of one organ we [also must] understand [the existence] of others, for we cannot conceive of hands without feet, without a stomach or without other parts.[9]

Jerome then proceeds to his own allegorical interpretation according to which the rivers symbolize the saints or the prophets who announce the advent of Christ.

Judging by his own comment on this verse in the Book of Psalms, Rashi must have been aware of Jerome's interpretation, for he writes:

> *Let the rivers clap their hands:* The prophets spoke in a language appealing to the ear; They did not mean to imply that the rivers [literally] have hands. This is merely a figure of speech meant to convey [the idea of] joy and gladness.

It is significant to note that the only other Biblical passage in which the expression "clap their hands" occurs is in the Book of Isaiah (55:12), "And all the trees of the field shall clap their hands." However, it seems that Rashi found no reason to comment on that verse.

In its rendering of Psalm 96* the Vulgate prefaces the psalm with a superscription which is not found in the Hebrew original: "A Song of David, when the house was [re]built after the captivity." In his *Tractatus sive Homiliae* Jerome continues: *"Sing to the Lord a new song* [Verse 1 of the Hebrew original]: Who is to sing? 'Sing unto the Lord, all the earth.' Now if this were to refer [merely] to the Temple in Jerusalem, O Jew, why should all the earth be called upon to [sing] praise?"[10] Jerome then goes on to explain this psalm in mystical terms. Rashi, however, remarks (on Verse 1): "This psalm refers to the distant future, as is proven by its concluding passage, *For He has come to judge the earth....* In every instance where the expression *shir hadash* ['a new song'] occurs [in the Biblical text] it refers to the distant future." It is noteworthy that Rashi offers no comment on the meaning of *shir hadash* in connection with Psalm 33:3 ("Sing unto Him a new song"), where the expression occurs for the first time in the Book of Psalms. In his comment on Psalm 40:4 ("And He has put a new song in my mouth"), as we shall see shortly, he interprets "a new song" as referring to the song of praise which the Children of Israel sang at the Red Sea.[11] He does not attempt to explain *shir hadash* when it occurs in Psalm 144:9 ("O God, I will sing a new song unto Thee") and Psalm 149:1 ("Hallelujah. Sing unto the Lord a new song"). It is only in the case of the opening verse of Psalm 96, upon which Jerome seems to go out of his way to comment, that Rashi states his own views at some length.

---

*In the Vulgate, where Psalms 1 and 2 are rendered as one chapter, this is Psalm 95.

In his commentary on Psalm 40, Rashi is in sharp disagreement with Jerome. Jerome focuses on Verses 7 and 8 ("Sacrifice and meal-offering Thou hast no delight in.... Burnt-offering and sin-offering hast Thou not required. Then said I, 'Lo, I have come with the roll of a book which is prescribed for me...'"):

> *Burnt-offering and sin-offering hast Thou not required. Then said I, 'Lo, I come.'* In the beginning of the book [this] is written about me [i.e. Christ]. Now that the superstitious old law has been abolished and Thou hast exchanged the sacrifices and the sacred rites of the Jews for the religion of the spiritual evangel, I [Christ] come into the world with joy. And of me it is written: In the beginning was the Word, and the Word was with God, and God was the Word.[12]

Rashi seems to have been aware of this Christian argument in support of the abrogation of the "old law" and its replacement with a "new" one, for in his commentary on Psalm 40 he singles out this particular passage for detailed explanation as follows:

> [Verse 7] *Sacrifice and meal-offering Thou hast not required:* On the day of the Giving of the Law, [as it is written in Exodus 19:5]: "And now if you will indeed hearken to the voice of the Lord," etc. and likewise [in Jeremiah 7:22]: "For I spoke not to your fathers, nor commanded them, etc. concerning burnt-offerings or sacrifices... "I [i.e., the Lord] said: "If any one of you should offer up a sacrifice" [Leviticus 1:2]. I did not obligate them nor place a burden upon them; your regular offerings and additional offerings merely give Me pleasure.

> [Verse 8] *Then [said I]:* At the time of the Giving of the Law I [the Lord] told thee: Lo, I have come to thee with the covenant handed down [to you] regarding "[All that the Lord has spoken] we will do and obey" [Exodus 24:7], and this word is the written testimony about Me in "the roll of the book," the Torah of Moses.

Perhaps it was to counter Jerome's mystical, homiletic interpretation of these two verses that Rashi chose to relate Psalm 40 to a historic fact; namely, the Exodus from Egypt. According to Rashi's explanation, the "pit" in Verse 3 ("He brought me up from the tumultuous pit and the miry clay") refers to Israel's captivity in Egypt, the tumult alludes to the roaring of the Red Sea, and the "miry clay" denotes the mud in that body of water. The "new song" in Verse 4 ("and He has put a new song in my mouth") is an allusion to the song of praise which the Children of Israel sang following their miraculous deliverance at the Red Sea, which is referred to in Verse 6 ("Thy wondrous works"). "Thy thoughts toward us" in Verse 6 indicates the farsightedness of Divine Providence in having the Israelites wander through the wilderness for 40 years to allow time for the regeneration of the forests of the Promised Land, which had been cut down by the Emorites when they learned of the impending entry of the Israelites.

In Psalm 80 Jerome confines his comments to two verses only; i.,e., Verses 16 and 19 ("... upon the son [of man] whom Thou madest strong for Thyself.... Quicken Thou us and we will call upon Thy name"): *And upon the son of man whom Thou didst confirm for Thyself:* It is obvious that he is speaking of the advent of Christ. And finally, the verse which follows points to his resurrection, saying: *Thou wilt quicken us and we will call upon Thy name.*"[13] Rashi interprets "the son" in Verse 16 as being Esau[14] and the "quickening" as referring to Israel's return from exile.[15] It is interesting to note, however, that the Targum Jonathan interprets the "son" as being the Messiah: "...and because of the king, the Messiah, whom Thou hast made strong for Thyself."[16]

According to Jerome, the "king" in Psalm 21:2 ("O Lord, in Thy strength the king rejoices") is Christ, *rex regum et dominus dominantium,* the "king of kings and lord of lords." Rashi, in order to forestall any association of this passage with Christ, "the anointed," rejects even the interpretation of the Rabbis who consider "the king" as the Messiah. He insists that the verse refers to King David, not to a future Messiah: "Our Rabbis interpret 'the king' as being the Messiah, but it is correct to interpret it as referring to [King] David himself, as an answer to the *minim* [sectarians]." According to Rashi, the crown cited in Verse 4 of the psalm ("Thou settest a crown of fine gold upon his head") is placed upon the head of David: "And He [i.e., the Lord] took the royal crown and it shall be upon the head of David." Jerome interprets the "crown" as "the crown of the Lord, the gathering of the Church from various nations, of which Paul speaks as 'my joy and my crown.'"[17]

According to Jerome's etymological analysis of the Hebrew

word *mahalat*[18] the opening verse of Psalm 88 ("...upon *Mahalat Leannot*") refers to the *mysterium* of the Church gathered together from among the nations so that many different places, regions and mores may unite into one chorus (Heb.: *mahol,* "dance", i.e., "chorus") to sing praises to God.[19] In Jerome's view, the entire psalm refers to the Savior.[20] Rashi, on the other hand, interpreting *mahalat* in its most straightforward connotation of "sickness," regards the psalm as referring to the unfortunate nation of Israel, which, sick with love for God, is now suffering the hardships of exile.[21]

Proceeding to Verse 4 ("For my soul is sated with troubles and my life draws near to the grave"), Jerome writes that it was Christ, not David, who spoke of his troubled soul. In his view, Christ means to say, "I bear the sins of many; therefore I am suffering for all of them."[22] Rashi, however, once again points out that this verse, like similar passages elsewhere in Scripture, does not refer to an individual but to the whole people of Israel: *"For my soul is sated with troubles:* This refers to the [entire] community of Israel."

Jerome continues: *"Thou hast put mine acquaintances far from me* [Verse 9]: During the passion of the cross even the apostles fled from me [i.e., from Christ]." He interprets "Thou hast made me an abomination to them" as *"They have made me an abomination to themselves,* [with] the Jews, naturally, saying, 'Crucify him! Crucify him! We have no king but Caesar!"[23] Rashi, however, insists that here, again, it is not an individual, but the entire Jewish people, that is speaking. It is the Jewish people, "whom the nations once respected but now despise." Thus, Rashi's responses, both direct and indirect, to Christological interpretations of Scriptural text are quite obvious.

Commenting on Psalm 99, Jerome points out what he considers an illogical sequence of three psalms — 93, 97 and 99. In his opinion, the order of these psalms should be reversed. (He understands the three opening words which all three psalms have in common, "The Lord reigns [lit., "has reigned"]," as referring to the rule of Christ). Psalm 99, "The Lord reigns, let the peoples tremble," should come first. (Actually, the Latin rendering, *irascantur,* is not "let the peoples tremble" but "let the peoples be angry"). This should be followed by Psalm 97, "The Lord reigns (lit., "has reigned"), let the earth rejoice." Psalm 93, "The Lord reigns (lit., "has reigned"), He is clothed in splendor," should come last.[24] Nevertheless, Jerome finds even in the allegedly illogical sequence a basis for Christological teachings; namely, that the patriarchs, the prophets and the believers are the "garment" in which Christ is clothed.[25] They surround him like a girdle that encircles the body. Jerome bases his "girdle" interpertation on Jeremiah 13:1-11, where Jeremiah is instructed to put on a girdle, then take it to a cave near the Euphrates river and hide it there, where it rots. According to Jeremiah, the girdle symbolizes the Jewish people (Verse 11). Jerome holds that the Lord then must have proceeded to make a new girdle for himself, for the Lord certainly could not remain naked. The new girdle was made from the Gentiles (i.e., by their conversion).[26] Once the Lord is clothed in His splendid new garment (Psalm 93), let the earth rejoice (Psalm 97) but let the peoples (meaning the Jews and the non-believers) be angry (Psalm 99).[27] Referring to Psalms 97 and 99 Jerome declares:

> Let the earth, the whole earth, rejoice; [Psalm 97]; that is, all those who believe. And the Lord has reigned, let the peoples tremble [or "be angry", Psalm 99]: The Lord has suffered; the Lord has been crucified... [But] O the kindness of the Holy Spirit! He did not say, "Let them perish," but only, "Let them tremble." He sought to point out their fault, not their punishment.[28]

Rashi sees no connection between Psalms 93, 97 and 99 except that each of them refers to another prediction for the future of the Jewish people. According to his interpretation, Verse 1 of Psalm 93 states that, in the distant future, it will be said that "the Lord has reigned,"[29] Verse 1 of Psalm 97 implies that the Lord will reign once the rule of Amalek has been removed (cf. Ezekiel 35:14, which is construed as referring to Amalek: "When the whole earth rejoices, I will make thee desolate.")[30] Verse 1 of Psalm 99, "Let the peoples tremble," refers to the battle of Gog and Magog, when the nations of the earth will be perturbed.[31]

Rashi explicitly refutes Jerome's interpretation of various

passages in Psalm 16. Jerome understands the superscription *mikhtam* (מכתם) as a composite of two words: *mokh* (מך), meaning "lowly" or "humble," and *tam* (תם), which may be rendered either as "simple" or as "perfect." Jerome states, "From this we understand that one word denotes [three qualities, namely] 'simple,' 'immaculate' and 'perfect.' However, each one [of these exists] in combination with humility," [32] Accordingly, Jerome construes Psalm 16 as a memorial to the passion of Christ.

Rashi is aware of this analysis of the word *mikhtam;* indeed, he specifically refers to it in his commentary on Verse 1 of this psalm, but he rejects it out of hand:

> The structure of this verse does not concur with that interpretation. There is a psalm [Psalm 58] with the superscription *le-David mikhtam.* In that case it would be possible to explain it as [meaning], "To David, who was humble and perfect," but here [where] it is written [in reverse order] *mikhtam le-David,* it is not possible to explain it in this manner. I say, therefore, that this [i.e., *mikhtam*] is one of the terms [employed] to denote a melody and rhythm.

Rashi insists that it is King David who speaks here, and that he is addressing himself to the entire community of Israel.[33] According to Jerome, Verse 4 was not uttered by King David but by Christ. In Jerome's interpretation, this verse does not read, "Their drink offerings of blood will I [i.e., David] not offer," but, "I [i.e., Christ] shall not convene their meetings for blood offerings." The Church Father explains this to mean that "Never again shall they offer Me sacrifices as [they did] under the Old Law; rather, it shall be the spiritual religion of the New Testament."[34]

Commenting on this verse, Rashi retorts: "May grief multiply for those who deny Thy existence and who rush, with awe, to worship another god. I [i.e., David] shall not be like them, offering blood libations to idols, and I shall not take the name of idolatry upon my lips." A strong reaction, indeed, to the interpretation offered by Jerome.

Due to a misreading of the word אדני (*adoni*) in the opening verse of Psalm 110 ("The Lord says to my lord") as *adonai,* Jerome associates Psalm 110 with Christ, who is given the divine appellation of *adonai* (*Dixit Dominus domino meo...*). Rashi, in keeping with the interpretation of this text by the Rabbis, explains *adoni* in this psalm as referring to Abraham, to whom this courtesy title ("my lord" or "my master") was accorded, for instance, by Ephron the Hittite (Genesis 23:11).[35] Rashi's interpretation of Verse 4 of this psalm, "Thou art a priest forever, in accordance with the order of Melchizedek," is consistent with his explanation of the opening verse. Jerome associates Melchizedek with Christ, but Rashi bases his interpretation on the Rabbinic tradition (Nedarim 32b, Rabbenu Nissim *ad loc.*) that Melchizedek is identical with Shem, the direct ancestor of Abraham. Rashi notes to Verse 4 that God says to Abraham: "So that thy sons may inherit from Shem, thy father's father, the ministry and kingship that were given to him." It is significant that Rashi explains the word *kohen* (priest) in the context of this passage as denoting high office (ministry), rather than priesthood, as substantiated in II Samuel 8:18, "...and David's sons were chief ministers (*kohanim*)."[36]

Jerome's comment on Verses 4-7 is as follows:

> *Thou art a priest for ever, after the manner of Melchizedek:* Let us say only this: Why should he say, "after the manner"? *After the manner:* Thou shalt never be a priest after the manner of the Jewish sacrifices, but a priest after the manner of Melchizedek. Just as Melchizedek, king of Salem, offered bread and wine [following the slaughter of Chedor-laomer, as told in Genesis 14:17-18], so shalt thou offer thy body and thy blood, true bread and true wine. It is this Melchizedek who gave us those *mysteria* which we have. It is he who said, "He who will eat my flesh and drink my blood." According to the order of Melchizedek did he pass on to us his sacrament.[37]

In order to forestall any chance that Rabbinic tradition might be cited in support of such Christological interpretations, Rashi toward the end of the psalm completely revises his own commentary. He now appears to be unhappy with the Rabbinic tradition that Melchizedek was the progenitor of priesthood (even in the sense of ministry), and comments as follows on Verse 7, the closing verse of the psalm: "This psalm should be interpreted as referring to David." In this vein, Rashi's ingenuity shines forth in his emphasis on the preposition על in Verse 4, "after the manner of Melchizedek." The meaning of this preposition, according to Rashi, is not "after the manner" of Melchizedek but "above" or "beyond" the ministry of Melchizedek. Rashi seeks to point out that whatever one's view of Melchizedek's identity, the appointment to royal status accorded to David outranked the ministry of Melchizedek:

> Which of the ministries [he comments on Verse 4] is higher than [that] of Melchizedek? It is royalty which is higher than priesthood by thirty degrees. [Royalty] is above the priesthood of Melchizedek, who was a priest to *El Elyon* [the deity above all other gods]. And if you should argue that he [i.e., Melchizedek], too, was a king — [then know that] the kingship of Melchizedek is no kingship [at all] as far as Israel is concerned.

The examples cited above would demonstrate that many of Rashi's commentaries on Biblical passages were indeed direct, deliberate reactions to the challenges of Christian interpretations. We have no documentary proof, of course, that Rashi actually read the Latin commentaries which he refutes. Yet, given the proximity and the close relations in which Jews and Christians lived together in Troyes during Rashi's time, there is good reason to assume that Rashi must have had at least second-hand knowledge of the views expressed by the Christian commentators. This hypothesis seems to be borne out by other cases in point from various books of the Bible which would require a much more extensive study to enumerate.

NOTES

1. Solomon Zeitlin, "Rashi," in *American Jewish Year Book, 5700*, New York, 1939, pp. 115 ff; J. Rosenthal, מחקרים ומקורות, Vol. I, Jerusalem, 1967, pp. 101-16; I. Baer, "Rashi and the Historical Reality of His Time," *Tarbiz*, Vol. X (1950), p. 221 f.

2. The Hebrew terms variously used by Rashi to refer to those who reject the basic tenets of Judaism are *minim* ("heretics" or "sectarians"), and *m'sitim* ("instigators" or "proselytizers").

3. Cf. J. Rosenthal, *op. cit.*, pp. 101-07.

4. *Monumenta Germaniae Historica*, Vol. IV, ed. Gerlinde Niemeyer, Weimar,

1963. See also J.P. Migne, *Patrologia Cursus Completus, Series Latina*, Vol. 170, pp. 803-36.

Hermanus, who was originally named Judah ben David HaLevi, was born in Cologne and frequently traveled to Mayence on business. When still a young man, he lent money to Ekbert, bishop of Munster, without receiving a pledge in return. His parents then sent him, accompanied by his tutor Baruch, to the bishop's court to collect the pledge. In the course of the 20 weeks he spent at Ekbert's court, Hermanus had the opportunity to attend the bishop's sermons and to take part in the religious disputations. It seems that soon after his return home, Hermanus showed definite leanings toward Christianity. He traveled to Worms, where he preached Christian ideas to the Jewish community. He was baptized about 1128 and five years later became a member and eventually prior of the Premonstratensian Order in Scheda, Westphalia. His autobiography, *Hermani Opusculum de conversione sua*, which first appeared in print in the year 1687 (ed. Johann Benedikt Carpzov), includes a description of Jewish life in Germany.

5. Urban T. Holmes, Jr. and Sister M. Amelia Klenke O.P., *Chrétien, Troyes and the Grail*, University of North Carolina Press, Chapel Hill, North Carolina, 1959, p. 12.

6. See Chapter 1, Note 18.

7. See Chapter 1, Note 23.

8. Solomon Zeitlin, in "Rashi," p. 124, remarks that, on the basis of his inspection of a manuscript in the library in Moscow the actual reading of this comment should be: "Many of the disciples of Jesus apply this passage to the Messiah but, in order to refute the *minim*, this passage should be applied to David himself."

9. S. Hieronymi Presbyteri *Tractus Sive Homiliae in Psalmos*, ed. D. Germanus Morin, Turnhout, 1958. (Hereafter: TH), p. 116: *Flumina plaudent manu simul. Interrogamus Iudaeos, qui secundum litteram intellegunt. Flumina manus habent? flumina voces habent? flumina pedes habent? flumina ventrem habent? Dicat aliquis: non est scriptum de ventre, de pedibus. Sed ego tibi dico: ex uno membro intelligimus et cetera; non enim possumus intellegere manus sine pedibus, sine ventre, sine membris ceteris.*

10. TH, p. 149: *Quando domus aedificabatur post captivitatem, canticum David. "Cantate Domino canticum novum." Qui cantate? "Cantate Domino omnis terra." Si de templo Hierosolymae dicitur, o Iudaee, quomodo omnis terra provocatur ad laudem?*

11. *A new song*: The song of the [Red] Sea.

12. S. Hieronymi Presbyteri Opera, *Commentarioli in Psalmos*, Turnhout, 1959. (Hereafter: CP), p. 207: *Holocaustomata et pro peccato noluisti; tunc dixi, Ecce venio. In capite libri scriptum est de me. Quia sacrificia et caeremonias Iudaeorum, ablata superstitione legis veteris, spiritalis evangelii religione mutasti: propterea laetus in mundum venio. Et de me scribitur: In principio erat Verbum, et Verbum erat apud Deum, et Deus erat Verbum.*

13. CP, p. 219: *Et super filium hominis quem confirmasti tibi. Manifeste de Xpisti loquitur adventu. Denique et resurrectionem ipsius sequens versiculus ostendit dicens: "Vivicabis nos, et nomen tuum invocabimus.*

14. On Psalm 80:16: *"And upon the son of man whom Thou madest strong for Thyself:* And upon Esau who was the beloved son of his father, who called him 'my son.'"

15. On Psalm 80:19: *"Quicken Thou us:* From the exile."

16. ועל מלכא משיחא דחילת לך

17. CP, p. 197: *Corona Domini, ecclesiae ex variis gentibus congregatio est, de quo Paulus... ait: Gaudium meum et corona mea.*

18. TH, p. 399: *Meleth sermo Hebraicus est, interpretatur autem chorus.* ("*Meleth* is a Hebrew word and is to be interpreted as 'chorus.'")

19. TH, p. 399: *Nam mysterium praefiguratur ecclesiae de diversis gentibus congregatae, ut de diversis locis et de diversis partibus et moribus unus chorus Dei laudum efficiatur.* ("For the *mysterium* of the Church assembled from various nations is presaged here so that, from many different places, regions and mores there may be formed one single chorus of God's praises.").

20. TH, p. 400: *Ex persona Saluatoris psulmus hic dicitur* ("This psalm is recited with reference to the Savior").

21. Rashi on Psalm 88:1: *"Upon Mahalat Leannot:* About [the people of Israel] sick with love and unfortunate on account of the sufferings of exile."

22. TH, p. 400: *Quiu repleta est malis anima mea. Multorum peccata porto, ideo pro omnibus doleo.*

23. TH, p. 402: *Longe fecisti notos meos a me. In passione crucis etiam apostoli me fugerunt. "Posuerunt me abominationem sibi." Iudaei scilicet, dicentes, "Crucifige, crucifige talem: nos non habemus regem nisi Caesarem."*

24. TH, p. 167: *"Dominus regnavit." Videtur quasi ordo sibi esse contrarius. Debuit enim primum dicere. "Dominus regnavit, irascantur populi" et postea dicere, "Dominus regnavit, exultet terra" et in ultimo, "Dominus regnavit, decorem indutus est.* ("'The Lord has reigned.' It seems that this is contrary to the logical order. It should be said first, 'The Lord has reigned, let the peoples tremble,' and after that, 'The Lord has reigned, let the earth rejoice,' and finally, 'The Lord has reigned, He is clothed in splendor.'")

25. TH, p. 167: *Patriarchae et prophetae quasi Xpisti vestimentum fuerunt.* ("The patriarchs and the prophets will be the garments of Christ").

26. TH, p. 167-68: *Non est nudus, non potest esse sine lumbari, non potest esse sine veste: priori populo perdito, facit sibi vestem de populo gentilium* ("He is not naked; He cannot go without a girdle [or loincloth]; He cannot be without a garment: When the erstwhile people perished, He made Himself a garment out of the Gentiles"). Following this act, *exultet terra,* let the entire earth rejoice.

27. TH, p. 167-68: *Dominus regnavit, irascantur populi. Sive de Iudaeis sunt, sive de*

gentibus quicumque non credunt, irascantur ("The Lord reigns, let the peoples be angry. Whether it be the Jews, or the nations that do not believe, let them be angry").

28. TH, p. 168: *Exultet terra, universa terra hoc est, omnis credentium populus. "Dominus regnavit, irascantur populi." Dominus passus est; Dominus crucifixus est....O clementia Spiritus sancti: Non dixit, pereant, sed, irascantur. Vitium voluit significare, non poenas.*

29. Rashi on Psalm 93:1: *"The Lord has reigned:* They will say this in the future."

30. On Psalm 97:1: *"The Lord has reigned:* When the dominion will be taken away from Amalek."

31. On Psalm 99:1: *"Let the peoples tremble:* The reference is to the war of Gog and Magog."

32. TH, p. 364: *Ex quo intellegimus, unum verbum et simplicem et immaculatum et perfectum sonare, ita tamen ut semper singulis humilitas praeponatur.*

33. "David says to the community of Israel, 'Thou shouldst say [to the Lord: Thou art my Lord].'"

34. TH, p. 371: *"Non congregabo conventicula eorum de sanguinibus": Nequaquam mihi ut in veteri lege offerent hostias, sed erit novi testamenti religio spiritalis.*

35. On Psalm 110:1: "Our Rabbis explain that this refers to our father Abraham, and I interpret [this passage] accordingly. The Lord said [this] to Abraham, whom people addressed as *adoni,* as in 'Nay, my lord, hear me' (Genesis 23:11)."

36. On Psalm 110:4: "The meaning of [the word] 'priest' includes [both] priesthood and rulership as in (II Samuel, Chap. 8), 'and David's sons were chief ministers.'"

37. TH, p. 225: *"Tu es sacerdos in aeternum secundum ordinem Melchisedech." Hoc solum dicamus: quare dixerit, "secundum ordinem"? Secundum ordinem: nequaquam sacerdos eris secundum victimas iudaicas sed eris sacerdos secundum ordinem Melchisedech. Quomodo enim Melchisedech, rex Salem, obtulit panem et vinum, sic et tu offeres corpus tuum et sanguinem, verum panem et verum vinum. Iste Melchisedech ista mysteria, quae habemus, dedit nobis. Ipse est qui dixit: "Qui manducaverit carnes meas et biberit sanguinem meum": secundum ordinem Melchisedech tradidit nobis sacramentum suum.*

CHAPTER SIX

Rashi, the Bible and the Talmud

It is in his commentary on the Talmud, even more than in his commentary on the Bible, that Rashi's ingenuity truly comes to the fore. Rashi's commentaries on the Bible and the Talmud accurately reflect the basic differences between these two treasures of the Jewish people.

Judaism is a philosophy of life. Its objectives and ideals are anchored in the Bible. But it is the Talmud that maps out the road to the attainment of these ideals. The Bible and Talmud set out from two opposite points of departure. The Bible (the Torah) originates from a superhuman source; here, the ideals of Judaism are set down in writing as immutable tenets. The Talmud, motivated by the complexities and ever-changing conditions of life, attempts to reconcile the exigencies of life with the postulates of the Torah. It seeks to teach the Jew how to shape his life in consonance with the Torah at all times and in varying circumstances. The Bible sets forth the ideal; the Talmud educates the Jew so that he may know how to fulfill it. The Bible illustrates the teachings of Judaism; the Talmud states what these teachings demand in terms of everyday living.

The Jew is not satisfied to understand merely the text or its philosophical basis; he wants to know how the teachings enunciated in the text will relate to his own life. This is the singular way in which Jews "read" or "study" the Bible, and it is this unique approach that in fact constitutes the essence of the Talmud. Consequently, it seems only logical and necessary that this dual purpose — the theoretical understanding of the Biblical text, on the one hand, and the realization of the Biblical ideals in practical life, on the other — should require two different techniques of interpretation on the part of the commentator.

In his commentary on the Bible Rashi sought to elucidate the religious basis of the Bible and to stir up those human feelings which are basic preconditions for the free-willed acceptance of any system of law. Rashi's commentary on the Bible is an appeal to the heart rather than to the intellect, a labor to construct emotional foundations for unquestioning readiness to obey and observe the laws of the Torah. The quest for perfection of character, based on the love and fear of God, the love of His people and of the Law which God gave to His people — these are the ideals which Rashi emphasizes in his commentary on the Bible. He was, of course, also an ingenious exegete, utilizing a variety of linguistic and grammatical techniques to interpret the text and its nuances. But an arid exegesis alone, concerned only with the explanation of words, could hardly have fulfilled Rashi's purpose — to instill into the hearts of his students those qualities of humility and unquestioning loyalty to God and His people which Rashi prized above all things. Hence Rashi intertwined his exegesis with ingenious moral allegories which he culled from the rich Midrashic literature and which he frequently displayed in a new garment, in a novel formulation, thereby incidentally leaving upon them the imprint of his own personality and philosophy. By this personal touch he imparted to ancient tales enduring warmth and timeless validity. Seemingly trivial occurrences are presented by Rashi in most moving words intended to touch the student's heart and to make him understand that nothing happens without the design of Divine Providence.

Commenting on a simple conversation between Jacob and

his son Joseph (Genesis 48:7) in which Jacob on his deathbed recalls the death of Rachel and her burial ("And as for me... Rachel died unto me in the land of Canaan on the way... and I buried her there on the way to Ephrath"), Rashi reformulates a beautiful story from Pesikta Rabbati III, 41 in order to forestall any criticism that might be made of Jacob's action and to confirm in the reader's heart the unshakable conviction that there is a reason and purpose for everything that happens in the lives of men and in the history of nations. In his commentary, Rashi has Jacob use the device of prophecy in an apology to Joseph for asking him to take his remains to Canaan for burial even though he, Jacob, did not bury Rachel in Canaan:

> And as for me, when I came from Paddan [Genesis 48:7]: Although I am troubling thee to take me for burial to the land of Canaan — and I did not do this for thy mother which I could easily have done since she died quite close to Bethlehem... do not imagine that it was the rains which kept me from taking her to Hebron for burial. It was the dry season, when the ground is riddled and full of holes like a sieve. And yet *I buried her there* [i.e., on the way to Ephrath]; and did not carry her even [the short distance] to Bethlehem to bring her to the city. I know that thou dost feel resentment against me in thy heart. Know, however, that I buried her there by [Divine] command, so that she may help her children when Nebuzaradan will take them into captivity. When they will pass along that road [on their way to exile] Rachel will come forth [from her grave and stand] near her tomb and weep and seek mercy for them, as it is written [Jeremiah 31:15 ff.]: "A voice is heard in Ramah [Rachel weeping for her children]," etc. And the Holy One, blessed be He, will reply to her, "There is a reward for thy work... and thy children shall return to their own border."

The dramatic dialogue between God and Abraham prior to the *akedah* — the binding of Isaac upon the sacrificial altar ("Take now thy son, thine only son, whom thou lovest, even Isaac..." Genesis 22:2) — reflects Rashi's compassion for the father who is about to sacrifice his son. Rashi does not conceal the fact that Abraham was torn by deep conflict. But when Abraham finally becomes convinced that God wants him to offer up Isaac as a sacrifice, he is ready to submit without hesitation to the postulates of his ideal:

[The Lord] said to him [i.e., to Abraham], "I beg of thee, stand firm for Me in this trial so that people will not say that the previous trials were not real tests." *Thy son:* [Abraham] said to Him: "I have two sons." He answered him: "Thine only son." [Abraham] said to Him, "This one [Ishmael] is the only son of his mother [Hagar] and that one [Isaac] is the only son of his mother [Sarah]." [The Lord] then said to him, "The one whom thou lovest." [Abraham] said to Him, "I love both of them." [Whereupon the Lord] said to him, "Isaac." Why did He not disclose this to him at the very first? In order not to confuse him suddenly, lest his mind become distracted and bewildered [and in his confused state of mind he might involuntarily consent and then there would have been no merit in his sacrifice], and so that he might value the [Divine] command more highly and that he might receive a reward for [the increasing sacrifice demanded by obedience to] each and every word uttered [by the Lord].

Whenever Rashi seeks to impart moral values in a more direct manner, he does not categorically command or forbid an act, but rather suggests, or illustrates, the advantages of the behavior regarded as desirable. Thus, Biblical law (Deuteronomy 14:1) forbids tattooing or the making of incisions of any kind upon one's body. To this, Rashi notes: "You are the children of the Omnipresent and it is therefore fitting for you to be pleasant looking, not cut about and with your hair torn out." The importance which Rashi attached to esthetics in personal appearance and dress is evident also in his comment on Proverbs 31:23, where the husband of the "woman of valor" is described. *"Her husband is known in the gates:* He stands out among his friends because of his beautiful garments."

Rashi's brilliant grandson Rabbi Jacob ben Meir Tam declared that though he could equal Rashi in his commentary on the Talmud, it would be beyond his capacities to match his grandfather's commentary on the Bible.[2] Rabbenu Tam was a genius but he could not achieve the complete blending of heart and intellect reflected in Rashi's Biblical commentary.

In his comments on the Biblical text Rashi left a measure of individual latitude to the student, for there can be no uniformity when it comes to man's personal faith and his private confrontation with the Almighty. Since the impact of any text on the reader will depend in great measure on the manner in which it is presented and interpreted, it is indeed not surprising that many outstanding Jewish leaders credit Rashi's commentary on the Bible for their own love of their people and for their personal commitment to Judaism. Hayyim Nahman Bialik, the most influential Hebrew poet of modern times (1873-1934), once wrote (1905):

> What is a nation of scholarship and spirituality? One which has one or two books which are precious to it and from which it educates itself. Such a book for the *entire* [Jewish] nation is the Pentateuch with Rashi's commentary; the Gemarah and its commentaries [perform a similar function] for a *majority* of the nation. A Jew who studied "Humash and Rashi" was no longer an ignoramus but was imbued with the spirit of Torah throughout his life. I do not know whether our own age will present us with such a creation as the Pentateuch with Rashi's commentary, but without it there is no cure for spiritual decadence or for the lack of love of Torah.[3]

Rashi put his very heart and soul into his exegetical writings.[4] Since each individual forms his own impression of a person or concept, depending on subtle and frequently irrational psychological factors, the impact of Rashi's teaching will not be the same on all his readers. Rashi's objective in his Bible commentary was to present the straightforward meaning of each word in its context,[5] but the perception of that straightforward meaning is left, as it must be, to the individual student.

The interpretation of the Talmud, however, requires a different approach. A word intended to stimulate thoughts or to motivate ideas is a very personal matter, with the individual reader or listener free to endow it with a variety of interpretations. Not so the word that is intended to spell out rules for action or behavior. It is within the power of such a word to build a whole community, or to destroy it. Though the Talmud, like the Bible, contains the religious and philosophical teachings of Judaism, it primarily reflects the development of a code of Jewish practice elaborated by means of logical argument. The study of the Talmud is of value only if it leads to action. Because of this emphasis on action and practice there can be no room for ambiguity or vagueness in the conception or interpretation of Talmudic language, because the observance and enforcement of Jewish law is dependent upon the proper interpretation of the Talmudic text. Hence, in his commentary on the Talmud, Rashi's appeal is to the intellect rather than to the heart; he painstakingly explains every possible problem or concept in order to avoid even the slightest chance of misinterpretation. Not impeded by the sanctity of his text — as he was in the case of the Bible — Rashi sometimes selects a *variatio lectionis* that can stand the test of internal evidence.[6] He applies a variety of methods with the sole aim of presenting a clear, unambiguous picture of the practical implications of a Talmudic passage. In some instances he moves from the general to the particular, and vice versa in others. In some cases he moves from the linguistic vantage point to that of conceptualization; in others the reverse seems to him more reasonable and intelligible. He seeks to relate new facts to old ones, to proceed from the known into the unknown.

Rashi's pedagogic insights enabled him to utilize sound educational principles which were not formulated in the history of education until centuries after his time.[7]

However, before he could approach the gigantic task of commenting on the Talmud, Rashi had to overcome numerous difficulties. The very style in which the Talmud presents itself is a unique phenomenon in the history of literature. The Talmud is not a systematically written, evenly edited literary work. In fact, it represents a mass of "oral" legislation which was never meant to be set down on paper. It is clearly stated in Gittin 60b that "words handed down in writing are not to be transmitted orally, and [conversely] words transmitted orally are not to be handed down in writing." The first breach of this injunction apparently took place during the time of Rabbi Akiba (ca. 100 C.E.). The cruel persecution which the Jews suffered under the Emperor Trajan and which gave rise to the heroic Jewish revolt against Rome under the leadership of Simon Bar Kokhba plunged the Jewish community of Palestine into confusion. In such difficult periods oral traditions are in danger of being forgotten; also, the previously uninterrupted chain of living tradition may be abruptly broken. It therefore became necessary to take two basic precautions against these very real threats to Jewish survival. First, the laws of the Oral Tradition had to be collected and categorized into a code that would be accepted by all Rabbinic schools. Disseminated by a uniform method of teaching and study, such a code, it was hoped, would help avert the danger that the Oral Law would be forgotten. Secondly, the authority of the Oral Law had to be secured against the eventuality that the Jewish people would be widely dispersed. To this end, the personal authority of the transmitting teacher had to be transferred to the Law itself.

The accumulated material that had been handed down from one generation to the next was critically examined, and the wheat separated from the chaff. The body of material which stood the test of authenticity was gathered by Rabbi Judah the Prince (Yehuda HaNasi) and collectively referred to as the Mishnah. We do not know exactly when the Oral Law was finally perpetuated in writing. It is generally accepted that this was the work of Rabbi Judah the Prince himself. There are those, however, who maintain that the Mishnah was written down only much later, along with the Gemarah, which serves as both commentary and supplement to the Mishnah.

In any event, like so many other developments in the history of the Oral Law, the breach of the prohibition against putting the Oral Law into written form was brought about by the tragic fate of the Jewish people. War, persecution and dispersion disrupted the regular, steady interaction between teacher and disciple which is a *sine qua non* for the study and preservation of any oral tradition. The ban against writing down the Oral Law had to be transgressed so that the Law itself might survive. Nevertheless, the Rabbinic authorities who put their hands to this task were constantly aware that they were party to the violation of an explicit injunction. Hence, when the Oral Law was set down in writing it was done in a manner that would preserve its "oral" character as much as possible. This could be achieved only by recording the spoken words of the Oral Tradition in their original, colloquial form, without recourse to "editorial" changes and literary niceties. The written text of the Oral Law was not intended to produce a new written code but only to reproduce the spoken word so as to preserve it from oblivion. As a result, the Talmudic text is not a smoothly-flowing presentation. Each word or phrase serves merely as a mnemonic or "shorthand" device to help both teacher and student remember the finer details of the Law.

Naturally, such a style has serious shortcomings. Speech is much more economical and concise than writing, for the simple reason that words as such are not expected to express everything that is in the speaker's mind. The words used to express thought will inevitably reflect the concrete circumstances under which they were uttered. In oral communication, a seemingly insignificant bodily gesture accompanying a word may express a complete thought. This is particularly true in discussions among scholars at Talmudical academies. "Even the everyday talk of Talmudic scholars requires careful study," we read in Avodah Zarah 19b. Interrogatives such as "Why?" or "How do you know?", when posed by the Sages in the Talmud, may be so pregnant with meaning that it would have taken several sheets of paper to convey it adequately in writing. The spoken word recast into "literary" form cannot reflect the situational richness that accompanied it when it was originally uttered. Also, the written word can communicate neither intonation nor emphasis. The same spoken word may have a variety of connotations, depending on how it is pronounced. It may imply question or answer, doubt or surprise. What an orator may be able to express by simple gestures or voice modulations may require a comprehensive statement from the reporter who commits the orator's words to paper for a wider, absent audience. The Talmud could not reproduce the rhythm or the inflection of the speech of the Sages whose rulings it records; hence, each word in the Talmudic text can serve only as a cue for the student's memory. This written cue, if it is to have any meaning, must be "reconstituted" into the spoken word.

Herein lies the reason why it is impossible to study the Talmud without special training and guidance. Due to its mnemonic character, the Talmudic text can be meaningful only to those whom it can remind of previously learned material. This "reconstitution" from written shorthand into oral communication is what we mean by "learning" the Talmud. The Talmud cannot be read silently; it must be put into speech and accompanied by oral comments. The traditional singsong *(niggun)* of Talmud study is the oldest and most original form of commentary. It is the transformation of the rigid, written word of Talmudic text into the living word of the Oral Law, with the *niggun* serving as acoustic punctuation.

Rashi's genius as a commentator on the Talmud lies in his ability to intuit the full meaning of the words uttered by the Sages and to convey it in his written commentary on the Talmudic text. The well-known saying that "without Rashi, the Talmud would have been forgotten in Israel"[8] is fully justified. For centuries no one was able to understand the Talmud without Rashi's commentary. His ingenuity enabled him to sense the milieu of the Talmud and become a participant, as it were, in the Talmudic discussions. Thanks to his sensitivity, he succeeded in resolving textual problems by means of the guiding particles with which he supplemented seemingly incoherent Talmudic passages.

The Talmudic text has no punctuation marks that would show where one statement ends and the other begins, which expressions belong together and which should be interpreted separately, or to indicate whether a sentence is a question or a declarative statement. Rashi injects himself, as it were, into the Talmudical discussions and senses whether a statement in the text is a question or a declarative sentence. If the former, he adds in his commentary the parenthetical expression *bitmihah* ("interrogative"); if the latter, he writes *b'nihuta* ("declarative").[9] Frequently, in the heat of the scholarly debate, it is difficult to tell who is asking a question and who is answering it. This is a problem which further complicates the study of the Talmud especially for the uninitiated. In such instances Rashi, in his commentary, helps guide the student through the maze of the Talmudic exchanges by adding the phrase "So-and-So asks" or "So-and-So answers." Traditionally the Talmud has been called *Yam haTalmud*, literally the "[uncharted] sea of the Talmud," and Rashi may rightfully be described as the self-assured captain who expertly guides the inexperienced seafarer to his destination.

It would be futile to attempt to categorize Rashi's methodology in his approach to the Talmud. The main objective of his commentary is to clarify the stenographic Talmudic text so that the Jew who subordinates his life-style to the demands of Jewish Law may understand what it is that the Law requires of him. Rashi's commentary is free of all sophistry and mental gymnastics. Unlike many products of later scholarship, Rashi's comments were not motivated by the wish to indulge in scholarly pyrotechnics but by his judgment that a given Talmudic statement was in need of explanation. He was not interested in presenting his own Rabbinic novellae but only in re-presenting the given text of the Law. He had sharp criticism for those who had forgotten the straightforward laws (*halakhot*) "because they were too much involved in hair-splitting (*pilpul*)."[10] He rejects one suggested explanation for the reason that while it delves very deeply into the subject matter, it is not tenable.[11] One cannot help discerning a note of scorn in Rashi's remark to one explanation (in connection with the slaughtering of sacrifical animals): "This is a faulty explanation [devised] by an individual who has a sharp mind but is a hair-splitter"[12] Rashi sought to bring the student as close as possible to the ideas set forth by the Sages, so that the student might actually be able to picture himself as a listener in the scholarly discussion to which the Talmudic "shorthand" alludes.

Rashi is sensitive to the mood of the Talmud, not merely to its logic. In many instances he admits, "This is an explanation which I derived intuitively [lit., "from my heart"],"[13] or "this is the explanation of my teachers but my heart hesitates [to accept it]."[14] Elsewhere he bluntly states, "I say that this is an error, that the reader was mistaken and that he did not know how to explain it."[15] Sometimes Rashi is surprised at explanations offered by his teachers and feels compelled to reject them: "This is how it appears to me and I am surprised at the explanation suggested by my teachers."[16] Frequently, in a humbler vein, Rashi indicates his disagreement with an interpretation by the phrase, "but it seems to me that..."[17]

In view of the foregoing it would appear contrived, if not presumptuous, to attempt to class Rashi's commentary in terms of one specific methodology or approach. Only an outsider who comes to a text with preconceived notions will seek to apply to it one rigid, uncompromising methodology. Not so a mind like Rashi, who lived and walked, as it were, with the scholars cited in his text, and indeed was able to immerse himself so deeply into their mentality that he became, in fact, their partner, reacting to situations which confronted them and commenting upon their reactions in turn, whenever and wherever common sense and necessity seemed to demand it. It therefore should not be surprising to note that Rashi's approach to the Talmudic text represented not one, but a combination of many methods.

In numerous instances, Rashi temporarily defers the explanation of a difficult concept by a terse statement to the effect that "this will be explained later on." With the same ease he explains *aggadot* (narrative material introduced by the Sages to illustrate the dry text of legal discussion) which, probably due to the unedited form in which they are reproduced, seem grotesque and tend to rob their authors of their credibility. For instance, in connection with prayers recited when entering and leaving a bathhouse, implying that one's ablutions may entail physical danger, Rabbi Abbahu is quoted (Berakhot 60a) as saying that on one occasion, when the floor of a bathhouse gave way, he, Abbahu, stood on a pillar and miraculously managed to keep one hundred and one men from falling and being buried beneath the rubble by supporting them all with one arm. Rashi explains: What Rabbi Abbahu really meant to say was that he managed to support one or two men with one arm, and that these men in turn started a human chain, each man supporting the next, up to the one hundred and first man, so that all these men could emerge from the ruins relatively unharmed. Elsewhere (Bekhorot 8a), in a discussion of the circumstances under which a mass resembling a "clean" fish discovered within the body of an "unclean" aquatic creature might be regarded as a *bona fide kosher* fish ingested by the unclean host and the circumstances under which it must be considered a forbidden growth or fetus belonging to the "unclean" creature, a statement is made that the gestation period of a rattlesnake is seventy years. Rashi explains this piece of Talmudic shorthand to mean that a rattlesnake is able to bear young until it reaches the age of seventy.

In the same manner, Rashi seeks to explain Talmudic statements which, due to the stenographic style of the text, sound unlikely or altogether unintelligible. Thus, according to Rashi, Dama ben Netinah (Kiddushin 31a) did not wear a garment made of gold (*sericum*) but merely one embroidered with gold threads. The statement in Tractate Yoma (75a) that "he who puts his eye in the cup sees the whole world as one smooth plain" is interpreted by Rashi to mean that to a drunkard everyone's property appears ownerless and free for the taking. Explanatory words or phrases such as "not really,"[18] "even" or "even if"[19] are inserted almost unnoticed into the text of Rashi's commentary in order to attach helpful nuances to Talmudic statements which at first glance sound illogical. In many instances ambiguous suffixes and verb forms in the text can be properly understood only if they are communicated orally. Rashi's written comments seek to reproduce concomitant intonations and gestures which he feels accompanied the spoken words of the Sages.[20] Thus, Rashi's sensitivity to, and his familiarity with, the world of the Talmud have enabled him to reconstruct the Oral Tradition on which the Talmudic text is based. It is therefore no exaggeration to say that were it not for the commentary of Rashi, the Talmud would have remained a closed book to the Jewish people.[21]

An additional difficulty encountered by Rashi was the task of establishing an authoritative, authentic version of the Talmudic text. In our own age of abundant paper and efficient, accurate typesetting machines, it is difficult to understand the problems of an earlier age in reproducing accurate versions of an original text. Parchment was a precious, rare commodity which only the very wealthy could afford to buy. Many responsa of that period reflect the value and scarcity of books.[22] The shortage of books reached a point where prayer books were in such short supply that certain prayers had to be omitted from the synagogue service because the worshippers were not sufficiently familiar with them to be able to recite them by heart.[23] Whoever wanted to possess a book had to copy it out for himself from another copy; this obviously was not an easy task.

A student of the Talmud was concerned first and foremost with acquiring a text of the entire Talmud or at least of as many tractates as possible. Since the copyists who worked with Talmudic texts were not always Talmudic scholars, and since the Talmud has no counterpart of the Masoretic tradition which establishes the authentic text for the Bible, many mistakes found their way into the Talmudic text in the process of countless copyings. In addition, many copyists undertook on their own initiative to "improve upon" passages which seemed to them obscure, but since they lacked familiarity with the subject matter they only succeeded in corrupting the original text. It is therefore not surprising that, in an attempt to check the proliferation of corrupted Talmudic texts, Rabbenu Gershom found it necessary to impose a *herem* (ban) on what he called "text-improvers."[24] Also, copyists frequently added their own notes or comments in the margins of the parchment sheets. Later copyists, unaware that these notes were not part of the original text, incorporated them into the text, thereby creating additional damage and confusion.

In view of the foregoing, it was necessary for Rashi to locate an authentic text before he could write an authoritative commentary on the Talmud. As already noted in Chapter One, Rashi's search for such a text led him first to Rabbenu Gershom's Talmudical academy in Mayence. Rabbenu Gershom had not only written commentaries on the Talmud but had also attempted to establish an authentic Talmudic text. Commenting on Sukkah 40a Rashi asserts that he had "received from his teacher a certain reading... [and] tried from his early youth to reconcile their words with the spirit of the Talmud but was unable to do so. He then found this other reading in the manuscript of Rabbenu Gershom of blessed memory." He compared various manuscripts[25] and frequently corrected the text in his commentary in accordance with the version transmitted to him by his teacher.[26] He also consulted other Rabbinic sources,[27] relying on a corrected, accurate tractate of the Mishnah[28] or on earlier editions.[29] We know of at least one instance in which Rashi's uncanny scent for mistakes in the Talmudic text led him to an older edition which confirmed his suspicion. He proudly showed it to his teachers, who, he recalls in his commentary on Arakhin 12b, were pleased with his discovery.[30] Rashi also tested extant Talmudic texts by internal evidence, on the basis of which he then decided which of two contradictory readings was the correct one.[31] In many instances, he emended readings on the basis of Geonic responsa, with which he was thoroughly familiar.[32] Rashi did not always find such documentary support for the emendations he submitted in his commentary on the Talmudic text, but it is the measure of his greatness that, even without this support, he had the courage to reject readings which in his opinion were incongruous with the general tone and spirit of the Talmud.[33] Only great men motivated by a selfless search for the truth can muster the courage to suggest such changes. To Rashi, the Talmud was not a mere work of literature which could be treated cavalierly. It was the basis of Jewish life and the treasure house of the Jewish spirit. In short, Rashi viewed the Talmud as a sacred book. But the sacredness of the Talmudic text did not mean that the errors which had obviously crept into the text had to be retained inviolate. Thus, commenting on Hullin 74b, he states: "Although this is the reading of all the [extant Talmudic] texts, the truth of the matter is that this is a mistake and that there is no sage who could justify this... This mistake must have occurred due to haste."[34]

Nevertheless, Rashi exercised the utmost circumspection in proposing emendations to the Talmudic text. Often, when he found two Rabbinic sources contradicting each other, he refrained from making a choice between the two.[35] In some cases he even commented on both readings without taking sides, leaving the decision for future commentators to make.[36] At times we can detect an undertone of annoyance when Rashi says, "This reading is mistaken and has crept into the text due to commentators who erred; not being sufficiently familiar with the meaning of the text, they permitted this error to creep into their reading."[37] In another instance, Rashi deletes a question which he considers to be a marginal note inserted by a student and then mistakenly incorporated into the text by a copyist.[38]

In this manner Rashi carefully and reverently weighed and tested the various readings which he found in extant Talmudic texts and, in his commentary, presents us with an authentic text of the Talmud, free of errors and copyists' transmogrifications. It is interesting to note that many of the readings suggested by Rashi in his commentary have found their way into some editions of the Talmud: later copyists at times incorporated Rashi's comments into the text as if they had been uttered by one of the Sages themselves.

NOTES

1. *Pes. Rab. III,4:* And since he [Jacob] blessed [his sons] and made them into tribes, he spoke about the matter of Rachel [Jacob] said to [Joseph]: "Why did thy mother not join me in my grave?" Since Joseph was greatly disturbed about this, his father began to reassure him: "Even as thou wouldst have wanted thy mother to join me in my grave, so I, too, would have wanted it...." [Joseph then] said to [Jacob]: "Perhaps the fact that thou didst not bury her [in the grave of the Patriarchs] was due to the [heavy] rains." [But Jacob] said to him: "No, [when I traveled] the distance to Ephrath it was [the time] between Passover and Shevuoth, when the ground is [riddled] like a sieve, so that it is easily negotiable." Thereupon Joseph said to him: "Command me now and I shall disinter her and bury her together with thee." [However] Jacob said to him: "Thou canst not do this, my son, because I buried her [at the place where she now lies] solely at the command [of God]. I, too, wanted to take her up [to the Cave of Mahpelah] and bury her there, but the Holy One, blessed be He, did not permit it, as it is written, *And I buried her there* [Genesis 48:7]... Because God foresaw that the Temple was fated to be destroyed and His children would be destined to go into exile. [On their road to exile] they will pass the tomb of the Patriarchs and plead with them to pray in their behalf, but [the Patriarchs] will be unable to help them. Since they will be passing on that road they will then come and embrace the tomb of Rachel, and she will plead [in their behalf] for mercy from the Holy One, blessed be He. She will say: "Master of the Universe! Listen to my weeping and have mercy on my children. O grant my request!" And the Holy One,

blessed be He, will then immediately listen to her prayer. How so? For thus wrote Jeremiah: "Lamentation, and bitter weeping, Rachel weeping for her children," and he writes, "and there is hope for thy future... and thy children shall return to their own border." And this mollified [Joseph] for the fact that his mother was not buried together with [Jacob].

2. S. M. Chones, *op. cit.*,7a: "Whatever explanations my master, my grandfather, gave on the Talmud,even I could offer, but I fear that I could not match his commentary on the Bible."

3. C. N. Bialik, *Letters*, (Hebrew), ed. F. Lachover, Tel Aviv, 1935/39. Letter dated 22nd Adar I, 1905.

4. Leopold Zunz, *Toledot Raschi*, Hebrew translation by Samson Bloch, Warsaw, 1862, p. 26.

5. Commentary on Genesis 3:8: "I, however, am concerned only with the plain sense of Scripture and with such *aggadot* as explain the words of Scripture in a manner that fits in with them."

6. On Shabbat 77a concerning the quantity of wine that must not be carried from one domain to another on the Sabbath: "There are some who erroneously assume that 'one quarter' means one quarter of a *log* [a quantity equal to the contents of six eggs] and not one quarter of one quarter.They are in error and our Rabbis did not explain it in this manner. Proof of this can be adduced from Tractate Nazir 38a."

Ibid., 85b, on the meaning of the word *keranot:* "This is how it seems to me, but my teachers did not explain it in this manner. Instead, they explain that *keranot* are borders. But I have great hesitation regarding this explanation. Also,in the entire Talmud (*Shisha Sidrei Mishnah*) I have [noted] that *keranot* is defined only as 'corners.' I have found support [for my view] in the work of Rabbi Simon the Elder, my mother's brother, who heard it from Rabbenu Gershom, Father of the Exile. The answer of Rabbenu Isaac ben Judah,who interprets it as meaning 'triangular,' does not seem right to me."

7. Johann Pestalozzi (1746-1827) was the first in the modern age to stress the educational principle that the foundation of teaching is the student's observation (R. H. Quick, *Essays on Educational Reformers*, New York, 1892, p. 368). Many of Rashi's explanations are based on personal observations from life, which he communicates in a most graphic fashion and which are readily understandable to the student. (See Chapters 7-10 in the present study). Rashi would first explain concepts which appeared to him less difficult and from there proceed to ideas which seemed more complex. It was not until the 17th century that John Amos Comenius (1592-1671) formulated the educational principle, "From the simple to the complex and from the known to the unknown." The fact that Rashi must have employed drawings and diagrams in many of his explanations is apparent from RaSHBaM's remark (on Numbers 34:12) that "our teacher, my grandfather, made a comment [here] and drew the outlines" and from the word *ka-zeh* ("like this") which Rashi

adds in many of his Talmudic comments (e.g., Hullin 124a, Avodah Zarah 72b, Bava Metzia 25b, Menahot 63a, Rosh HaShanah 17b).

8. Menahem ben Zerah, Introduction to *Tzedah La-Derekh.*

9. E.g., Ketubot 111a; Bekhorot 8b; Zevahim 15a, 15b; Bava Metzia 7a; Bava Kamma 86b, Sukkah 5a.

10. On Temurah 15b: ששכחו מתוך פלפול הלכה האיך

11. On Pesahim 19a: יורד לעמקי תהום וא״א להעמידו

12. On Hullin 81a: ופירוש משובש הוא מאדם חריף ומפולפל

13. E.g. on Gittin 33a: כך אני מפרש בכל מקום מלבי

14. E.g. Shabbat 92b: כך לשון רבותי ולבי מגמגם
Ibid. 15a: ורבותי מפרשין בלשון משה רבנו ולבי מגמגם

15. On Shabbat 86b: ואומר אני שהוא שיבוש והגורס טעה ולא ידע לפרש

16. E.g. on Shabbat 101b: כך נראית שיטה זו בעיני ועל מה שפירשו רבותי תמהתי

17. a. In Shabbat 10a, regarding the best time of day at which people should have their meals, the Talmudic text states that if one eats after the sixth hour in the morning it is "like a rock thrown into a skin bottle." To this Rashi comments: קשה לגוף ולי נראה לא קשה ולא יפה ("[This means] bad for the body, but to me it seems that it is neither bad nor good").

b. In Pesahim 54a the Talmud enumerates the things which were created at dusk on the sixth day of Creation, among them *mikhtav.* To this Rashi comments: חקיקתן וצורתן כך שמעתי. ולי נראה כתב זו היא צורתן והמכתב הוא עט וחרט ("[*Mikhtav* means the art of] engraving and its form. This is what I heard but it seems to me that *k'tav* would be the art, while *mikhtav* refers to the pen and the stylus").

18. To the statement in Shabbat 10b that enmity arose between Joseph and his brethren on account of two *sela'im* of silk, and to the statement in Sanhedrin 7b that sixty mighty men stood around the bed of King Solomon, Rashi comments: לאו דוקא ("Not really" or "not exactly").

19. a. To the statement in Ta'anit 28b concerning the days of the year on which an individual (worshipping without a congregation) must recite the entire Hallel, Rashi notes: אפילו יחיד ("Even an individual").

b. To the statement in Bava Metzia 7a that if two people find an object "they must divide it between themselves. If it is a gilded cloth" Rashi notes: כלומר אפילו היא מוזהבת חולקין ("It must be divided equally between them even if it is a gilded cloth").

20. E.g. to the statement in Pesahim 8a that a balcony may be searched for leaven *l'orah* Rashi indicates that this means not by candlelight brought to the balcony but by the natural daylight that illuminates the balcony. (*L'orah* can be read either as "light" or "by its light").

21. Isaac ben Sheshet, *She'elot uTeshuvot RIBaSH*, par. 394 (beginning).

22. Joel Miller, *op. cit.*, No. 29, p. 15; A. Berliner, *Beitraege zur Geschichte der Raschi Commentare*, Berlin, Rosenstand, 1903, p. 1.

23. *Mahzor Vitry*, 221, p. 358: "I have noted that the verses of the Musaph service were never recited on the festivals in our localities because people do not know them by heart."

24. Rabbenu Tam, *Sefer HaYashar*, Zhitomir, 1869, Introduction. See also S. M. Chones, *op. cit.*, pp. 208b and 210a.

25. E.g. Shabbat 29a, where Rashi explains the term *bukhia* as a hollow tile stove called *tiules* in Medieval French. He adds that the reading *be-tafi* mentioned in other books also refers to a stove.

26. E.g. on Zevahim 56a: כך הגהתי מספרו של רבי ("Thus I have emended it according to the book [written] by my teacher").

27. E.g. on Shevuot 34b: וכן דרך תנאים וספרי וספרא ("And this is the way of the Tannaites, of the Sifre and the Sifra").

28. E.g. on Shevuot 35a: וכן כתוב ונקוד בסדר משנה מוגהת ודווקנית ("And thus it is written and punctuated in an emended, accurate [text of a] Mishnaic tractate").

29. Shevuot 36b: וכן מצאתי לשון בבלי בספרים ישנים ("And thus I found the text of the Babylonian Talmud in ancient books").

30. It is stated in Arakhin 12b that the people of Israel counted seventeen Jubilees between their arrival in the Promised Land and their departure into exile. The Talmudic text attempts to explain this calculation with a statement opening as follows, "These three years of their expulsion by Sennacherib." To this, Rashi notes that the word "three" must have been inserted into the text erroneously and that the text should read simply, "These years of their exile by Sennacherib." Rashi adds:

כך הבנתי מלבי וישרה בעיני אבל לא שמעתיה ואחרי כן מצאתי ספר ישן מוגה שכתוב בו כן והודעתיו לרבותי וישרה בעיניהם ("I have understood this intuitively [lit., "from my heart"], and it was correct in my eyes but I had not [actually] heard it [from another authoritative source]. [But] subsequently I found it in an ancient, emended text where it is written so, and I notified my teachers of it and it was right in their eyes.")

31. E.g. on Zevahim 120a: ה"ג במסכת מעילה והכי נמי גרסינן לה ("This is the reading in Tractate Me'ilah and so we shall read it here as well").

In Sanhedrin 86b it is stated that unlike a scholar who has misled his community (*zaken Mamre*), a mere student whose explanations lead a community astray is not considered guilty of a capital offense. The question is then asked how one is to determine whether the person who misled his community is to be classed as a scholar or as a mere student. Rashi, basing his interpretation on Avodah Zarah 19b, explains "שאינו ראוי להוראה עד שיהיה בן מ'" ("A student is not fit to be a teacher until he has reached the age of forty").

32. a. With reference to Shabbat 135b. Here, in connection with a statement by Rabbi Assi that only those male infants who were born naturally (i.e., not by Caesarean surgery) must be circumcised on the eighth day, the

Talmudic text states that this is an argument among the Tannaites. Rashi says:

ה״ג הא מילתא בשאילתות דרב אחאי ("This is the reading also in the She'iltot of Rav Ahai [of the Geonic era]").

b. With reference to the question in Makkot 9b whether a manslayer who hated his victim is permitted to go to a City of Refuge, the opinions are divided between Rabbi Judah the Prince and other authorities. Rashi maintains:

אין לך שונא גולה כך מצאתי גירסא בתשובות הגאונים ("One who hated [his victim] does not go to the City of Refuge. [This is the ruling which] I found in the Geonic Responsa").

c. Defining felt shoes mentioned in Betzah 15a, Rashi says:

ראיתי בתשובות הגאונים שרגילין ללבשן תחת מנעליהן ("I saw in the Geonic Responsa that these were worn under one's shoes").

d. In connection with a growth on the lung of beef cattle which would render the animal unfit as food (Hullin 47a), Rashi notes:

ובתשובות הגאונים הבבלים מצאתי כן ("And I found it thus in the Responsa of the Babylonian Geonim").

33. With reference to the assessment of the worth of a person (Arakhin 17b), Rashi notes:

ואני שמעתיה כמות שהיא כתובה בספרים ופירושה כמו שפירשתיה ואין שיטת הש״ס כן ("I heard it as it is written in the texts and the explanation is as I have given it, but the spirit of the Talmud is not so").

34. אע״פ שהוא בכל הספרים אמת הדבר שהוא שבוש ולא יש חכם אשר יושיבנו על כנו. ואגב שיטפא דגירסא אישתבשו.

(The comment refers to the Talmudic statement that an unborn live calf embryo found in the womb of a cow that has been killed by ritual slaughter may be eaten without subjecting it to separate *shehitah*, but that the *helev* [suet] is forbidden. The text asks, "What *helev*?")

35. In connection with two contradictory opinions (Haggigah 19b) regarding the combination of water from waterholes on different levels so as to obtain the quantity of water required for a ritual bath, Rashi notes:

ובלשון הספרים איני יכול להעמידה דא״כ מתניתא קשיין אהדדי ומאי חזית דציית לבתרייתא ("I cannot maintain it from the way it is written in the texts because [we have here] two statements that contradict one another. Why should you follow the latter of the two?")

36. a. In connection with a statement by Rabbi Eliezer (Hullin 4a) that matzot baked by Kuthites must not be eaten on Passover "because they are not expert in watching [the matzot carefully]." Rashi comments:

ל״ג ולמאן דגריס הכי מפרש ("We do not read it thus. However, if one reads it thus, this [i.e., R. Eliezer's statement] is the explanation.")

b. Rav Hisda quotes (Zevahim 115b) the Biblical verse, "And he sent the young men of the Children of Israel..." (Exodus 24:5). To this Rashi notes: נראה בעיני שהספרים חסרים כאן ולא ידעתי מה, ואם אין חסרים זהו פירושו ("It seems to me that something is missing here, and I do not know what it is. However, if there is nothing missing, then this is the explanation").

c. With reference to questions of defilement and purity the Talmudic text (Haggigah 20b) mentions two cases that seem similar and poses the question, "What is the difference between the two?" To this Rashi notes: לא גרסינן, ואי גרסינן הכי פירושו ("We do not read it thus. However, if one reads it thus, this is the explanation...")

d. With reference to a question (Temurah 3a) concerning burnt offerings brought by an idol worshipper, Rashi notes: וללא''א דכתיב בספרים ול''ג עליהן משמע הכי ("And according to a second version which does not include the word[s] 'upon them' (or 'with them'), the explanation is as follows").

37. גירסא זו הכתובה בספרים משובשת היא וע''י פרשנים טועין שלא היו בקיאין בשמועה ופירשוה בשיבוש בתוך הגירסא וכך הדעה ולא יותר.

(The comment concerns an argument between Rabbi Ishmael and other Rabbinic authorities [Keritot 4a] about the punishment of one who eats the suet of an ox, a sheep and a goat).

38. With reference to the principle stated by Rabbi Ishmael that a violation of a negative commandment not involving action is not punishable by flogging, Rashi found the reading: "There would be a difficulty in the third chapter of Tractate Makkot. To this Rashi comments: לא גרסינן ותלמיד טועה שהוקשה לו כתבה בגליון ספרו; קשיא לו הך דאלו הן הלוקין וכתבוה סופרים בגמ' והתלמיד טועה... ("[The words] 'in the third chapter...' do not belong in the text; a student who was in error and who had difficulty wrote it into the margin of his text and the copyists [mistakenly] incorporated it into the text. However, the student was in error...."). Rashi then proceeds to clear up the misunderstanding.

Part IV

THE WORLD THROUGH RASHI'S EYES

In his commentaries on the Bible and the Talmud Rashi rendered a unique service to the Jews of his own generation. He sought to make not only the philosophical and ethical concepts of the Bible and of the Talmud but also the practical aspects of Biblical and Rabbinic law understandable to his contemporaries by relating these concepts to their own everyday lives. Biblical and Talmudic allusions to customs, mores, dress, food, arts and crafts, medical advice, folk wisdom and an unending variety of other human notions and phenomena served Rashi as bases for comments designed to link the universe of the Bible and the Talmud with the ideas, customs and habits of medieval West European Jewry. Rashi's comments were meant to speak not merely to the Jewish savant but also, if indeed not primarily, to the "ordinary" Jews of Rashi's day, irrespective of educational, social or vocational background.

Rashi's endeavors in this regard have yielded one significant by-product which has placed subsequent generations — and not Jews alone — eternally in his debt. With his comments, he constructed for generations of future students a spellbinding, convincing picture of life and work in medieval Western Europe as he and his contemporaries observed it. Thanks to its geographic centrality and economic significance, the city of Troyes was an ideal source for Rashi's observations. Rashi's comments reveal the commentator as anything but a scholarly recluse: they reflect a remarkably open mind with a keen sense for the practical aspects of life.

In the following five chapters, which comprise the fourth section of this book, the author has attempted to cull from Rashi's commentaries random aspects of life, work and behavior typical of the Jews in Rashi's world. It is hoped that this presentation, which in the context of the present book can be little more than an outline, will motivate interest in further study.

The notes to these chapters should be of additional interest because they show the Biblical and Talmudic contexts for Rashi's observations. They quote Rashi's commentaries together with quotations or abstracts of the Biblical and Talmudic passages to which the commentaries refer. Thus, the notes should provide further insights into Rashi's manner of relating the timeless Biblical and Talmudic heritage to the era and to the world in which he found himself.

CHAPTER SEVEN

Behavior, Manners and Dress

Rashi's commentaries display a keen sensitivity to human behavior and to human reactions linked with the phenomena of daily life. Rashi's aim, it seems, was to show that many of the behavior patterns and mannerisms he describes were much the same in his day as they had been a thousand years earlier because they are quasi-automatic responses to age-old stimuli. Thus, commenting on Caleb's silencing the Children of Israel concerning Moses in the wilderness (Numbers 13:30), Rashi notes that if one desires silence, it is customary to say, "Sht."[1] In connection with a statement in Lamentations 2:15 that the onlookers will "hiss and wag their head" when they behold the sad fate of Jerusalem, Rashi points out that it is common for people to "blow air with their mouths" (whistle?) at the sight of a disaster.[2] To the vision of Rabbi Eleazar ben Pedat related in the Talmud (Ta'anit 25a) Rashi comments that one can awaken a sleeping person by snapping one's fingers.[3] To the lament that the Jewish people stretched out its hand to the ancient kingdom of Egypt (Lamentations 5:6) Rashi remarks

155

that a person who is about to fall instinctively stretches out his hand for support.[4] Where the Talmud (Sukkah 52a) tells of the anguished pose struck by Abaye, Rashi says that when a person is troubled and immersed in thought he will lean against a doorpost (as if seeking to steady himself).[5] Elsewhere in his Talmudic commentaries Rashi notes that one who is in distress plucks or tears at his garments in utter frustration.[6] To the Talmudic statement (Shabbat 10a) that when Rava prayed he "clasped his hands," Rashi adds that a student when confronted by his angry teacher will clasp (or wring) his hands in apprehension.[7] Where the Talmud suggests the behavior proper when visiting the sick (Shabbat 12b), Rashi advises that one should sit still without turning either to the left or to the right, a pose which he characterizes as that of one who is shy and fearful.[8]

With regard to commonly used gestures, Rashi, commenting on Proverbs 1:24 ("I have stretched out my hand but no man attended"), explains that the ancient way of beckoning to another person to come closer was to extend one's hand toward the person wanted (instead of moving one's hand in one's own direction).[9] It is interesting to note that this is still the gesture used by Arabs and by Sephardic Jews when motioning to another to come closer. Commenting on a gesture that passed between a father and son in the course of a scholarly debate (Mo'ed Katan 25a), Rashi states that one who wishes to communicate with another person when he does not want the others present to notice will touch the other person's foot.[10] In his commentary on the Biblical prohibition against tale-bearing (Leviticus 19:16) Rashi mentions that gossipers exchange private winks so the others present should not understand.[11]

Disapproval of another person was expressed in Rashi's day by a sound similar to clearing one's throat. (Rashi uses the onomatopoeic Hebrew *ar-ar* to indicate this choking sound, which he mentions in connection with the drinking of the bitter waters by a wife suspected of adultery.)[12] Approval of a vital, energetic individual was indicated by the statement, "This is a man alive!"[13]

Rashi acknowledges that individuals differ in their conceptions of what is proper and what is not. To the Talmudic statement (Gittin 90a in connection with legal justifications for divorce) that "people diverge in their attitudes as regards sensitivity to food and drink" Rashi notes, "There are people who are highly sensitive and reject food because of small defects, and there are those who are less sensitive. Likewise, opinions of people differ as to [what constitutes] lewdness. Some detest the smallest measure of lewdness, while others are less sensitive, and still others are not sensitive [to it] at all."

Concerning etiquette (Berakhot 53a) Rashi comments that it is the general custom for people to say, "To your health!" when someone sneezes.[14] Noting the courtesy extended even to slaves in the household of Rabban Gamliel (Berakhot 16b) Rashi points out that in his own day it was the custom to address people as "Master" or "Mistress" Such-and-Such.[15]

Living in an area where viticulture was widespread, Rashi probably had ample opportunity to observe the effects of strong drink. Where the Book of Proverbs (23:31) speaks of wine, Rashi notes that while the customer in a tavern is interested primarily in the cup of wine before him, the tavernkeeper is chiefly concerned with the contents of the customer's purse.[16] Commenting on Job 6:3 ("...therefore are my words broken") Rashi refers to the stammering drunkard whose words can hardly be understood.[17] In connection with the evils of overindulgence in food and drink (Pesahim 49a) Rashi aptly describes the *clochard* so often seen in certain sections of Paris to this day. A tramp, he says, folds his clothes beneath him and goes to sleep in the street. This, he continues, is also the custom of drunkards who are so inebriated that they cannot manage to go home to their own beds at night.[18]

Rashi was aware also of other examples of boorishness. In connection with a note in the Talmud about how Rabbi Judah the Prince would attempt to restrain himself from belching during prayer (Berakhot 24a) Rashi complains that people are in the habit of belching after a heavy meal and that as a result one can easily ascertain what they have eaten.[19]

Rashi's commentaries are replete with folk wisdom. In connection with a Talmudic statement (Bava Metziah 27b) that people tend to be superstitious about lending their wallets Rashi counsels that a man should never lend his wallet because one who lends his wallet sells his luck.[20] To the Talmudic dictum, "If thou wouldst be strangled, see that thou art hanged upon a tall tree" (Pesahim 112a) Rashi comments that if one wants his opinion to gain acceptance, he should cite it as the opinion voiced by an individual who is generally accepted as a great man.[21] Elaborating on the Talmudic concept of *hillul haShem*—"profanation of the Divine Name"—in Shabbat 33a, Rashi explains that a great man to whom others look for wisdom and guidance must be careful in his actions, for if he is not, others will think that if even this wonderful man seems to consider it proper to disregard the Law of God, *they* certainly do not need to subordinate their lives to it.[22]

Rashi clearly attached considerable importance to clean and appropriate clothing. Commenting on a reference to "glory" in Isaiah 10:16 (the same Hebrew word—*kavod*—is used for both "glory" and "honor"), Rashi notes that clothes honor the man.[23] He devotes particular attention to the care, washing and styling of clothes. Methods of laundering, perfuming and pressing are discussed in great detail in connection with a wide assortment of Talmudic passages. We learn from Rashi's commentaries to these passages that in his own day clothes were laundered in a pair of rectangular pits, about one cubit deep, which were dug in the ground. In one of these pits rain water was gathered; the other was filled with a mixture of rain water and dog excrement. It seems that the dog excrement was allowed to ferment so that it might act as a detergent. The laundry was soaked in the excrement mixture for a day or two and then transferred into the pit of rain water for scrubbing.[24] Rashi himself does not explain the purpose of the excrement. He admits he does not know why the excrement was used in laundering; he merely reports that he saw this method employed in Germany.[25] If the garments were to be dyed, they were first soaked in alum.[26] Garments were washed with their neck openings tied.[27] Clothes were scrubbed with both hands; the garments were folded in half and moved back and forth.[28]

After the clothes had been washed, they were perfumed—probably in order to remove any smell of dog excrement that still clung to them after they had been scrubbed in the pure rain water. The clean clothes were gathered and placed on a "laundry chair," a long board with many perforations, under which the perfuming agent was set. The clothes on the chair absorbed the perfume through the perforations.[29] The perfuming was usually done with spices which were placed over a fire underneath the "laundry chair"; the aromatic smoke thus produced would pass through the perforations and penetrate the clean clothes.[30] Silken garments (which presumably could not be laundered by the same method as linens) were perfumed by pressing a container of aromatics onto the material so that it might absorb the scent.[31]

Clothes were pressed by placing them between two long, heavy pressing boards (*makhbesh*). The upper board was lowered upon the clothes by means of pegs which were pushed into staggered holes in four rods fixed to the lower board — one rod at each corner. The space between the two boards was regulated so as to produce the pressure needed to press the clothes. The upper board was locked into place by the pegs.[32]

It seems that in Rashi's day the basic garments of men and women were much alike in cut and shape. The main garment for either sex was a shift; this was topped by an outer robe to which stockings were attached. The robe in turn was topped by a silken coat,[33] which was closed with cords hanging from the waist.[34] Puttees were wound around the legs.[35]

Trousers worn by the men of Rashi's generation seem to have resembled knee breeches because Rashi, in describing them, uses the German word *Kniehosen* (spelled in Hebrew letters).[36] A mantle or cloak was worn over the outer garments in cold weather; it consisted of just two flaps which were cut in a circular manner at the hem.[37] During the warmer season of the year this mantle was replaced by a thinner garment. This garment was folded back when the wearer sat down, revealing the garments beneath.[38] All garments were carefully hemmed.[39] The sewing, particularly in the case of silk,[40] was done with a very fine flax thread.[41] Because buttons apparently had not yet been invented, trousers were belted with a string pulled through a hem at the waist. The fit of the trousers around the waist could be tightened or loosened by pulling in or releasing the string as needed.[42] Since pockets were unknown in Rashi's day (they did not come into use until the 16th century) the handkerchief took the form of a scarf tied around the neck with ends hanging down in front so that the wearer could use them for wiping his mouth and eyes.[43]

Rashi gives more attention to the description of women's clothing than to men's garments. The reason for this may be, in part, that the Talmud, too, devotes much discussion to women's apparel. The many ornaments and accessories worn by women, particularly on festive occasions, were studied by the Rabbis with care to see whether or not a woman would be violating the prohibition against "carrying" on the Sabbath by wearing these adornments when she went forth from her home on the Sabbath day. As a result, Rashi had many opportunities to describe the women's apparel of his own day in his commentaries.

The women of Rashi's generation kept their cloaks in place around the neck by means of a strap which was sewn to one edge of the garment's neckline and which they would twist around a precious stone (or even a lowly nut) attached to the other edge.[44] Gowns were closed with pins or brooches.[45] Straps on a lady's garment might be decorated with gold or studded with precious stones.[46] Women also wore belts made entirely of gold platelets or with jewel-studded gold inlays.[47] Belts were tied with fringes attached to either end.[48] When women dined, they covered their gowns with a kind of bib. This bib had a loop at its upper edge through which was threaded a strap that was knotted around the neck. Rashi adds that these straps would be pulled rather tightly so as to make the flesh of the woman's neck protrude and make her look plump; apparently, a fleshy neck was considered attractive in a woman in Rashi's day. Rashi assures us, however, that since the strap was wide and soft, it could not cause any injury to the woman's neck or throat.[49] Some women wore sleeves slashed in such a way as to expose their bare arms. Rashi disapproved, describing this fashion fad as imitating the Gentile women of France "whose [bare] flesh can be seen from their sides."[50] The Talmudic passage to which this comment refers states that if a woman wears such immodest garb it is sufficient reason for her husband to divorce her. Women wore a special apron around their hips which looked like a pair of short pants; this garment was worn for the sake of modesty.[51]

Among the miscellaneous other accessories worn by women in his day Rashi describes a kind of veil which extended around the forehead and which covered the wearer's eyes. He notes that this covering over her eyes sometimes caused the woman to fall asleep.[52]

Women in Rashi's time parted their hair in the middle.[53] The hair might be intertwined with ribbons, which were sometimes embroidered with gold thread.[54] When a woman saw a white hair on her head, she would pluck it out so that she should not look old.[55] Women wore wigs to make their hair appear thicker and fuller. Women with thin hair[56] wore hairpieces plaited through their own hair. Some wore these simply to enhance their natural beauty.[57]

Since married Jewish women, according to Jewish law, were not permitted to appear in public bareheaded, they developed an interesting variety of head coverings. Some wore woolen caps or snoods topped by a thin decorated kerchief,[58] which was frequently pulled over the eyes. The problem remained what to do about wisps of hair which kept creeping out from beneath the kerchief. Some women wore small lace headdresses which covered their hair completely.[59] Others twisted unruly wisps around a hairpin which they then pushed beneath the lace headdress.[60] Still other women wore, as a kind of ornament, a thin gold headband or tiara across the forehead to cover their front hair from ear to ear. Sometimes this headband was not made of gold but merely of silk interwoven with gold threads.[61] In either case, the headband apparently was intended to keep the hair in place. Some women in Rashi's time wore hats made from the ribs of feathers[62] which may have resembled the straw hats of our own day.

It is interesting to note that, in striking contrast to the

attention given women's headgear, Rashi's commentaries contain almost no references to head coverings worn by men. The reason for this may be the fact that, contrary to popular notion, the prohibition against married women being seen bareheaded in public was regarded as much sterner than that against men appearing with their heads uncovered.[63] However, there is one Talmudic comment by Rashi that seems to refer to a man's hat. This headpiece appears to have been shaped like a writing reed, tapering off from its middle into a pointed top.[64]

Rashi's commentaries include numerous references to footwear. Some shoes in his day were made with soft uppers and tied with leather laces threaded through four loops. Others were made of hard, unprocessed leather through which no laces could be pulled; however, these shoes somehow could be tied at the top.[65] The wearer pulled on the shoe with the help of a small loop or flap attached to the back of the heel.[66] Some shoes had wooden soles to which the leather uppers were nailed. The soles were reinforced with iron tips. There were shoes which were open both at the front and at the back and into which the wearer could slip from either end.[67] Some shoes were open-backed.[68] Others had soles which were thicker on one side than on the other; the soles then had to be leveled by means of nails hammered into the thinner side so that the wearer could walk properly.[69] Sometimes lighter footgear — apparently socks or slippers — was worn under heavier overshoes to give the wearer added protection when the ground was wet.[70]

In Rashi's day, no less than in our own, women enjoyed wearing jewelry. They wore around their necks small flasks of gold or silver which, in addition to being decorative, contained the oils and perfumes with which the wearers liked to anoint themselves.[71] Strings of pearls were popular.[72] Sometimes amulets were used as pendants.[73] Women's mantles were fastened with golden clasps[74] and gowns were closed at the neckline with semicircular chokers.[75] Ladies pierced their ears for earrings, inserting threads or little chips of wood into the holes to keep them open.[76] Even little girls had their ears pierced and the perforations kept open in this manner, although, as a rule, they did not begin wearing earrings regularly until they were older.[77] Rashi tells us that in his time earrings, rings and bracelets were made by goldsmiths[78] and sold by peddlers who went from door to door offering their wares to the ladies.[79] The women kept their jewelry in special boxes or etuis[80] which were decorated with inlay work and studded with little nails.[81]

The women of Rashi's era used mirrors to inspect themselves. According to Rashi, mirrors were apparently regarded as meant for the use of women only.[82] Creams and ointments known to women in Rashi's world included a lime compound used as a depilatory,[83] a powder rouge,[84] a kind of facial mask made from dough to add color to the cheeks,[85] a blue powder for coloring the eyelids[86] and an eyeshadow which was applied around the eyes in order to make them appear larger.[87] Women also used perfumed powder.[88]

In general, the women in Rashi's community, particularly in the cities and larger towns, were carefully guarded and protected. Important ladies owned special "boxes" or carriages in which they were taken wherever they wanted to go.[89] Commenting on a Talmudic reference to blue eye-paint in connection with a prohibition against "carrying" on the Sabbath, Rashi makes a distinction between city girls and young girls who live in villages. The village girl, he explains, does not need so much protection for her chastity as her sisters in the city because there is little fun or lightheadedness in villages with a small population. This is why girls in villages are permitted to keep their faces uncovered and to use eye-paint on both eyelids instead of on just one.[90] At least one other reason why the chastity of village girls was considered to be less threatened than that of their city sisters was that villagers all knew one another well, so that reports of any improper conduct in a village would spread quickly and result in social ostracism for the girl.

NOTES

(Biblical and Talmudic passages are printed in italics; abstracts of such passages, and Rashi's commentaries, in Roman type).

1. *And Caleb silenced the people concerning Moses:* It is customary for one who wishes to silence others to say, "Sht."

2. *They hiss:* [The act of] blowing air with one's mouth. People do this at the sight of something important being destroyed.

3. *He thereupon snapped [his fingers] at my forehead:* A sound produced by snapping one's middle finger and thumb and brushing the fingernail.

4. *We have given the hand to Egypt:* If a man falls and wants to get up he stretches out his hand to someone standing beside him so that the latter should help him.

5. *He leaned [in deep anguish] against a doorpost:* He leaned against the doorpost like one who is immersed in thought and troubled.

6. Megillah 26a [A discussion of the borders of the tribal territories]: [*The land of Benjamin] touched lightly [upon that of Judah]... and Benjamin fretted over it:* One who is in distress plucks and rubs at his garments.

7. *He clasped his hands:* He clasps his hands with his fingers like one who feels uncomfortable because he is afraid of his teacher.

8. *[He] must wrap himself about [in a spirit of reverence]:* Like one who sits in fear, without turning to either side.

9. *I have stretched out my hand:* To motion to someone to come closer, just as one puts out his hand in the direction of another to signal him to come closer.

10. *His father tapped him with his sandal:* As one who surreptitiously touches the foot of his friend [when he wants to communicate something to him] without the others noticing.

11. *Thou shalt not go up and down as a tale bearer:* It is the way of all those who go about gossiping to wink with their eyes and to suggest slanderous statements [by innuendo] so that [the] others [present] should not understand them.

12. Sotah 18b [A description of the ordeal of the bitter waters for the wife suspected of adultery].
Rashi: "One who chokes because of [having taken] a drink [too quickly] makes a noise that sounds like *ar-ar.* It is a way of expressing [the idea that] a calamity has struck."

13. II Chronicles 23:11:
A man alive: When people see an active person, they say, "This is a man alive!"

14. *It was not their custom to say* marpe *[To your health!] if someone sneezed in the house of study [because that would constitute an interruption of the studies]:* If someone sneezes, it is customary to say to him, "To your health!"

15. *Usually slaves were not addressed as "Father or Mother Such-and-Such," but in Rabban Gamaliel's household they were addressed this way:* Just as we today address a person as Master or Mistress Such-and-Such.

16. *When it gives its color in the cup:* [The spelling here is] not *kos* ["cup," but]

kis ["purse"]. He who drinks casts his eye upon the cup, but the tavernkeeper [keeps his eye] on the man's purse.

17. *Therefore are my words broken:* Like one who does not have the strength to utter an intelligible word... a stammering drunkard.

18. [Rabbi Shemaya describes a scholar who overindulges in food as] *A folder of garments and a man who lies down and sleeps:* This is what drunkards do: instead of going home to sleep in their beds, they fold their garments beneath them and go to sleep [wherever they happen to be].

19. [When Rabbi Judah the Prince felt the need to belch during prayers he would put his hand to his chin in an effort to restrain himself]: Rashi: Sometimes one emits through his mouth a gust of air because he has eaten too much. This has the smell of the food he ate."

20. *A purse [is] not lent... because people are superstitious about it:* A man who lends his wallet sells his luck.

21. *If thou wouldst be strangled, see that thou art hanged upon a tall tree:* If thou wishest to [utter an opinion] which thou wouldst have others accept, cite it [as an opinon stated by] a great man.

22. Rashi: "If a great man from whom people learn is not careful in his actions, lesser people will denigrate the Torah because of his behavior. They will say: 'This one understands that there is nothing worthwhile in the Torah and in its commandments.' In this manner the name of God is profaned."

23. *And under his glory:* Clothes honor the man.

24. Bava Bathra 17a [Discussion of what constitutes an infringement upon a neighbor's property]:
A man should not dig a washing pool: He digs a rectangular pit one or more cubits deep and then fills it up with rain water to wash clothes. There were two pits. The one was for soaking [the laundry] for one or two days in dog excrement. This pit was called *mehamtzan* [fermentation pit]. The other one was for scrubbing the laundry and was called *nidyan* [washing pool].

25. Ketubot 77a [A list of occupations which make a man obnoxious to others so that he may be compelled by the Court of Law to grant his wife a divorce];
One who collects dog excrement: I do not know for what purpose they needed it,but I saw in Germany that clothes would be soaked in this for a day or two.

26. Menahot 42b [A reference to the dyeing of the blue thread used in making the *tzitzit*]:
Color... dye: Dyers soak [the] clothing [to be dyed] in alum.

27. Shabbat 48a:
It is permitted to untie the neck of a shirt [on the Sabbath when it is returned by the launderer]: It is permitted [on the Sabbath] to untie the collar which the launderers usually tie up.

28. Zevahim 94b [A reference to the manner in which the blood of sacrificial animals is washed off]:
Rubbing: Rubbing one side against the other just as launderers do, holding a garment in both hands and rubbing it.

Niddah 62a [A reference to the manner in which the stains of menstrual impurity are washed off]:
To rub: Between two hands as launderers do, folding the garment surface to surface and rubbing one surface against the other.

29. Shabbat 88a:
[A launderer's chair upon] which one piles the clothes: This is a long, perforated board. The perfume is placed underneath and the clothes absorb the perfume through the perforations.

Shabbat 123b: [Objects which may or may not be handled on the Sabbath]:
A launderer's basket: A copper vessel made like a sieve with many perforations. It is used by launderers who place it onto the clothes and spray water on the clothes through it. Others say that perfume is placed under it and the clothes above the basket absorb the perfume by way of the perforations.

30. Shabbat 18a: [If one places a perfume brazier under garments which will continue to absorb the perfume all day long it is not considered a violation of the Sabbath]:
Perfume: Frankincense and other kinds of spices placed onto a fire for the purpose of perfuming clothes.

31. Betzah 23a:
It is forbidden to invert a cup of aromatics on silken garments on a festival: To invert a cup of aromatics over a silken garment in order to perfume it with the aromatics in the cup.

32. Shabbat 141a:
One may undo a householder's clothing press [on the Sabbath]: Two long, heavy boards. The clothes are arranged on the lower board. The upper board is then lowered to press the clothes with the help of pegs. There are rods with holes fixed to the four corners of the lower board. The upper board has perforations in each of its four corners [into which the rods fit] and it moves up and down on the rods. In order to press, the [upper board] is lowered and a peg is placed into the hole in the rod so that the board cannot move.

33. Menahot 39b [A discussion on the precepts of wearing *tzitzit*]:
A [silken] garment: A robe made of silk taken from a cocoon.

Exodus 28:4 [Description of the High Priest's vestments];
A robe: A kind of robe similar to a shirt except that the shirt is worn next to the body while this robe is referred to as an outer [lit.: "upper"] garment.

34. Shabbat 59b [A discussion of what accessories may be worn outdoors without violating the prohibition against "carrying" on the Sabbath]:
Fringes, tassels: Short straps used for tying and fastening.

35. Pesahim 11a:
One may wind a hollow belt or fascia [to tie a broken cord of a bucket]: [Old French] *Faissoles* — puttees which are wrapped around the legs.

36. Shabbat 120a [Discussion of permissible ways of handling clothing on the Sabbath]:
A pair of breeches: Called *Kniehosen* [knee breeches] in German.

37. Menahot 41a [What garments must have *tzitzit* inserted]:
A cloak: Mantel in the vernacular. Like those of ours which are cut round and have only two corners at the bottom [instead of four].

38. Betzah 38b [Digression in a scholarly discussion. Rabbi Abba made a remark which made his colleagues smile. Rabbi Abba therefore asked them, "Did I take your cloak from you?" an idiomatic expression meaning, "Have I said anything wrong?"]:
A woolen cloak: A handsome wrap which one wears underneath his cloak. When one sits down, he folds back this cloak, revealing this wrap.

39. Shabbat 29a [Discussion of ritual purity and impurity of garments]:
Hem: It is the custom of tailors to make a hem [in their garments]; that is, they fold the edge of the cloth a little and stitch it down.

40. Shabbat 20b [Discussion of garments which must have *tzitzit* attached]:
Garment of inferior silk: A coat made of soft silk which peels. This occurs quite frequently in silk.

41. Me'ilah 18a [Discussion of a garment which is Temple property]:
Cloth of a fine, downy texture: The finest flax... so thin that it can easily be rolled [tightly enough to be] stored within a nutshell.

42. Menahot 35a [Discussion of laws relating to *tefillin*]:
A loop: Similar to what we have on [the waist of] our trousers so that the belt is not fixed to the garment but can be either tightened or loosened.

43. Shabbat 120a [Discussion of ways in which clothing may or may not be handled on the Sabbath]:
The scarf around his neck: Its end[s] hang in front so that he can wipe his mouth and eyes with it.

44. Shabbat 65a [How a woman may go out on the Sabbath with a weighted cloak and not transgress the prohibition against "carrying" on the Sabbath]:
A woman may weight [her cloak] with a stone: Those who wear a cloak attach a strap on one end opposite the neck, and on the other end there is a stone or a nut. The strap is then wound around the latter so that the cloak will not drop [from her shoulders].

45. Shabbat 62a [Discussion regarding accessories which a woman may or may not wear when going out on the Sabbath because of the prohibition against "carrying" on the Sabbath]:

A brooch: Nuska: so called because it pins together the openings of a cloak.

46. Shabbat 59b [Discussion regarding accessories which a woman may or may not wear when going out on the Sabbath because of the prohibition against "carrying" on the Sabbath]:
Wrought metal: A strap decorated with gold or precious stones.

47. Shabbat 59b [Discussion regarding accessories which a woman may or may not wear when going out on the Sabbath because of the prohibition against "carrying" on the Sabbath]:
Belt: A precious belt. Some make these of gold platelets; others, with golden inlays studded with precious stones.

48. Song of Songs 7:6: *And the king is held captive in the tresses thereof:* The fringes of the belts with which the belts are tied.
Shabbat 111b [Discussion of ways in which clothing may or may not be handled on the Sabbath]:
Band: A wide belt, with threads hanging from its ends for tying.

49. Shabbat 57b [Discussion regarding accessories which a woman may or may not wear when going out on the Sabbath because of the prohibition against "carrying" on the Sabbath]:
Catella: A precious garment hung around a woman's neck over her breast to protect her clothes from food while she eats. It has loops for straps similar to [those at the waist of] our trousers through which a wide belt is pulled. She rolls this garment around the belt because it is rather wide; she then ties the belt around her neck, tying it very tightly so that her flesh protrudes and makes her look plump. Since the belt is smooth and wide, it does not hurt her.
Shabbat 59b [Same discussion as in Shabbat 57b]:
A band with trinkets: A garment with loops similar to those at the waist of trousers. [The woman] inserts a wide band into [the loops] and ties the garment around her neck. The garment hangs over her breast. This is a precious [garment] and is painted with gold leaf.

50. Gittin 90b [Discussion of legitimate grounds for divorce]:
With her armpits uncovered: At the elbows in the manner of the Edomite [i.e., Gentile] women in France whose [bare] flesh can be seen from their sides.

51. Shabbat 92b [Discussion regarding accessories which a woman may or may not wear when going out on the Sabbath because of the prohibition against "carrying" on the Sabbath]:
A woman who wraps an apron around herself: Short pants which are worn for the sake of modesty.
Yevamot 24b [Suspected infidelity]:
The woman within is fastening her sinnar *[apron]:* Similar to pants; women wear it for the sake of modesty.
Shabbat 13b [Discussion of ritual purity]:

An apron [interposed between husband and wife in bed during her unclean period]: An apron worn by women; it extends from her thighs down.

52. Ketubot 17b [Legal aspects of marriage]:
Hinuma: A veil upon [a woman's] head which covers her eyes just as is done in these parts. Sometimes she falls asleep under it because her eyes are covered [by it].

53. Mo'ed Katan 9b [A woman is permitted to groom herself on the intermediate days of festivals]:
She [plaits her hair]... and makes a part: She parts her hair on one side or the other.

54. Isaiah 3:20:
The headtires... and the sashes...: Short ribbons used for tying the hair. Some embroider these with gold thread.

55. Shabbat 94b [Men are forbidden to wear female garments and to use feminine ways of making themselves more attractive]:
A woman's garment: It is the way of women to be aware of such things and to beautify themselves [by plucking out their white hairs].

56. Shabbat 64b [Accessories which a woman may wear when going out without transgressing the prohibition against "carrying" on the Sabbath]:
A wig: A switch of hair worn by a woman to make her own hair appear thicker.
Arakhin 7b [Discussion of whether it is permissible to derive gain or benefit from the wig of a woman who has died]:
A wig [One may derive benefit from the hair of a woman who was executed for a crime]: Women attach the hair of other women to their own.

57. Sanhedrin 112a [How to dispose of the hair of a woman who lived in a "condemned city;" i.e., in a city where, according to Biblical command (Deuteronomy 13:13 ff.), everything must be destroyed because its people were evil]:
A wig: Hair of other women worn by a woman to beautify herself.

58. Gittin 20a [Discussion of materials legally acceptable for use in preparing a legal document]:
[The document is invalid] if the writing is on a cap: A woolen hat or cap worn by women under beaded scarves.
Shabbat 57b [Accessories which a woman may wear when going out on the Sabbath without transgressing the prohibition against "carrying" on the Sabbath]:
A woolen cap: A hat beneath [a woman's] snood with which she adorns herself.

59. Shabbat 57b [Discussion regarding accessories which a woman may or may not wear when going out on the Sabbath because of the prohibition against "carrying" on the Sabbath]:
Bizyune — that which imprisons her flying hair: A small headdress. After the woman has covered her hair by weaving beads through it, some wisps of hair

may still show from her beads. [These stray wisps are called *p'ruhei*, "flying," because they fly outside her hair covering]. She tucks them underneath her beads by means of a small headdress, thus preventing them from showing.

60. Shabbat 60a [Discussion regarding accessories which a woman may or may not wear when going out on the Sabbath because of the prohibition against "carrying" on the Sabbath]:
A woman tidies her hair with it: [She takes the] hair that shows from beneath her beads and winds these wisps around a pin which she then sticks under her snood so that [the wisps] will not show.

61. Shabbat 59b [Discussion regarding accessories which a woman may not wear when going out on the Sabbath because of the prohibition against "carrying" on the Sabbath]:
A tiara: Which she fastens to her forehead from ear to ear. Some are made entirely of gold plate; others, of silk interwoven with gold threads.

62. Shabbat 74b [Refers to the prohibition against plucking feathers or wings from a bird on the Sabbath]:
[He transgresses] because of clipping [which is forbidden on the Sabbath]: Hats are made also from quills and from birds' wings [stripped of their] feathers.

63. See *Shulhan Arukh*, Even HaEzer 21:2 and Orah Hayyim 91:3.

64. Hullin 18b [Description of the projecting point of the Adam's apple of an animal to be slaughtered for meat]:
The projecting point: It actually resembles a sort of hat, tapering from the middle to the top until it becomes as pointed as a kind of *calamus* [writing reed].

65. Yevamot 102a [Discussion of the shoe used in the *halitzah* act]:
Shoe lace: The term *na'al* denotes both a sandal and a shoe. *Min'al* is Rabbinic Hebrew; *na'al* is Biblical Hebrew.... Two straps are pulled through its loops as if to make two shoes, one on top of the other. A sandal, by contrast, has neither ties nor double straps on its loops because it is hard and the strap would not hold it together. However, it can be tied at the edge of its opening to make it fit tightly.

66. Shabbat 112a [Laws regarding the permissibility of tying articles of personal apparel on the Sabbath]:
The handles of his sandals: Flaps toward the back of the foot for holding the shoe while one puts it on.

67. Shabbat 60a [Accessories which may not be worn outdoors on the Sabbath because it would entail a transgression of the prohibition against "carrying"]:
A nail-studded sandal: Wooden clogs with leather uppers attached to the clogs with nails.... They are studded with nails like horseshoes. [This sandal] has two openings and can be put on from either side.

68. Yevamot 103b [The shoe used in the *halitzah* act]:
Also a sandal which consists only of a sole: An open-backed shoe.

69. Shabbat 60b [Discussion regarding accessories which may or may not be worn on the Sabbath because of the prohibition against "carrying" on the Sabbath]:
An inclining sandal: The sole is not even; it is thicker on one side than on the other. When one walks on it, it inclines to the thinner side and it must be raised so as to be even with the [thicker] side.

70. Yevamot 102b [The shoe used in the *halitzah* act]:
[A sandal] sewn with flax: Sewn with thread like the kind we use [nowadays]. *With slippers:* Worn under heavy shoes to protect the foot from water.

71. Gittin 69b [Digression: A discussion of a cure for worms]:
An amuletful of phyllon: A nut-shaped case which women wear in a little container attached to their necklaces. It is made of gold or silver and contains a mixture of oil and fragrant spices, which is called phyllon and resembles the leaves of vines.
Pesahim 42b [Articles which must be put aside as "leaven" during Passover]:
Women's cosmetics: This includes blue and red paints and perfume pendants which they hang around their necks.
Yoma 75a [The tradition that cosmetics for the women were sent down from Heaven to the Children of Israel in the wilderness along with the manna]:
Cosmetics for women: Which they crush with a mortar and use as fragrance to please their husbands.

72. Kiddushin 22b [Symbolic interpretation of the Biblical law under which a slave who refuses to accept his freedom in the year of release must have his ear pierced as a symbol of his bondmanship]:
In a symbolic manner: Like a string of pearls and perfumed spices around the neck of a woman to serve as an ornament.

73. Sanhedrin 68a [Discussion of ritual defilement]:
An amulet: Made of leather and filled within. It is hung around the neck like a piece of jewelry.

74. Isaiah 3:23 [The prophet's description of the accessories and jewels worn by the "daughters of Zion"]:
Clasps: Buckles made of gold, with which women fasten the cloaks wherewith they cover themselves.

75. Sotah 7b [How the jewelry is to be removed from a wife suspected of adultery]:
Necklace: A kind of semicircular choker with which she fastens her garment.

76. Shabbat 57a [Accessories which a woman may wear when going out without transgressing the prohibition against "carrying" on the Sabbath]:
With threads which are [inserted] through their ears: Put into her pierced ears to prevent the holes from closing up.

77. Shabbat 65a [Articles which a little girl may wear when going out, without transgressing the prohibition against "carrying" on the Sabbath]:
The little girls: Who pierce their ears but do not wear earrings until they are grown up. They place threads or chips into their ear [lobes] to prevent the holes from closing up.

78. Kiddushin 82a [Occupations which were considered undesirable for men because they involved dealing with women]:
A goldsmith: One who makes bracelets, earrings and rings for women.

79. Sanhedrin 100b [Peddlers who do business with womenfolk are often beaten up by jealous husbands]:
Itinerant peddlers: He travels around the city with women's jewelry which he sells [to the women].

80. Shabbat 62a [Discussion of prohibition against "carrying" on the Sabbath]:
A balsam phial: In which to keep [the ring]. Some explain that this phial is sealed and that she reseals it after she has opened it.

81. Hullin 25a [Unfinished articles are not susceptible to ritual defilement]:
Drilled with a pick of iron: Neither the nails nor the decorative tile have yet been put in, as is done in the boxes [used by] women.

82. Job 37:18:
...which is strong as a molten mirror: Similar to the mirrors used by women.

83. Shabbat 78b [Discussion of quantities which, if carried out of a private domain on the Sabbath, involve a violation of the prohibition against "carrying" on the Sabbath]:
For smearing the smallest of girls: They were smeared with lime to remove hair from their bodies.

84. Mo'ed Katan 9b [What cosmetics are permissible or forbidden during the intermediate days of festivals]:
She may put rouge on her face: This is a paint which reddens [the cheeks].

Shabbat 64b [What cosmetics must not be used on the Sabbath]:
She must not rouge her face: This is *tinfanol* in Old French. It is red in color.

85. Shabbat 94b [What cosmetics must not be used on the Sabbath]:
[She] likewise [transgresses a Sabbath law] if she paints her face: If she smears upon her face a kind of paste which leaves the skin red when she peels it off.

86. Mo'ed Katan 9b [What cosmetics are permissible or forbidden during the intermediate days of festivals]:
If she paints [lit. "blues"] her eyelids: If she puts on a blue color on her eyelids in order to make them look more beautiful.

87. Jeremiah 4:30:
...That thou enlargest thine eyes with paint?: Eyeshadow makes the eye appear larger.

88. Ketubot 48a [Does the court of law have the authority to charge a man for cosmetics purchased by his wife during his absence?]:
Cosmetics: Perfumes from the spice-peddler's powder with which women beautify themselves.

89. Eruvin 14b [Ritual purity and defilement]:
A large box or chest: Similar to the box suspended on a wagon used by distinguished ladies.

Eruvin 30b [Conveyance by which a priest can travel over graves without incurring ritual impurity]:
A chariot for women: A chariot shaped like a box.

Bava Kamma 98b [Discussion of torts]:
A box: The box of the chariot made for use by women.

90. Shabbat 80a [Discussion of quantities which, if carried out of a private domain on the Sabbath, involve a violation of the prohibition against "carrying" on the Sabbath. This passage speaks of quantities of eye-paint sufficient to cover one eyelid. The Talmud then asks: Why speak of only one eyelid? Do women not color both their eyelids? One of the answers is that girls and women living in cities should color only one eyelid out of considerations of personal modesty. Women in the provinces, however, may color both their eyelids]:
The women in the provinces [may color both their eyelids]: Girls who live in villages do not need [to worry] too much [about] modesty because there is no lewdness or lightheartedness there. Also, there are not so many people. Therefore they do not need to cover their faces and they may color [lit, "blue"] their eye [lids].

CHAPTER EIGHT

Health and Medicine

The beginnings of medical science in Europe are generally associated with the School of Salerno, Italy, which was founded during the ninth century. However, this school, the oldest center of medical knowledge in Europe, did not reach its peak until the twelfth century.[1] Most of the advances made in medicine during the time span between the passing of ancient Greece and the period of Rashi originated in Asia and Africa. The treatises describing these developments were predominantly written in Arabic; as a result, they were inaccessible and hence unknown to most Europeans of Rashi's day.

It can therefore be said with a fair degree of certainty that Rashi's acquaintance with medical science is based primarily on the Talmud. Because Judaism has always placed great stress on the importance of human life and its preservation, the Talmudic text is replete with laws, customs and opinions regarding health and hygiene. Indeed, many Rabbinic discussions on laws not directly related to the human body or its care digress into the field of health rules and folk medicine. In his commentaries on both the Bible and the Talmud Rashi gives much attention to diseases and their cures. He interprets passages on health and medicine in terms of the knowledge which was available in the Europe of his day and which had hardly advanced beyond the level of folk medicine known in the Talmudic era.

It is perhaps due in part to his numerous explanations of diseases and cures that some authorities regarded Rashi as a *rofe* (physician, literally, "healer").[2] But though the symptoms of disease recorded in Rashi's commentaries and in part familiar to us in our own day show his keen gifts of observation, the remedies he offers naturally lack the refinements of later medical progress and largely fall into the category of folk medicine.

Since post-mortem examinations of human bodies are generally forbidden by Jewish law, whatever knowledge Rashi had of human anatomy was probably derived from his familiarity with the anatomy of cattle, which in many respects resembles that of man. It was necessary for Rabbinic authorities to be conversant with the anatomy of cattle in order to ascertain whether a slaughtered animal was fit for consumption as meat under Jewish law. However, Rashi's grandson Rabbenu Tam, who may be assumed to reflect his grandfather's teachings in his own writings, cautions against equating diseases of animals with those afflicting humans because humans, unlike animals, have *mazal*[3]; that is, man is subject to the irrational factor of "luck" which makes his body's reactions to disease and injury unpredictable and frequently defies generally accepted principles of medicine. Rashi's realization of this difference between humans and animals may account for the rather sparse references in his writings to diseases of the lungs although pulmonary diseases and abnormalities are primary reasons for the ritual disqualification of animals slaughtered for food under the laws of *shehitah*.

A superficial study of Rashi's commentaries would indicate that he did not think too highly of physicians. However, his motivation in this respect was not the same as that of religious sects such as the Karaites, who felt that it was wrong for men to attempt to cure the sick because this meant thwarting the will of God. The Talmud has no objections to the help which a physician can give the sick. "Is it not common sense," one passage reads, "that if a man has a pain he visits the *assia* [healer]?"[4] The duty of the Jew to do everything in his power to preserve human life is explicitly stated in the widely-quoted principle that *pikuah nefesh dohe Shabbat:* whenever there is danger to human life, even such basic Jewish laws as those of Sabbath observance may be suspended.[5] This being the attitude throughout Jewish law, Rashi would hardly have found it justifiable to reject the value of medical treatment *per se*. His own reservations about physicians are expressed in his commentary to a Mishnah which suggests that one should not teach one's son to be a physician.[6] He maintains that physicians are not sufficiently concerned about their patients and consequently give them the kind of food which is fit only for healthy people. Also, physicians lack humility before God, so that sometimes they inadvertently cause a patient's death and do not give sufficient attention to patients who are poor.[7] Commenting on the Rabbinic tradition that King Hezekiah banned a certain *Sefer HaRefuot* (Book of Remedies), Rashi, who held that sickness was inflicted on man by God to teach the patient a moral lesson, suggests that the king banned the book because he wanted to encourage the sick to pray for Divine mercy.[8] In another commentary on this tradition, Rashi notes that patients relying on the Book of Remedies were cured so quickly that they did not become properly humbled by their sickness.[9] As regards the advice given in Tractate Sanhedrin that a scholar should not reside in a city where there is no *rofe*, Rashi defines the term *rofe* to denote not a physician but a *mohel* (circumciser).[10] He gives the same definition for *rofe* in connection with a statement in Tractate Bava Bathra that it is obligatory to provide accommodations for such a person.[11]

On the other hand, Rashi seems to have respected good physicians. Commenting on a dispute in Tractate Avodah Zarah about whether a heathen should be permitted to circumcise a Jewish infant, Rashi holds that under certain circumstances a Gentile surgeon who is known for his expertise may be trusted to perform a circumcision on a Jew since such a man would not want to endanger his good reputation by mutilating his patient.[12]

Disease has not changed materially over the centuries. What has changed is the recognition of symptoms and the remedies devised to provide cure or relief. As medicine progressed, our concern with diseases and their cure has become more accentuated. Diseases of the heart were known to man since time immemorial. Rashi knew that both physical hunger and lack of emotional fulfillment can affect the heart. Referring to a Talmudic statement that the hearts of R. Hisda and Rabba, the son of R. Hunah "grew faint" after these men had sat all day long as judges in legal disputes, Rashi explains that the faintness had come upon them because they had not eaten all that day.[13] If a person prolongs his prayers in the expectation that they will be answered more readily if he does so, and his hopes then remain unfulfilled, his disappointment will cause him "an ache in the heart."[14] Rashi describes a victim of a heart attack as screaming in pain and unable to catch his breath.[15] The physician and pharmacologist David I. Macht (1882-1961) interpreted two of Rashi's comments on Biblical texts as suggesting the symptoms of coronary occlusion or angina pectoris. Rashi regards these symptoms as a punishment for disobedience to the word of God and as retribution for Israel's enemies. Commenting on Deuteronomy 28:28, "The Almighty shall smite thee with hardness of heart *(timhon ha-lev)*" Rashi explains *timhon* as being synonymous with *otem* (stoppage or obstruction).[16] Commenting on Lamentations 3:56, where Israel's foes are cursed, "Thou wilt give them hardness of heart *(meginat ha-lev)*," Rashi notes that a painful pressure, like that of a *magen* (a heavy shield), causes an obstruction or "stopping up" of the heart.[17] He also knew that the cessation of an audible heartbeat or palpable pulse did not necessarily imply that death had set in.[18]

Rashi describes the condition known today as hiatal (or diaphragmatic) hernia which can cause symptoms mimicking a heart attack: shortness of breath and a pressure "like a fist" can occur if the fleshy partition beneath the heart is bent "toward the inside." While he does not mention any remedies to cure or relieve genuine heart disease, he recommends a variety of herbal medicines to relieve the symptoms arising from the diaphragmatic disorder.[19]

Rashi discusses numerous health rules and remedies to avoid or relieve ailments of the digestive tract. In connection with a Talmudic statement about the evils of getting angry on a full stomach, Rashi recommends that one should fill his stomach one-third with solid food, one-third with liquid and leave one-third empty.[20] One should not eat when one is angry because of the danger that one's stomach may burst if one fills it to capacity while in a state of emotional turmoil.[21] One should not indulge excessively even in food which one enjoys.[22] The Talmud cites *tibbul* (literally, "dip") as a food which should be taken regularly to prevent stomach trouble. Rashi tells us that this is bread soaked in vinegar or wine.[23] He underscores the Talmudic dicta that one should drink plenty of water after meals[24] and that changes in dietary habits lead to intestinal disorders.[25] To the statement in Tractate Sanhedrin that more people die from "delayed calls of nature" than from starvation, he notes that more people succumb to intestinal disorders than to the "hyderikon" (dropsy or edema) caused by hunger.[26] To Abaye's opinion, cited in Tractate Ketubot, that dates eaten after a meal have a beneficial effect on health, Rashi discreetly implies that they have laxative properties.[27] Remedies for intestinal troubles which, according to Rabbinic law, may be applied to the abdomen even on the Sabbath included a heated cloth or vessel to be placed on the abdomen[28] and a "hot cup" on the navel. This "hot cup" is described by Rashi as a cup filled with hot water and then emptied. While the air inside the cup is still hot from the water, the cup is inverted and placed on the patient's navel. The cup then pulls the intestines into their proper alignment by suction.[29]

Blindness, and hence any disease of the eyes, is the subject of much apprehension and discussion in Jewish tradition. According to a statement in Tractate Avodah Zarah, a blind person is among the four classes of individuals who are regarded as dead.[30] As a consequence, Rashi's commentaries contain interesting information on various ocular diseases.

Commenting on Psalm 6:8, "My eye wastes away because of grief," Rashi describes a visual disturbance in which the eye is clouded and one sees everything as through a glass.[31] He may be referring to a condition sometimes set off by emotional stress without a discernible physical disorder being present in the eye. In connection with remedies which may or may not be applied to the eye on the Sabbath, Rashi cites several conditions which may affect eyesight. One disease, referred to in the Talmudic text as *barkit* (*barak*="brightness," hence apparently a euphemistic term), is characterized by the formation of a membrane, a "protruding cataract," which covers the eye; it was treated with the blood of a woodcock.[32] White spots forming in the iris were treated with the blood of a kind of bat; the blood of this animal was rather thin and easily penetrated the eye.[33] Commenting on the law in Leviticus 21:20 that one who has a "speck [*tevalul*] in his eye" may not perform priestly duties in the Temple, Rashi defines *tevalul* as a condition in which apparently the white and black parts of the eye are not properly defined; for instance, a white line extending from the sclera (the "white of the eye") through the iris.[34] With reference to the use of collyrium as an eyewash, he says that collyrium has the disadvantage that, when applied to the eye, it congeals until it becomes like glue (Old French: *glosier*) and obstructs the patient's vision. Water is the ideal eyewash because it does not cloud vision, is immediately absorbed, can be wiped away easily and leaves no crust on the eye.[35] A painful eye was "cooled" by the application of a metal object to the eyelid, or of a metal ring around the eye.[36]

Rashi's commentaries contain several references to the care of the teeth and the mouth. In connection with suggestions in Tractate Shabbat on how a toothache may be treated on the Sabbath, he notes that wine made from unripe grapes is harmful to the teeth and that vinegar may loosen the teeth.[37] During the Talmudic period, and apparently also in Rashi's day, tartar was removed from teeth by cleaning and scraping the tooth at the gumline.[38] Both the Talmud and Rashi knew of removable false teeth made of gold or silver.[39] Halitosis was evidently a matter of great concern. Commenting on a passage in Tractate Ketubot listing physical defects which make a man so repulsive that he may be compelled under the law to give his wife a divorce, Rashi defines the term "polypus" as an unpleasant odor emanating either from the nose or from the mouth.[40] Elsewhere, he notes that it is not pleasant to talk to someone whose stomach is empty because the person will have bad breath.[41] He mentions the custom of women to keep a long pepper, or ginger, or cinnamon in the mouth to sweeten the breath.[42] Rashi describes scurvy (*zafdinah*) as a condition which begins with bleeding of the gums when the patient eats and which eventually spreads to the intestines.[43]

Rashi's commentaries include details regarding the treatment of the newborn. To a statement in the Talmud about circumstances under which one may assist in a delivery on the Sabbath, he remarks that the umbilical cord must be cut in order to prevent the baby's intestines from dropping out when the baby is picked up.[44] He explains Verse 4 of Ezekiel 16,"Thou wert not salted," as referring to the ancient custom of rubbing a baby at birth with salt in order to harden and strengthen its body.[45] He also mentions the practice of anointing the skin of newborn infants with oil.[46] The baby was then wrapped in swaddling clothes, into which he was tied with a kind of belt or girdle. This was done in order to "set his limbs," which were believed to be soft and dislodged at birth.[47] Sometimes the child's spine had to be straightened by manipulation.[48] If a newborn infant gives no sign of life — and here Rashi adds that the baby may be alive even if his heartbeat is not audible — he should be fanned.[49] An infant boy whose body is red; that is, one whose blood has not yet been absorbed by the flesh but is still on the under-surface of his skin, must not be circumcised because all his blood would flow out.[50] If an infant cannot suck at his mother's breast because his mouth is not strong enough to do so, burning coals should be placed near his mouth to warm it so that it may gain strength.[51] Commenting on laws relating to a woman's ritual impurity following childbirth, Rashi describes a Caesarean birth apparently produced by a drug which opened the mother's abdomen without surgery.[52] As for the training of the newborn infant,

Rashi apparently believed that the child must be taught to be right-handed.[53]

In his commentaries Rashi lists numerous folk remedies for scorpion stings and insect bites. A scorpion sting was to be covered with the gall of a white stork. In addition, the patient had to drink some of this stork gall mixed with beer.[54] Another remedy for the sting of a scorpion was to place a crushed spider on the affected area.[55] A hornet sting should be covered with the crushed remains of a fly.[56] An interesting first-aid measure for choking described by Rashi is the re-setting of the laryngeal muscle by suspending the patient in an upside-down position.[57]

Commenting on the laws of Passover, Rashi warns patients against becoming too much accustomed to taking drugs because drugs may become an expensive habit.[58]

As bandages or dressings for wounds Rashi lists combed flax[59] and flaked wool.[60] Dry wadding or a dry sponge was used to protect wounds or inflamed areas from irritation by coarse clothing.[61] Relief from calluses on the soles of the feet could be obtained by tying a coin to the callus.[62]

Rashi's commentaries include descriptions of diseases which are obviously serious but for which the modern-day equivalent is unknown. Commenting on a passage in Tractate Shabbat he defines *askara* as a disease which begins in the intestines, ends in the throat and was called *bon malant* in Old French.[63] (The *Arukh Completum* refers to this sickness as *bubons malignes* and identifies it with *"boesartige Druesengeschwuere"*; i.e., malignant tumors of the glands.).[64] Elsewhere, Rashi says that sometimes *askara* is not discovered until it has spread to the oral cavity, in which case it is fatal.[65]

"Hyderikon" (dropsy or edema) occurs in three forms. The most serious of these is one in which the flesh swells and becomes hard to the touch; it is a punishment for '*averah*' (sin) — probably sexual promiscuity. The second form, *shains* in Old French, is characterized by an accumulation of fluid between the flesh and the skin, giving the skin a transparent, glassy appearance. The Talmud attributes it to hunger. The third and last type, which the Talmud ascribes to witchcraft, results in emaciation.[66]

Rashi's commentaries include references to two organic diseases of the brain. One of these is epilepsy, which Rashi explains as a condition that causes the patient to fall to the ground.[67] The other, identified in the Talmudic text as ra'atan, is described both by Rashi and in the text itself in terms which seem bizarre today. The disease is caused by an insect that has somehow settled in the victim's brain. One of the symptoms is a discharge or drainage to the outside, because the patient is surrounded by flies. Rashi notes that the flies which feed on this discharge are dangerous because they can transfer ra'atan to another person. The cure related by Rashi is hardly less strange then the description of the disease. His remedy is a mixture concocted from a plant called *polion* (mint), wormwood,[68] the rind of a nut tree, shavings from a dressed hide, a lily, and the skin of young dates. The patient is taken into a hermetically sealed chamber enclosed with walls that have a thickness of seven and one-half bricks. There, the plant and herb mixture is poured over the patient's head until his skull is sufficiently soft to be opened with a surgeon's knife. The insect is removed from the exposed brain by lifting each of its legs separately, carefully separating each leg from the brain tissue by placing a myrtle leaf between the insect's leg and the patient's brain. If one were to attempt to pluck the insect from the brain by grasping its body, it would dig its legs into the patient's brain and perforate the delicate membrane.[69] The description of this brain surgery, if it may be characterized as such, makes *ra'atan* appear like a malignant growth in which the "tentacles" or "legs" of the tumor have burrowed into the brain tissue and must be removed with the utmost care if the brain itself is not to be destroyed in the process.

A much more commonplace ailment which afflicts many people in our own day is the *shigaron* mentioned in Tractate Gittin. It is explained by Rashi as a disease of the hips and thigh called *hanche* in Old French.[70] This, obviously, is sciatica.

The Talmud knew of prosthetic aids such as artificial legs.[71] According to Rashi's description cripples in his day apparently did not walk or lean on the artificial limb but used crutches for locomotion. "One whose leg was amputated makes a sort of artificial leg which was a receptacle into which he places the stump of his thigh. However, he does not lean on this but uses for support a stilt tied to his thigh and rests his hands upon a crutch."[72] Those who had legs but could not move them, due to, say, paralysis, had special wooden or leather supports which they tied to their legs and which enabled them to drag along their legs as they moved with the aid of hand crutches.[73] The hands would be protected by special leather gloves or hand coverings.

Rashi was well aware of the psychological and environmental factors which contribute to health or help cause illness. Anxiety about the future, such as uncertainty about one's livelihood and fear for one's personal safety,[74] sap at a man's energies. Financial pressures rob the individual of the clear mind he needs in order to pursue his studies.[75] Fear and anxiety cause dryness in the mouth[76] and shortness of breath.[77] The angry man breathes heavily through his nose and looks "hot."[78] His face takes on a yellowish color.[79] One who longs for a loved one sighs whenever he thinks of him.[80] Pleasant sights such as lush gardens and peacefully flowing rivers, Rashi comments to a passage in the Book of Proverbs, refresh the heart.[81] The best environment for a man is the water and the air to which he has become accustomed. A change to an environment which he has not previously experienced will be detrimental to his health.[82] A person in distress should go out of doors and get some fresh air to relax his mind.[83] To the Talmudic dictum that city life is difficult Rashi comments that this is so because cities are overcrowded and dwellings are built too close to one another, robbing the inhabitant of good, clean air. The environment is healthier in smaller localities where houses are surrounded by gardens and orchards and the air is good.[84]

NOTES

(Biblical and Talmudic passages are printed in italics; abstracts of such passages, and Rashi's commentaries, in Roman type).

1. George Sarton, *Introduction to the History of Science, Vol. II, Part I,* Baltimore, 1931, p. 69ff.

2. S.M. Chones, *Toledot HaPosskim*, Warsaw, 1910, p. 8:
"According to the great French writer [Georges-Bernard] Depping [1784-1853] (in his book *History of the Jews* [actually *Les Juifs dans le moyen âge*]) he [i.e., Rashi] also was well acquainted with philosophy, which he studied from the books of the Jews, the Greeks and the Arabs. He was also a great *rofe*. The [author of] *Shalshelet HaKabbalah* wrote that he compiled a book on medicine, and the [author of the alphabetically arranged bibliography] *Sifthei Yeshenim* [Amsterdam, 1680] wrote at the end of the [entries for the] letter *resh* that he himself had seen this book in manuscript form...."

Gedaliah Ben Yihya, *Sefer Shalshelet HaKabbalah*, Warsaw, 1881, p. 22b:
"...there is in the *Sefer HaShorashim* [the grammar lexicon by David Kimhi] a reference to the root *taphash*, from which it appears that Rashi was knowledgeable in the field of medicine."
[Rashi explains that *taphash* ("fattening" of an organ, in this case the heart) causes a person to become *tipesh* (a fool)]

Theophile Boutiot, *Histoire de la ville Troyes et la Champagne meridionale*, Troyes, 1870, Vol. I, p. 250:
"*Cet homme célebre est Raschi, plus connu sous le nom de Jarchi. Il était fils d'Isaac, homme de mérite, chef de l'académie juive établie a Troyes...* (This famous man is Rashi, better known by the name of Jarchi. He was the son of Isaac, a man of merit, head of the Jewish academy established in Troyes...)."
p. 251:
"*Jarchi étudia en outre de la Bible et du Talmud, la grammaire, l'histoire, les langues, la médicine et l'astronomie* (Jarchi studied, among other things, the Bible, the Talmud, grammar, history, languages, medicine and astronomy)."

Boutiot seems to have confused Rashi either with Solomon of Lunel, who was mentioned by the traveler Benjamin of Tudela, or with the grammarian Solomon ben Abba Mari of Lunel, who was active during the second half of the fourteenth century. Both these individuals were known by the Hebrew cognomen *Yarhi*. (Lunel was derived from the French *lune* and translated into Hebrew as *yareah*, "moon".)

3. Zevahim 116a, Tosafoth: "Rabbenu Tam used to make a distinction between the diseases of men and those of animals because man [as distinct from animals] has *mazal*."

4. Bava Kamma 46b.

5. Yoma 85b, Shabbat 132a.

6. Kiddushin 82a: *One should not teach his son to become... a physician.... The best of physicians are destined for Gehenna....*

7. Rashi: "Because he is not afraid of his patient and feeds him with the food of the healthy. He is not humble [lit., "he does not crush his heart"] before the Omnipresent and he sometimes causes the death of a human being. It is also within his ability to heal the poor but he does not [always] do so."

8. Berakhot 10b:
[King Hezekiah] hid away the Book of Remedies: So that they might pray [to God] for mercy.

9. Pesahim 56a:
[King Hezekiah] hid away the Book of Remedies: Because their hearts did not submit to their disease since they were cured at once.

10. Sanhedrin 17b:
A scholar should not reside in a city where the following ten things are not found.... [A] rofe: To circumcise [male] infants.

11. Bava Bathra 21a:
Rofe: A circumciser.

12. Avodah Zarah 27a:
An expert physician: He will not [want to] damage his reputation by mutilating the [infant's] penis.

13. Shabbat 10a:
Their hearts grew faint: They grieved because they were unable to study Torah that day... However, it seems to me that this is not the correct explanation for "their hearts." Rather, this means that their mood became affected... due to fasting because they had not eaten all that day.

14. Berakhot 32b:
If one prolongs his prayer and thinks too much about it: He expects that his prayer will be fulfilled because he has prolonged his prayers, and he is then disappointed. His hope has gone for nothing and this causes an ache in his heart when a man yearns for something and his desire is not fulfilled.

15. Bava Kamma 80a:
There was once a certain person who suffered from his heart... He groaned: Plidrer in Old French. He was screaming because of heart pain and was unable to catch his breath.

16. David I. Macht, *The Heart and Blood in the Bible,* Baltimore, 1951, p. 33.

17. Macht, *op. cit.,* p. 28.

18. Yoma 85a [A discussion of signs indicating the cessation of life pertinent to the circumstances under which an attempt might be made on the Sabbath to retrieve a victim pinned under wreckage]:
Rashi: "One says that one notices by the heartbeat whether there is life and whether his pulse is beating there. Another says [one notices it] by the nose, because sometimes life can be recognized not by the heartbeat but by [whether the person is] breathing."

19. Avodah Zarah 29a:
Istumcha of the heart: Fleshy partitions beneath the heart; this is the diaphragm. Another explanation: it is the lobe opposite the heart and is called *nivlah.* Sometimes it tends to bend toward the inside and impedes breathing. It is like a fist.

Agdana: a bitter herb. [Rashi lists a number of herbs used to relieve the symptoms and then adds:] These should be taken with wine.

20. Gittin 70a [A digression in a discussion of circumstances under which a husband may divorce his wife]:
Eat one-third: Fill thy stomach one-third [with solid food], drink one-third and leave one-third of thy stomach empty.

21. *Ibid. And leave one-third for when thou art angry:* And thy stomach will be filled with anger. Stop eating [then], for if thou wilt fill it with food and drink and thou wilt become angry, thou wilt burst.

22. *Ibid. Do not indulge too freely in a meal which gives thee pleasure:* Withdraw thy hand from it and do not fill thy belly.

23. *Ibid. Tibbul:* To dip bread into vinegar or bread into wine.

24. Berakhot 40a [Digression in a discussion of blessings to be recited over various foods]:
He who makes his food float in water: He drinks a great amount of water after his meal until the food [in his stomach] floats in the water.

25. Sanhedrin 101a:
Change in routine: He who changes his routine and eats more than he is accustomed to eating — this is the beginning of intestinal disorder.

26. Shabbat 33a [Discussion of illnesses that are considered as punishments for sins]:
Many are those killed by delayed calls of nature: More people die from intestinal diseases than from the *hyderikon* of hunger.

27. Ketubot 10b [Objections to a statement by Rav that one should not hand down a legal ruling after having eaten dates]:
Abaye said: Mother told me: Dates... after a meal [are] as a bar to the door:... The rule is that they are good after a meal.

28. Shabbat 40b:
Above the intestines: If one has pains in his intestines a vessel or cloth is heated for him and placed there. It helps.

29. Shabbat 66b:
An inverted cup: A cup [filled] with hot air; namely, one from which hot water was poured out. It was placed on the navel of a person who had pains in his intestines. The cup takes hold of the flesh, pulls the intestines toward it and restores them to their [proper] place.

30. Avodah Zarah 5a:
Four [kinds of persons] may be regarded as [if they were] dead: the poor, the blind, lepers and the childless.

31. *My eye wastes away because of grief:...* An eye whose light is dimmed and it appears [to the person] as if he were seeing through a glass in front of his eyes.

32. Shabbat 78a:

For the outside: The blood of the woodcock is used for a *barkit* which protrudes.

33. *Ibid.*

Yarod: Tevalul; however, I saw [it defined] in the Tosefta [as] *havarvar;* namely, thin white spots that form in the eye.

The blood of krushtena: This is a bat called *telpha.*

For the inside: The bat is found in populated areas. It [i.e., its blood] is used [as a cure] for *yarod* because it is absorbed in the eye.

34. *Tevalul:* Something that blurs the eye; for instance, a white line which extends from the white of the eye and intersects the iris, which is the ring surrounding the pupil, called *fronila* [prunelle]. This line intersects the ring and runs into the black.

35. Shabbat 78a: [Discussion regarding the minimum quantites of liquid which, if carried out of a private domain on the Sabbath, involve a violation of the prohibition against "carrying" on the Sabbath.]:

All liquids: All liquids with which collyrium is rubbed on…. *And form drops:* They cover the eye and obstruct vision because they become thick and congealed like glue, which is called *glosier. Except for water:* Which is better than all of them because it cures and does not dim vision and is absorbed immediately, [can be] wiped off quickly and forms no crust on the eye.

36. Sanhedrin 101a:

An article may be placed over the eye on the Sabbath [in order to protect it]: People place a metal object upon the eye in order to cool it, or—as people with eye complaints do—place a ring around the eye.

37. Shabbat 111a:

Acid: Wine from unripe grapes is harmful to the teeth. *If there is no wound, vinegar weakens:* The juncture between the teeth and the gums becomes loose.

38. Kiddushin 24b [A discussion of the right of a slave to freedom if his master injures him]:

If his master is a physician and [the slave] asks him to… drill his tooth….: To clean and scrape [it] around the gumline.

39. Nedarim 66b:

She has an inserted tooth: Her tooth has fallen out and she put another one in its place…

Shabbat 64b [Whether wearing a removable false tooth could constitute a transgression of the prohibition against "carrying" on the Sabbath]:

An inserted tooth: She places it into her mouth from another place; it is made of gold.

Ibid.: The Sages prohibit: According to another explanation, the inserted tooth is a tooth [taken] from another human being.

Shabbat 65a:

The Sages forbid [wearing the tooth on the Sabbath only if it is a gold tooth]:…: Because it looks different from the other teeth and she might be ridiculed [lit., "made to feel ashamed"] so that she might take it out and carry it.... However, it seems to me that the reason [for the prohibition] is that [the tooth] is so precious and she might [take it out to] show it [to others]. Therefore it is forbidden [to wear it on the Sabbath] but a silver [tooth] is not so important, so she will not boast of it.

40. Ketubot 77a:

One who has a polypus: What is a polypus? A bad smell from the nose. In the Tosefta [it is explained as] a bad smell from the mouth.

41. Berakhot 44b:

If one ate vegetables before the fourth hour [of the day] it is forbidden to talk to him. Why? Because his breath smells: Because the time for a meal has not yet come and the smell is unpleasant to people who talk to him before he ate a meal, since his stomach [lit., "his body"] is empty.

42. Shabbat 64b [A woman does not violate the prohibition against "carrying" on the Sabbath if she goes out with a long pepper, ginger or cinnamon in her mouth to sweeten her breath]:

Pepper: The woman places a long pepper into her mouth [if it] smells bad; [she may also use] ginger or cinnamon [for this purpose].

43. Avodah Zarah 28a:

Zafdinah: Begins in the mouth and ends in the intestines.

What are its symptoms? If he puts anything into his mouth, blood will come out from between his teeth.

Yoma 84a:

Zafdinah: A disease of the teeth and gums. It starts in the mouth, ends in the intestines and is dangerous.

44. Shabbat 128b:

We tie up the umbilical cord: Of the newborn infant which is [quite] long, for if [the cord] is left untied the baby's intestines will drop out when he is picked up.

45. Thou wert not salted: This teaches [us] that a newborn infant is salted so as to strengthen its flesh.

46. Shabbat 119b:

"Touch not My anointed ones [I Chronicles 16:22] "These are the babies: Because it is customary to anoint newborn infants with oil.

47. Shabbat 66b:

[It is permitted on the Sabbath] to swaddle: To swaddle a newborn infant. [One] swaddles him in cloth and ties him with a belt in order to set his limbs which are soft and dislodged at birth.

Shabbat 147b:

To swaddle: As is done with a newborn infant to straighten his limbs in order to avoid curvatures.

Sotah 11b [Regarding the tradition that God sent someone down from

Heaven to straighten the limbs of the newborn Hebrew infants in Egypt]:
To smooth: As is done with newborn infants to settle their limbs, correcting
them as they became dislodged during birth.

Shabbat 123a:
Or straighten an infant['s limbs]: To smooth out the limbs. The limbs are loosened
at birth and need to be reset.

48. Shabbat 147a:
One must not straighten an infant's limbs [by manipulation on the Sabbath]: The meaning
is, "Thy hands have shaped me" (Cf. Job 10:8)... One corrects and resettles
the bones and vertebrae of his spine in accordance with the measurement[s]
of his body.

49. Shabbat 134a:
If an infant does not breathe: If no breath is discernible because there is no pulse as
is the way with all men,
He should be fanned with a fan: He should be fanned with a fan that is called *van*
[in Old French].

50. Shabbat 134a:
Who is red: His entire body is red because his blood has not been absorbed in
his flesh. All his blood is still on the under-surface of his skin and if one were
to circumcise him all his blood would run out.

51. Shabbat 134a: [Remedies which Abaye's mother administered to
babies with various ailments]:
If an infant cannot suck, his lips are cold: He cannot suck because his lips have
become cold and he has no strength to suck.
Let them bring a vessel of burning coals: Coals on a board or in a vessel.
And held near his nostrils: And place it close to his mouth.
So as to heat it: To warm his mouth so that he may [be able to] suck.

52. Niddah 40a [Discussion of ritual impurity following childbirth]:
For a fetus born by way of the mother's abdomen: With the aid of a drug that opened
her abdomen; the fetus was removed and she was healed.

53. Shabbat 88b:
To those who turn to the right [the Torah is an elixir of life]: Those who occupy
themselves [with the Torah] with all their might and make an extreme effort
to learn its secrets; just as a person who uses his right hand because this is
the more important [of the two hands].

54. Ketubot 50a: [Abaye's mother had a cure for a child six years of age
who has been stung by a scorpion]:
The gall of a stork: The gall of a stork called *vashto.*
Rub it in and drink it: Use it as an ointment and [also] let him drink it with beer.

55. Shabbat 77b [God created every living thing for an express purpose]:
[God created] a spider for the scorpion: For a scorpion sting, a spider should be
crushed and placed upon [the affected area].

56. *Ibid.*

[God created] a fly for the hornet: One who was stung by a hornet should crush a fly and apply it [to the affected area].

57. Shabbat 66b:

One may reset [a laryngeal muscle] on the Sabbath [to prevent choking]: When a muscle in the throat became dislocated, the patient was hung upside down in order to straighten his neck. This resembled hanging.

58. Pesahim 113a:

Do not take drugs: Do not become used to taking drugs because thou wilt become accustomed to them; thy desire will ask for them and thou wilt waste money.

59. Shabbat 50a [Discussion of whether one may go out wearing this dressing without violating the prohibition against "carrying" on the Sabbath]:

Pekorin: Combed flax which is placed upon a wound.

60. *Ibid.:*

Tsipah: Flaked wool which is applied to a wound.

61. Shabbat 134b [Remedies permitted to be applied on the Sabbath]:

Dry wadding or a dry sponge: [May be used on the Sabbath] because it is not done for medicinal purposes but in order to prevent the rough clothing from irritating the wound.

62. Shabbat 65a [Women may go out on the Sabbath with a coin tied to a callus]:

A callus: A wound on the sole of the foot. A coin is tied to it as a cure.

63. Shabbat 33a [Croup as a punishment for slander]:

Askara: A disease that begins in the intestines, ends in the throat and is called *bon malant* [in Old French].

64. Nathan filius Jechielis, *Arukh Completum,* New York, 1955, Vol. I, p. 182a.

65. Taanit 19b [Calamities such as an epidemic of croup, for which the Bet Din declared a public fast and had the shofar sounded]:

Askara: Sometimes it is discovered in the mouth of a man and he dies.

66. Shabbat 33a [Dropsy as a punishment for sin]:

Hyderikon: The [form of the] disease due to sin is thick: the flesh swells and becomes hard.

Swollen: Shains [in Old French]: the skin swells on the flesh; there is water between the flesh and the skin and the body looks like glass and is soft.

Caused by witchcraft, thin: The body becomes thin and emaciated.

67. Shabbat 61a [One suffering from epilepsy is permitted to carry an amulet on the Sabbath]:

Epilepsy: A disease in which one falls to the ground. It strikes the head and the brain.

Ketubot 77a [Which physical defects in a marriageable woman are considered as private and invisible, and which ones are visible and accordingly well known]:
Epilepsy: A disease which causes one to fall to the ground.

68. HaMetargem to Ketubot 77b: *Veludna:* Wormwood; a kind of herb [used as] a cure for intestinal diseases.

69. Ketubot 77b:

Afflicted with ra'atan: A person who has an insect in his brain and who is pursued by flies.
Phyla: A herb called polion.
Veludna: Alyashena [in Old French]
Nut skin: The rind of a nut tree.
Hide shavings: Shavings from a dressed hide.
K'lil malkah: a lily.
The calyx of a red date tree: A rind which young dates have, similar to young nut trees.
Into a house of marble: Of marble; that is, a place where no air can enter.
Seven bricks and a half: The walls had a thickness of seven and one-half bricks.
Taken to him: The mixture is poured upon him.
Until the cranium is softened and then the skull is cut open: His skull becomes soft and is ready to be opened with a knife.
Tarfei: Leaves.
Lifts each leg: He lifts its leg, for if he would grasp [the insect] by its body to remove it, it would bury its legs in the brain and perforate the membrane.
Beware of the flies of those afflicted with ra'atan: The flies that settle on him are dangerous and carry the same disease to others.

70. Gittin 69b [Circumstances under which a divorce may be given]:
For shigaron: A disease of the hips and the thigh called *hanche* [in Old French].

71. Cripples are permitted to go out [on the Sabbath] with an artificial leg (Shabbat 65b).

72. Yevamot 102b.

73. *Ibid.:*
With supports for his legs: One who must use his hands for moving about and has to drag his [useless] legs makes cushions of wood or leather to tie to his legs.

74. Gittin 70a:
Three things weaken a man:... Anxiety about the future; for instance, worries about making a living or fear of an enemy...

75. Sanhedrin 26b:
Worry is conducive: Anxiety about one's livelihood is conducive to making one

forget his studies. If one figures, "I shall do thus and so and then I will succeed," this is conducive to destroying that very same thing because such planning is of no avail even in connection with the study of Torah; e.g., if one says, "I will complete such and such tractates by a certain day."

76. Rashi on Psalm 22:16:
My tongue cleaves to my throat: A man in distress has no saliva in his mouth.

77. Rashi on Exodus 6:9:
They hearkened not to Moses for impatience of spirit: A person in distress becomes short of breath.

78. Rashi on Exodus 15:8:
And with the blast of Thy nostrils: Whenever the breath of nostrils and anger are mentioned in Scripture... [it] denotes burning and fire. It means that when one is angry, his nostrils become hot and burning...

79. Rashi on Sanhedrin 105a: [In connection with a story about two dogs that were angry at one another and were attacked by a wolf]: As yellow as the face of an angry man.

80. Sanhedrin 63b:
They remember their altars just as they remember their children [cf. Jeremiah 17:2]: Like a person who longs for his son and sighs whenever he thinks of him.

81. Rashi on Proverbs 15:30:
The light of the eyes rejoices the heart: A thing that is desirable to see. The words mean what they say. *The eyes:* [Sights that] make the heart happy; for instance, a park or flowing rivers.

82. Rashi on I Chronicles 11:17:
O that one would give me water to drink of the well of Beth-Lehem: All water and air to which a man is accustomed is good for him; if he is not accustomed to them, they are harmful.

83. Sukkah 28b [Studying the Talmud in the Sukkah]:
One who feels uncomfortable: The air is good for him to refresh his mind.

84. Ketubot 110b:
City life is difficult: Because everyone lives crowded together there. The houses are close together and there is no air. In [smaller] towns [by constrast] there are gardens and orchards near the houses and the air is good.

CHAPTER NINE

Arts, Crafts and Industries

A visitor to the city of Troyes is intrigued by the many street names recalling trades practiced there during the Middle Ages. When city communities as we know them today first arose, craftsmen not only united in trade guilds to protect their vocational and economic interests but also lived and worked in close geographic proximity to one another. Streets, lanes and sometimes entire sections of medieval cities such as Troyes were occupied by artisans of one trade only, so that these locations took the name of the trade for which they had become known.[1] The Rue de la Grande Tannerie (Great Tannery Street) and the Rue de la Petite Tannerie (Small Tannery Street) seem to substantiate the importance of medieval Troyes in the manufacture of leather and parchment without which literary activity would have been unthinkable when Rashi compiled his commentaries. The Rue de l'Orfévrerie (Goldsmiths' Street) and the Rue de la Monnaie (Money Street) recall the jewelry and coin businesses of the city, and the Rue de la Corderie was the home of the beltmakers in Rashi's day.

193

Rashi's commentaries show his remarkable familiarity with the crafts and industries of his period and his world. His observation of the activities of artisans, tradesmen and shopkeepers in Troyes provided Biblical and Talmudic terms with graphic explanations which not only helped his contemporaries to an understanding of the Bible and Talmud in terms of their own day but also have given later generations interesting glimpses of life and work in medieval cities.

As already noted, the numerous tanneries of Troyes in Rashi's day occupied two entire streets, which were not far from the Church of St. Jean and led to the Place de la Tannerie.[2] Here Rashi may have had an opportunity to observe the preparation of "Cordovan" leather,[3] which he mentions in a commentary in Tractate Haggigah and which, as he notes in connection with other Talmudic passages, was treated with dog excrement,[4] gall-nut resin[5] and tree bark[6] during the tanning process. This type of leather, originally produced by the Moors in Cordova, was used particularly in the manufacture of ladies' shoes.[7] Rashi explains that, as a rule, the first step in the dressing of leather was to spread the hides on the ground to be trodden upon by passers-by,[8] and that cobblers and saddlers used a paste made of rye flour to glue sheets of leather together.[9] Leather workers usually traced an outline on the surface of the leather before cutting it. After this outline was checked and, if necessary, corrected, the leather was cut with a special cobbler's knife.[10] In the manufacture of shoes the leather was fitted onto a wooden last.[11] Sandals might be made of leather straps nailed to a wooden sole covered with leather.[12] Leather was used also to protect the stump of an amputated leg.[13] There was a special bootmakers' black for dyeing shoes.[14]

The silversmiths and goldsmiths of Troyes were widely known for their work as far back as the twelfth century.[15] In his commentaries Rashi describes methods used in the manufacture of silver and gold articles. It seems that silver was melted down and refined at the place where it was mined.[16] Silver was refined on hot cinders placed into a crucible of clay.[17] Silver vessels were decorated with floral patterns or engraved designs which were blackened with smoke from burning sulfur to make them visible.[18] Silver was polished with a sediment which was found in wine barrels and which Rashi calls "alum."[19] Broken silver vessels were soldered.[20] Quicksilver was kept in a container with a small opening, which was sealed with pitch or brimstone. A hole was made in the seal so that the needed quantity of quicksilver could be poured from the container.[21]

Gold was refined over a layer of glowing coals resting on a clay base. The coals were covered with a perforated clay vessel through which greenish-red flames escaped.[22] Also, gold was purified in a special crucible atop burning coals;[23] if no coal was available, the crucible was placed on a tripod and bran was used in place of coal.[24] Designs and ornaments were engraved or cut into gold with a goldsmith's stylus, which resembled the tool used by scribes for writing on boards or tablets.[25] Gold was beaten into various shapes and thicknesses and into gold leaf with a special mallet.[26] The gold to be beaten was placed on an anvil; the worker would strike the mallet alternately three times on the foil and once directly on the anvil so that the mallet would be smooth and the gold leaf would remain free of scratches and unbroken.[27] Gold leaf produced in this manner was used to ornament the pages of illuminated manuscripts.[28] Gold wire or thread was manufactured by the same process as copper needles.[29]

Blacksmiths in Rashi's day worked with a variety of tools. The fire in which the iron was forged was fanned with bellows.[30] The iron was cast in molds in much the same manner as gold and silver.[31] In the forging process the wastes were separated and discarded.[32] The iron was smelted, strengthened and hardened by plunging it into water directly from the fire.[33] The blacksmith's anvil was mounted on a block or on a tree stump[34] to which the blacksmith carried the iron with a pair of tongs.[35] Sparks flew as the hammer pounded the iron[36] to widen or to narrow it; holes were expanded,[37] indentations evened out and filled in, and dents were smoothed.[38] Thick bars of iron were flattened with strokes of the hammer; iron plates flattened in this manner were forged into weapons.[39]

Coppersmiths wore leather aprons to protect them from copper dust. These aprons were warm, not only because of their thickness but also because of their constant contact with the heated copper.[40] Copper, like silver, was smelted at the mine and had a rather unpleasant odor, which, Rashi points out, tended to adhere also to those who worked with it.[41] The copper was heated, flattened and hammered to form cauldrons or kettles.[42] While the kettle was still hot, it was filled with cold water in order to break up the bubbles which had formed on the copper surface from the intense heat. This process also served to harden the metal.[43] Rashi notes that when they were struck, cauldrons made of lead absorbed and retained sound longer than vessels of any other metal, presumably including copper.[44] Copper wire was drawn out to the desired thickness in the manufacture of copper needles.[45] Traveling coppersmiths in Rashi's day would move from town to town with collapsible composite rods or tools made of metal.[46]

Rashi considered certain tools as insignia by which craftsmen advertised their trade and their availability for employment. Thus, in connection with a Talmudic law forbidding carpenters to carry their "chips" behind their ears when going out at an hour close to the beginning of the Sabbath, lest they unwittingly come to transgress the prohibition against "carrying" on the Sabbath, Rashi notes that the "chip" and other artisans' tools mentioned in this particular Talmudic passage were not so much actual tools as they were symbols by which the artisans advertised their trade when they went out into the street.[47] Rashi defines the "chip" as a ruler similar to that used by a scribe; the carpenter used it to measure the size of boards.[48] Other carpenters' implements described by Rashi are the lathe,[49] which was used in shaping shutters and boards,[50] and various kinds of saws, a large one for lumber[51] and a small one for wood.[52] Both saws produced a very fine sawdust.[53] Rashi makes mention also of cabinet makers who decorated wooden covers and benches[54] and ornamented the sides of chests with circular grooves.[55]

Rashi knew that glass was manufactured from sand (silicon)[56] and makes reference to a long tube used by glassblowers to shape sheets of glass into all kinds of vessels.[57] Rashi admits that he did not observe this process personally but says he heard the glassblowers describe it.[58]

Pottery was not widely used in Western Europe during Rashi's time. According to at least one history text on daily life during the twelfth century, dishes during this period were made primarily of wood and metal.[59]

The manufacture of clay articles in Rashi's day was a rather complicated process, which can be reconstructed from Rashi's references in his comments on several Talmudic passages. First, the claystones had to be pulverized. The larger stones which remained intact had to be removed; the powdered clay was then sifted and mixed with water, kneaded and formed into a doughlike lump while the kiln was heated.[60] The lump was molded into the size and shape required for the article to be made.[61] Smaller utensils such as candlesticks were formed by hollowing out the lump of clay with one's hand.[62] Other pottery articles were shaped with the aid of a potter's wheel[63] resting on a wooden jack.[64] The article was then placed into the kiln.[65] Rashi makes mention of a glazing process involving the use of a lead-like material.[66] Pottery was made also from very soft soil called *Kreide* (the German for "chalk") found in the region of Troyes. Rashi adds that if this material comes into contact with an acid it will dissolve and become unfit for use.[67] Broken barrels were repaired with a gum extracted from trees. The same material was used to produce a resin used for repairing clay dishes. According to Rashi, this resin smelled like incense.[68]

Apart from the craftsmen who were experts in their trade, Rashi describes several trades which were regarded more casually in his day. The bloodletter lowered blood pressure by reducing the volume of blood in the body.[69] The bath attendant at the public baths kept the bath warm and collected tokens — usually worn-out or defaced coins — from the bathers so he could know how many patrons had to be provided with hot water and bath towels.[70] The barber plied his trade with a pair of scissors and a hair clipper.[71] He placed a towel on the knees of his customer to protect the latter's clothes from the falling hair.[72] According to Rashi, the barber's patrons were primarily male.[73] Women came to him only to bring their sons for haircuts.[74]

Rashi's commentaries contain few references to bakers, butchers or tailors. It seems that in his time most householders baked their own bread, prepared their own meat and sewed most of their own clothes. This appears to have been true particularly in the case of the Jewish community and of activities predominantly subject to Jewish religious strictures. Bread was baked mostly at home. The dough was prepared in a trough where it was allowed to rise overnight.[75] The finished loaves of bread adhered to the walls of the oven[76] and had to be pried loose with a peeling or scraping shovel.[77] Bread was stored and offered for sale in baskets woven from peeled willows.[78] Butchers, it was generally felt in Rashi's day, could not be trusted because they were too eager to make money[79] They frequently deceived their customers by stiffening the hair on the carcasses they sold so that the animals would look fatter than they actually were.[80] The butchers themselves would open the carcass[81] after it had been skinned and hung on iron hooks fastened to poles standing on the ground.[82] Rashi says that in order to make the animal easier to skin it would be thoroughly "watered" before it was slaughtered.[83] It is not clear whether this means that the animal was given large quantities of water to drink or whether the water was poured in liberal amounts over its hide. Rashi describes various types of butcher knives.[84] Not all butchers used scales, especially not the experienced butchers who knew how to assess the weight of a portion of meat by holding it in one hand and "weighing" it against a weight held in the other hand.[85]

Though, as already noted, clothes were mostly made in the home, certain tailoring work was entrusted to expert tradesmen. This was true particularly in the case of hairy material. The cloth would be stretched between two pegs and beaten thoroughly to straighten the hairs.[86] Rashi describes various kinds of tailors' stitches. The true expert could make several stitches with one single movement of his needle.[87] The novice could not even stitch a straight seam; his stitches looked so irregular that they resembled the bite of a dog's teeth.[88] Rashi suggests that one use a long thread, at least double the length of the needle, because it is not possible to sew if the thread is any shorter.[89]

Hunting was never popular among Jews, not only because animals killed by a procedure other than *shehitah* (ritual slaughter) are not permitted as food under Jewish law but also because the injunctions of Jewish law against causing unnecessary suffering to animals conditioned the Jewish people from the very outset against the sport of hunting. Most of Rashi's references to hunting deal with the trapping of birds. Bird hunters lay in wait for their quarry in cone-shaped huts[90] made of willows and reeds,[91] or they dug themselves caves from which they could observe and catch birds without frightening them away.[92] Birds also were trapped in nets spread in midair[93] or caught on small boards attached to the top of a hunter's rod and covered with a thick layer of glue. Birds that perched on the board would become stuck.[94] If the bird attempted to fly away, the weight of the board to which it was literally glued would cause the bird to drop to the ground and into the hands of a hunter.[95] Bird hunters on horseback carried falcons and decoys to attract their prey.[96] Big dogs[97] were used in hunting larger animals. A large animal might be trapped in a device which snapped shut when touched by the animal's foot or paw.[98] Another kind of animal trap was a straw-covered pit into which animals fell.[99]

Fox hounds, as well as other dogs, were kept as pets in Rashi's day. In a commentary on a law making Jews responsible for the Sabbath rest of their animals, Rashi notes that these pets wore collars as ornaments.[100]

Unlike hunting, fishing was always considered a legitimate pursuit among Jews. Rashi tells how fish in the water were guided along a special reed fence and channeled into an enclosure where they could be easily caught.[101] Another fish trapping device was a basket with an opening at either end, one wide and one narrow. The fish entered through the wide opening but only its head could pass through the other end. Struggling to swim back the fish was caught in the fibers of the basket which slid beneath its gills.[102] Baskets in which fish were trapped might be left submerged in the water to keep the fish alive until they could be sold or prepared for eating.[103] Rashi also makes a reference to a fishhook.[104]

It appears that while the Talmud records numerous scholarly discussions about hunters and hunting, Rashi was interested primarily in those aspects of animal trapping which seemed to him more relevant because they concerned animals permitted as food under the dietary laws.

NOTES

(Biblical and Talmudic passages are printed in italics; abstracts of such passages, and Rashi's commentaries, in Roman type).

1. Moritz Heyne, *Fuenf Buecher Deutscher Hausaltertuemer*, Vol. I, Leipzig, 1899, p. 304.

2. For a map of twelfth-century Troyes, see Urban T. Holmes, Jr. and Sister M. Amelia Klenke, O.P., *Chrétien, Troyes and the Grail*, Chapel Hill, North Carolina, 1959. For a map of Troyes in modern times, see Lucien Morel-Paven, *Troyes et l'Aube*, Troyes, 1929, p. 1.

3. Haggigah 4a [Enumeration of persons whose occupations exempt them from bringing offerings in the Temple on festivals]:
The scraper [defined as one who collects dog excrements for use in laundering or tanning]: And I say that it [i.e., dog excrement] is needed for the dressing of Cordovan leather, which is done with dog excrements.

4. Berakhot 25a [One who has just placed leather into dog excrements for tanning is not permitted to recite the *Shema* while he is near the leather]:
Rashi: This refers to the excrements of dogs and pigs, which are used in the dressing of hides.

5. Shevuot 42a:
Gall nut: "Gales" in Old French, used in the dressing of hides.
Shabbat 79a:
Gall nuts: Hides are prepared with pounded gall nuts just as is done here with a crushed bark called *tana.*

6. Shabbat 123a [Prohibition against moving a tree bark on the Sabbath]:
It must not be moved: Bark which is used in the dressing of hides.

7. John F. Benton, *The Memoirs of Abbot Guibert of Nogent*, New York, 1970, p. 65.

8. Pesahim 46a [Discussion on questions of ritual impurity. According to Talmudic law, hides to which bits of flesh still adhere are susceptible to ritual

defilement. However, once the hide has been subjected to the leather production process the flesh is considered non-existent and the hide is no longer susceptible to defilement on account of the flesh. The question is then posed at what point the production process can be said to have begun. Rashi explains the process]:

He trod on them: Hides are usually spread out on the ground to be trodden on by people. This is the beginning of the process by which hides are converted into leather.

9. Pesahim 42b [Prohibition against possessing shoemaker's glue on Passover because it is made from a "leaven" product]:

Shoemaker's paste: "Glud" in Old French. Leatherworkers [use it to] paste the hides together when they come apart or they join two hides together to make them stronger. Usually they add some oatmeal [to the paste].

10. Shabbat 75b [Prohibition against the tracing of outlines on the Sabbath. The tracing of outlines is one of the thirty-nine principal activities that must not be performed on the Sabbath.]:

The tracing of outlines: Leatherworkers usually trace an outline [on the surface of the leather] before cutting, lengthening, widening or shortening the hide. Only thereafter do they use the knife, cutting along the outline.

11. Sanhedrin 68a [A discussion of ritual impurity]:

Shoemaker's last: The last was made of leather. It resembled a shoe stuffed with hair, with the opening sewn up. Shoes were made in those days just as in our own [though] shoemakers [now] make them with a wooden last.

12. Betzah 14b [Prohibition against sending a pair of hobnailed sandals as a holiday gift]:

But not hobnailed sandals: Made of wood covered with leather and nailed [to the sole].

13. Shabbat 66a: [How may a cripple go out on the Sabbath with his supports and not violate the prohibition against "carrying" on the Sabbath?]:

With his supports: Supports for a cripple. He moves forward on both knees and ankles; a leather support is made [to cushion] the joints.

14. Megillah 19a [Boot blacking may not be used as ink for a megillah, mezuzah or tefillin:]

Bootmakers' blacking: A paste used for blackening shoes.

15. Joseph and Frances Gies, *Life in a Medieval City,* London, 1969, p. 80.

16. Gittin 69b [Silver dross mentioned as a cure for anal worms]:

Dross: "Cogilon" (Old French), derived from silver chips at the place where the silver is mined from the soil and is melted down.

Gittin 86a: [Silver dross mentioned as a cure for a certain kind of boil]:

Dross: Silver refuse which emerges from the place where it is melted at the time it is mined from the mountains. This is called "cogilon."

17. Proverbs 17:3:

The crucible is for silver: A crucible in which silver is refined. This is done with vegetable ashes placed on clay.

18. Shabbat 18a [It is permitted to place sulfur under silver vessels on the eve of the Sabbath to undergo the process of sulfuring all through the Sabbath]:
Sulfur: Underneath silver vessels decorated with floral engravings and various patterns. They are then exposed to smoke from [burning] sulfur; [as a result] the engravings become black and visible. This process is called "nieller" [in Old French].

19. Shabbat 50a [Vessels may be polished on the Sabbath with any polish except that silver must not be polished with white earth]:
Except silver vessels with gartekon: [Gartekon is] a kind of sediment found in wine barrels. This is called "alum;" it is used for finishing the silver vessel because silver is soft and this material makes it smooth.

20. Shabbat 16b [Discussion of ritual impurity in vessels]:
And soldered it: "Solder" in Old French. To repair silver in the place where it is broken.

21. Shabbat 78a [Discussion of quantities which, if carried out of a private domain on the Sabbath, involve a violation of the prohibition against "carrying" on the Sabbath]:
[As much as is needed] to make a little hole: A vessel in which molten [quick]silver is placed. Its opening is blocked with tar or pitch. A small hole is made in the seal to allow the [quick]silver to be poured out.

22. Haggigah 13b [Reference to the vision of Ezekiel 2:1 ff.]:
Like the flame that goes forth between the potsherds: Gold refiners perforate a clay vessel and put it over coals on which the gold is then placed, together with broken pieces of brick or clay. The flame which comes through the perforations in the vessel has many colors and keeps flickering.

Eruvin 104a [Discussion of the permissibility of sprinkling salt on the altar ramp on the Sabbath]:
One may sprinkle salt: Just as the fire that flares up among the shards on which gold is refined. They have holes and cracks and the flame that rises from amidst them has a greenish or reddish color. [Rashi's interpretation is an etymological one. He points out that the verb בזק ("to sprinkle") and the noun בזק ("flash" or "lightning") have the same root: ב-ז-ק].

23. Proverbs 27:21: *The refining pot is for silver, and the furnace for gold.*
The refining pot: [This utensil] is made for silver; the *koor* [crucible], for refining gold.

24. Shabbat 78b [Discussion of prohibitions against "carrying" on the Sabbath; reference to crushed bricks or stones used in making a peg for a tripod]:
For making a [tripod's] peg: [A tripod] for a crucible which was placed on a special stand. ...Where there is no coal available, gold is refined over burning bran.

25. Exodus 32:4: *And formed it [i.e., the golden calf] with an engraving tool:* A goldsmith's tool with which they engrave and cut figures into gold. [It is] like a writer's stylus that incises letters on tablets.

26. Shabbat 123a [Laws concerning the moving of an object on the Sabbath]:
The goldsmith's mallet: Must be smooth for beating the metal foil.

27. Shabbat 103a [Laws concerning work forbidden on the Sabbath]:
Because those who beat out the metal plates of the Tabernacle did so: They beat alternately three times on the foil and once on the anvil to smooth the mallet so that the mallet would not break the foil. I have also seen those who mint coins doing this in our place.

28. Joseph and Frances Gies, *op. cit.,* p. 83.

29. Hullin 30b [How the slaughtering knife should be "drawn" across the throat of the animal]:
Beaten gold: Drawn, since it is soft and it is drawn just as copper workers draw out the copper into the wire from which they make needles.
    Bava Metzia 83b [Ways of distinguishing between thieves and harmless individuals]:
He might have been rolling thin metal: He stretches copper and iron wires to make needles [without a hammer so as not to attract attention with the noise].

30. Ta'anit 12a [A self-imposed fast not undertaken before sunset on the previous day is likened to a pair of bellows filled with wind]:
Bellows: The bellows with which the blacksmith fans the fire. It is full of air.

31. Pesahim 54a [According to a tradition, tongs were among the objects created at twilight on the Sixth Day]:
Rashi: [The tongs were] made with a mold, by casting, just as silver and copper vessels are cast.

32. Shabbat 42a [It is permissible on the Sabbath to douse a lump of fiery metal in the street because it might cause a fire]:
A lump of fiery metal: That which is thrown out; the metal waste.

33. Yoma 34b [On the eve of Yom Kippur, if the High Priest was old or ill, a lump of hot wrought iron would be thrown into the cold water to heat the water before the High Priest used the water in the sacred ritual. The question is raised whether this act does not constitute a "hardening" of the metal which is forbidden on the Sabbath and on Yom Kippur]:
Hardening: When one plunges iron from fire into water it becomes harder and stronger.

34. Sanhedrin 52b [Description of execution by beheading]:
On a block: A piece of thick wood fastened to the ground just as those used by the blacksmiths.

35. Pesahim 54a [The tradition about the creation of tongs, see Note 31]:

Tongs made with tongs: This is done with another pair of tongs. He holds the metal with a pair of tongs and beats it with a hammer.

36. Bava Bathra 26a [If a flying spark from a blacksmith's anvil causes damage to property, the blacksmith is responsible]:
A spark: A spark which is emitted from iron when [the iron] is beaten with a hammer.

37. Shabbat 52b [Rings and halters beaten thin so as to fit loosely around the neck of an animal]:
Beaten: Beaten with a hammer until the hole stretches and widens to its full circumference.

38. Avodah Zarah 52a [Reference to the manufacture of appurtenances for idol worship]:
Knocked: Beat upon it with a hammer until it expands and fills in the notch.

39. Avodah Zarah 16a [One does not sell shields or metal shutters to idol worshippers because they might forge them into weapons]:
Because they forge [weapons]: Because they beat them until they become thin and then they forge weapons from them.

40. Hullin 57b [Defects that may make an animal unfit for food under Jewish law. R. Simon ben Halafta used a leather apron, such as that worn by copper workers, to wrap around a hen whose feathers were gone entirely. He placed the bird thus wrapped into an oven, and as a result the hen grew feathers even larger than those it had lost]:
Covering it with a piece of apron used by metal workers: He wrapped [the bird] into a piece of material worn by copper workers to protect them from the fine copper particles. It is made of leather and is always warm because of its thickness and [because of its constant contact with the] copper.

41. Haggigah 4a [Among those persons whose occupation exempts or disqualifies them from bringing offerings in the Temple on festivals are copper smelters, to whom the unpleasant odor of the metal adheres]:
The copper smelters: Who smelts the copper at the place where it is mined. They all have an unpleasant odor.

42. Ketubot 77a [A coppersmith is defined as one who may be compelled to give his wife a divorce because of the unpleasant odor which adheres to him]:
They hammer out cauldrons: They hammer and flatten copper and manufacture cauldrons. This has a bad smell.

43. Shabbat 41b [It is permissible on the Sabbath to pour a large quantity of cold water into a hot empty kettle in order to cool the kettle. However, the question is asked whether this act does not constitute a "hardening" of the metal, which is forbidden on the Sabbath]:
Is he not hardening it? If a metal vessel is hot and one pours cold water into it, the vessel is hardened... because the high temperature causes the metal to form bubbles and almost to break, and the cold water hardens these weak spots.

44. Sanhedrin 64a [A suggestion that the Evil Inclination which tempts one to worship idols be cast into a cauldron of lead and that the cauldron should then be covered so as to absorb his cries (cf. Zechariah 5:8)]:
Lead absorbs the sound: A cauldron made of lead absorbs sound and retains it longer than any other metal vessel.

45. Bava Metzia 83b (See Note 29):
Flatten: He stretches copper and iron wire to make needles.

Shabbat 123a [Discussion of circumstances under which a needle must be regarded as a "working utensil" which must not be handled on the Sabbath]:
In their shapeless form: Needles into which the eyes have [yet] to be put.

Hullin 30b [see Note 29].

46. Shabbat 47a [In connection with the prohibition against making a tool on the Sabbath, the question is asked whether it is permissible to dismantle a composite rod to its original, unopened state on the Sabbath]:
Copper workers: They go from city to city to do their work and have composite rods.

47. Shabbat 11b:
With a chip behind his ear: To me, however, it seems that all the things mentioned here are symbols which artisans carry on them when they go out into the street so that people can recognize their trade and offer them employment.

48. *Ibid.*:
A chip behind his ear: A long, straight piece similar to a ruler with which [the pages of] books are ruled; [it is] called *vira* in Old French. It is used to straighten boards, just as our carpenters do, by drawing lines.

49. Shabbat 97a [A discussion of the principle that wherever there is a gap of less than three handbreadths the areas so separated are considered for legal purposes as one single area. An attempt is made here to apply this principle to small mounds on the ground and to consider them as nonexistent as long as they are not higher than three handbreadths. The preliminary reason suggested for this attempted application is the fact that ground cannot be leveled by means of a planing tool. Rashi proceeds to explain the nature of the tool]:
A tool for planing: Two kinds of wood and iron implements, one inserted into the other, with which a width of board is evened and smoothed.

50. Shabbat 48b [Discussion of objects that may become ritually impure]:
A carpenter's plane: Shutters are smoothed with it. A piece of iron is placed into a wooden mold specially fitted for it. After the work is done, [the tool] is removed.

51. Shabbat 123b [Discussion concerning what utensils maybe handled on the Sabbath]:
Except a *massar:* A large saw made to cut lumber.

52. Shabbat 157a [See Note 51]:

The big saw: A saw of artisans for cutting wood.... It is made like a knife, full of notches.

53. Hullin 88b [The use of sawdust to cover up the blood of slaughtered animals]:
Sawdust: When carpenters use a saw, sawdust fine as dust is produced.

Bava Kamma 119b [If a carpenter works on the premises of another man, even the sawdust becomes the property of the proprietor]:
Sawdust: It is very fine and falls from the surface when the cut is made. It is as fine as dust.

54. Hullin 25a [Discussion of "unfinished" objects which cannot become ritually impure]:
To adorn with borders: Large carvings and engravings as are made on the top surfaces of chests and benches.

55. Exodus 27:5 [Description of the altar in the Tabernacle]:
The ledge around the altar: Making rounded grooves in the boards that form the sides of chests and wooden benches.

56. Megillah 6a [Discussion of Israelite tribal territories]:
White glass: Extracted from sand [of the district of Zebulon].

57. Sanhedrin 91a [The question is asked how the dead can be resurrected after they have turned into dust. The answer given is that if a glass vessel which is made by the breath of a mere mortal can be repaired when it is broken, then certainly a human being, made by the breath of God, can be revived. Rashi explains the glassblowing process]:
If a glass vessel, even though made by the breath of man, can be repaired when it is broken: When he makes it, he has a hollow tube into which he blows; this is [what I have] heard from artisans. They [i.e., the broken glass vessels] can be salvaged by melting them down again and using the material for making a new vessel.

58. *Rashi ibid.:* This is [what I have] heard from artisans.

59. Urban Tigner Holmes, Jr., *Daily Living in the Twelfth Century,* Madison, Wisconsin, 1952, p. 155 ff.

60. Shabbat 74b [Productive activities forbidden on the Sabbath; one who transgresses these prohibitions must bring sin offerings, one for each separate violation of the Sabbath involved in his act]:
He who [makes an earthenware barrel on the Sabbath must bring] seven sin offerings [because each of the acts that follow entails a separate transgression of the Sabbath law]: He grinds the stones, pulverizes them and removes the coarse pebbles from it... sifts them, kneads the clay... piles the clay when he makes the lump, to smooth it... and he burns it in the fire of the kiln.

61. Bava Metzia 74a [Laws of price fixing]:
[Potters' lumps of clay require] molding: He rolls it according to the size required, large or small, and impresses the shape of the vessel into it.

62. Betzah 32a [Work prohibited on a festival]:
One must not hollow out a lump of clay in order to make a lamp: To take one of the clay pieces from the potter in order to push one's fist into it, thus making a [well] to turn it into a candleholder.

63. Hullin 16a [Slaughtering done with a knife fixed to a potter's wheel]:
The potter's wheel: A potter's wheel which has a wheelwork whereby it can be turned as the vessel is shaped.

64. Sotah 11b [Discussion of a method of child delivery]:
A wooden block: A thick trunk on which [the potter] sits while he molds the clay to shape the vessel in accordance with the desired size.

65. Bava Metzia 74a [Laws of price fixing]:
And burns [the clay]: To harden it in a kiln.
Sukkah 7b [Discussion of kinds of structure that qualify as a sukkah]:
A sukkah shaped like a kiln: Round.

66. Pesahim 30b [Kashering of utensils for Passover]:
Glazed vessels: They are made of clay but are covered with lead.
Hullin 47b [Vessel used in examining the lungs of an animal after slaughter]:
A glazed earthenware plate: A bowl made of clay covered with lead... called "plumier;" i.e., sealing clay; it has an attractive appearance.

67. Proverbs 25:20:
Nitre: A kind of soft soil similar to our soil, called *Kreide,* which is hollowed out to make vessels. If an acid drops upon it, it dissolves and is spoiled.

68. Betzah 33b [Prohibition against making a utensil on a festival]:
Olive barrels: A broken barrel is plastered together with resin from which tar is made. This resin is called "rishna." Its scent is like that of frankincense. In Arabic it is called "mustaki" and it is used for repairing broken clay bowls.

69. Kiddushin 82a [A list of occupations which involve dealings with women and are therefore considered undesirable]:
A blood letter: One who lets blood.... he is called *gara* because he reduces (מגרע; pi'el inflection of the verb) the volume of blood.

70. Bava Metzia 47b:
Tokens [used] at [public] bathhouses: The bath attendant receives tokens from those who intend to use the baths in the bathhouse, so that he may know how many [bathers] there are and, according to their number, he may then warm the water and prepare towels. He receives small, defaced coins [as tokens].

71. Betzah 35b [Utensils which may become ritually impure]:
Hair clipper: A knife called *shahor* because it causes the hair to fall. The scissors have two knives... parts which can be separated from one another.

72. Shabbat 9b [Types of work which should not be begun shortly before the Sabbath]:

Barber's sheet: An apron placed upon [the patron's] knees to protect [his clothes] from falling hair.

73. Bava Metzia 97a [Laws regarding the borrowing of tools]:
A town barber: One who cuts the hair of the men in the town.

74. Kiddushin 82a [See Note 69]:
Barbers: Women need them for their sons.

75. Pesahim 30b [Laws regarding utensils for Passover use]:
The yeast dish: A vessel in which the woman soaks and leaves the yeast. She places [the yeast] into the dough and sometimes leaves it there overnight.

76. Ta'anit 22b [In a discussion of fasts to be observed in case of a natural disaster which affected a certain amount of grain]:
The question was asked: [Does the Mishna mean] as an oven full of grain or as an oven full of bread [which involves a smaller quantity than an oven full of grain]?: .... The bread does not fill the oven entirely. It just adheres to its walls.

77. Ta'anit 25a [In connection with the story of the poor woman whose empty oven miraculously filled up with bread]:
Mardeh: A scraper, "pala" in Old French. It is called *mardeh* [from "scraping off"] because the bread is scraped [with it] from the sides of the oven.

Shabbat 117b [May bread forgotten in an oven be removed on the Sabbath?]:
A baker's shovel: A tool with which bread is scraped from the wall of the oven to which it adhered.

78. Genesis 40:16:
...And behold, three baskets of hari *were on my head:* [Hari are] baskets woven of peeled willows. There are many of these in our country; they are used by vendors of fancy rolls.

79. Kiddushin 82a [Lists of occupations considered undesirable]:
The worthiest of butchers is a partner of Amalek: On his account, cases of doubt as to the *kashrut* of his meat arise because he is greedy [for money] and he offers [these meats of dubious *kashrut*] as food.

80. Bava Metzia 60b [Ethics of shopkeepers]:
An animal [carcass] must not be given an appearance of stiffness: He stiffens the hair of the carcass so as to make [the animal] look fat.... They inflate the intestines sold in the butcher shop so that they may appear wider and larger.

81. Hullin 50b [Laws relating to fatal diseases which, if found in a carcass after ritual slaughter, makes the animal unfit for consumption under the dietary laws]:
A certain part of the rumen: The *panca* [rumen] is the place perforated by the butchers when they remove the excrement from the part [of the carcass] from where the noxious matter flows.

82. Yoma 16b [Measurements of the Temple; there was to be a space of four cubits between the tables and the poles]:

Small poles: Low poles placed into the ground, to which iron hooks were attached on which the animals were suspended for flaying.

83. Shabbat 45b [Prohibition against "watering" an animal for slaughter on the Sabbath]:
One waters: The animal is watered before it is slaughtered so that it may be flayed more easily.

84. Betzah 31a [The chopping of wood is forbidden on festivals, except if it is done with a butcher's chopper, a tool not specifically made for chopping wood]:
Butcher's chopper: A butcher's knife similar to an ax, which is not a tool of the trade. Some make it with two cutting surfaces. The second [surface] looks somewhat like [that of] a saddler's knife.

85. Betzah 28a [In connection with weighing meat on a festival]:
A skilled butcher: One who knows how to assess the weight [of a portion of meat in one hand and to weigh it against a weight held in his other hand].

86. Shabbat 11b [A hatcheller must not go out with his cord in his ear shortly before the Sabbath]:
Cord: He fastens with it the two ends [of the cloth] and stretches [the cloth] on his pegs to beat it with sticks in order to raise its hair.

Hosea 6:9: *Just as a gathering of fishermen who gather in their fish, so is the gathering of priests who gang up to murder the people on the way:* The term *hakei* refers to the seams with which the hatcheller fastens the two ends of the cloth when he beats it with his stick.

87. Mo'ed Katan 10a [Discussion of the difference between the work of an ordinary person and that of a craftsman, and in what way sewing is permitted during the intermediate days of a festival]:
A needleful of stitches in one sweep: When he sews, he makes [a number of] stitches the length of the needle; then he pulls the needle from the garment, and in this way many stitches are made with one movement. Anyone who knows how to do this is indeed an expert.

88. *Ibid.:*
Sews tuck stitches: He does not stitch in a straight line but in separate stitches. This is called "dog-stitching" because the uneven stitches resemble the bite of a dog's teeth, which are widely spaced. He does not sew in the regular manner; namely, stitch next to stitch, but inserts the needle once at a higher place and once at a lower place. That is why it is called a "dog-stitch" because the teeth of a dog, too, are uneven, one tooth being higher than the other.

89. Bava Kamma 119b [Discussion of which part of a thread used by a tailor belongs to the proprietor of the article on which the tailor is working, and which part remains the property of the tailor]:
[The length of the needle and] beyond the [length of the] needle: [In this case it remains the property of the tailor] because if there is only as much of the thread left as the length of the needle, one cannot sew with it.

90. Sukkah 19b [A discussion of kinds of structure that qualify as a sukkah]:
Like a cone-shaped hut: A cave for hunters in which they lie in wait for birds. It is made like a round, tapering vessel. Its roof and walls are made of one piece.

91. Sukkah 3b [Laws regarding the *eruv* on the Sabbath]:
A guardhouse: A hut made of willows and reeds for guarding fruit or for bird hunters.

Bava Metzia 42a [Laws of negligence involving deposited money]:
A hut made of reeds: A small shelter, round, resembling a hat, made by bird hunters for lying in wait [for their quarry].

Shabbat 56b [Legend of the origin of Magna Graecia (Greek Italy)]:
A hut: A small shelter for hunters, made of reeds and willows.

92. Ta'anit 22a [Question of legal distinctions between disasters due to normal, natural causes, on the one hand, and "acts of God," on the other. The case under discussion is whether, if a land animal jumps on a roof and snatches a baby lying there, this accident should be regarded as a natural calamity or as an "act of God." It is argued whether, if the roof is not one which tops a house but one which covers a subterranean cave so that it is almost level with the ground, such an accident, too, should be regarded as an "act of God" or not. Rashi describes the kind of "cave" to which the text refers]:
Like the caves of hunters: A small cave dug by hunters in which to lie in wait for birds.

93. Hullin 51b [Need for a special examination of the organs of a bird trapped under unusual conditions, to see whether the bird has sustained any injury that makes it unfit for consumption under the dietary laws]:
A closely knotted net: A bird that fell into a net spread in midair.

94. Shabbat 80a [Discussion of quantities of paste which, if carried out of a private domain on the Sabbath, involve a violation of the prohibition against "carrying" on the Sabbath]:
Pasted: A small board topped with paste is placed on top of the hunter's rod. The bird perches on it and gets stuck. A large quantity of paste must be spread on the board for this purpose.

95. Hullin 52a [See Note 93]:
Affixed: Paste is smeared on a small board. When the bird perches on it, it is glued [to the board]. If it attempts to fly away with the board it drops to the ground.

96. Shabbat 94a [Discussion of whether placing a live bird on a horse's back to be carried by the horse constitutes a violation of the Sabbath]:
Falconers: Bird hunters who place upon a horse live birds, such as a falcon, in order to catch other birds.

97. Yevamot 59b [Reference to a question whether a *kohen* (priest) may marry a woman who was covered by an animal]:

A vicious dog: A big dog used for catching [other] animals.

98. Shabbat 18a [Discussion about Sabbath "rest" for utensils]:
What of the trap... which performs an action: A trap laid to catch animals by their paws. As soon as they touch it, the spring snaps shut by itself and catches [the animal's paw].

99. Ezekiel 19:4: *He was taken in their pit.*
Pit: A pit covered with straw. The animal falls into it.

100. Shabbat 51b [Man is responsible for the Sabbath rest of his animals]:
And all animals that wear collars: For instance fox hounds and small animals that wear collars as ornaments.

101. Bava Kamma 81a [Joshua permitted fishing in Lake Tiberias with a fishing rod provided that the fishermen did not spread a screen, which would interfere with shipping]:
Spread the sail: Fisherman insert pegs to make reed enclosures in the water for trapping fish.

102. Shabbat 18a [See Note 98]:
But what of the trap...: Baskets are made with a large opening [at one end] and a very small one [at the other]. The fish enters and puts out its head through the narrow end, but it cannot get its body out. When it attempts to pull back its head, the edges of the basket slide under its gills.

103. Ta'anit 24a:
When there is no [actual] catching required: For instance, if [the fish] was trapped in a basket and left [submerged] in the water to keep it alive, as is done by fishermen.

104. Shabbat 18a [See Note 98]:
In his gill: It is the fishhook which the fish swallows and it is stuck. The implement does not move.

CHAPTER TEN

Tools, Instruments and Utensils

In his commentaries on the Bible and the Talmud Rashi discusses medieval tools, instruments and utensils which he could have known only by actually watching them in operation, for we find them described in no other contemporaneous source and certainly not in the Rabbinic literature preceding Rashi. Rashi's knowledge of such details also attests to the harmony in which the Jews of Troyes and other districts of medieval France lived with their Gentile neighbors— a fact which is borne out also by the Responsa literature dating from that period.

As already noted, the Champagne province, of which Troyes was the capital, was a center of viticulture, where many Jews, probably including Rashi himself, owned vineyards.[1] As a consequence, Rashi had ample opportunity to observe the methods by which wine was produced and processed. The wine was decanted from barrel to barrel by siphons (*diofi:* from the Greek *diaphysso*, lit., "to drain entirely."). Rashi explains the siphon in his commentary on a statement in Eruvin 104a that siphons may be used on the Sabbath. "Wine is tranferred from one barrel to another by means of two pipes with obliquely cut ends. These ends are then fitted to one another. The [free] end of one of the pipes is put into the full barrel. Some of the wine is then drawn off by mouth suction by way of the free end of the other pipe. The mouth is then withdrawn from the pipe and the wine flows freely by itself [into the other barrel]." (The obliquely cut pipes were necessary because, obviously, neither rubber nor any other elastic material with which one could have produced bent piping was known at the time.)[2] In his commentary on Avodah Zarah 72b (regarding the handling of wine by heathens) Rashi gives a more detailed description of the siphoning operation,[3] As a matter of fact, Rashi's original version of this latter commentary seems to have included a diagram of a siphon, for the text of the commentary (see Note 3) contains the word *ka-zeh* ("like this"). However, the original copyist apparently omitted the drawing; that is why the diagram does not appear in extant editions of the Rashi commentaries.

Liquids were stored in a utensil called *arak.* Rashi describes the *arak* in connection with a statement in Eruvin 104a that it is permissible to cause water to drop from an *arak* (the Talmudic text apparently refers to a water clock) for a sick person on the Sabbath. The *arak,* Rashi explains, "is a vessel with a narrow opening and is made of metal. Its bottom has many small perforations. It is filled with water and then its upper opening is plugged. As long as this opening is plugged no water will leave the vessel. When the plug is removed,the water will leave [the vessel] drop by drop through the perforations."

Water was used as a weighing device. Rashi knew of water scales, which he describes in his commentary on Betzah 28a.[4] This instrument is a vessel "which has a scale *(sh'natot)* and other signs marked [on it]." The vessel was filled with water, and the scale "indicates how high the water has to rise in order to show the equivalent of one pound of meat — as tested beforehand." It seems that the product to be weighed was actually placed into the water, and its weight was measured by the amount of the water it displaced in the vessel.

For measuring liquids by volume a large earthenware vessel was employed. This vessel had raised markings which Rashi describes as resembling small nuts, to indicate the various measuring units. The markings were whitened with lime to make them visible.[5]

There also were mechanical scales. One type consisted of a vertical pole to which a horizontal rod and tongue were affixed. The pans were suspended on chains from each end of the horizontal rod.[6] Wood, wax and copper were weighed on wooden scales.[7] Goldsmiths and silversmiths used special small scales.[8]

Heavy loads of metal were apparently hoisted with a magnet, to which Rashi refers as a stone which "lifts metal without touching it."[9]

It seems that both solar energy and water power were utilized in Rashi's day. Rashi tells of glass vessels so shaped that, when filled with water, they could concentrate the heat of the sun in strengths sufficient to cause combustion. A pre-heated glass vessel was filled with water and exposed to the heat of the sun. The glass would then produce a flame which would set fire to chaff that was brought near it.[10] As for the harnessing of water power, Rashi makes reference to the wheel of a water mill.[11]

The use of individual cups or glasses for drinking purposes seems not to have been as common in Rashi's time as it is today. In his commentary on Avodah Zarah 72b regarding circumstances under which a Jew may drink wine from a container shared by a heathen, Rashi describes the *knishkanin* as a large container from the sides of which two or three pipes branched out, turning upward and running parallel with the walls of the container as far as the container's rim. When this container was filled with wine, these pipes were all filled to the same level and as many people could drink from the container as there were pipes. (According to the Talmudic text, Jews and heathens could drink together from such a container as long as each used a separate pipe.)

Hot water was kept warm in a container resembling the samovar of a later period (*muliar*: Greek *miliarion*). This container had attached to its side a smaller vessel in which coal was stored to provide a steady source of heat for the water.[12] In another comment on the same Talmudic passage (Shabbat 41a), which discusses permitted ways of using heated water on the Sabbath, Rashi describes a water-heating oven with two compartments. The water was kept "in the empty one, which is next to the coal compartment." Although this technique in principle is similar to the samovar-type arrangement, there is one difference in that "the wall in the oven between the two compartments is very thick, and since the oven is heated constantly, the heat of the wall keeps the water warm even when there is no more heated coal in the compartment." Another water-heating device, also explained by Rashi in connection with Shabbat 41a, was the *bei dudei* (a kind of double boiler), "a large, double-bottomed kettle. Coal is placed into the space between the two bottoms to keep the water warm in the upper part."

It appears that the principles underlying these water-heating utensils were utilized also in public bathhouses. There were holes through which hot air and water were channeled into the bathing chamber from underneath the floor.[13] The air and water were heated by a fire that burned outside and underneath the bathhouse.[14] There were also Turkish baths, where one could stand or sit without pouring water over one's body but just to warm up and perspire.[15] Bathhouses had stone floors.[16] A kind of shower bath may even have been known in Rashi's day; Rashi tells of an arrangement in which water dropped down from above and the bathers stood on planks beneath it to wash themselves.[17] A copper utensil which had tiny perforations like a sieve was used in sprinkling clothes with water, apparently for ironing.[18]

It is amazing to the modern-day reader to note the detail in which Rashi described the tools of his day and differentiated between them. He makes reference to a variety of needles used by various trades for specific purposes. The small needle (*mahat shel yad*; literally, "hand needle") was used to sew clothing but also to extract thorns from the flesh.[19] A very fine needle (*mahat sidkit*) was used to mend tiny rents in garments.[20] Sackmakers used large, coarse needles;[21] saddlers, an awl (*mahta d'ushkafa*) with sharpened ends that could cut the thread at the seams.[22] A "double needle" (*mahat d'talmiuta*) produced stitches which Rashi describes as resembling the furrows made by a plough in a field.[23] Rashi also mentions a needle used for tattooing. The person desiring the tattoo "first writes [the design] upon his flesh with a chemical or with red coloring matter. Then he tattoos his flesh [by tracing the design upon it] with a needle or a knife." The coloring matter then oozed in between the skin and the flesh, where it remained permanently visible.[24] Needles were manufactured from copper or iron wire drawn through holes of varying sizes. This work did not entail much noise and therefore could be performed also during the night.[25] It was mostly done by coppersmiths.[26]

Rashi's commentaries list an equally large variety of knives. Small table knives were used to cut or slice bread, meat and other foods in the home.[27] Some knives were ornamented with "horn-like" projections on the backs of their blades.[28] Butchers worked with various kinds of knives. A large one, which resembled a hatchet, could not be used for ritual slaughtering but was utilized in cutting the meat and breaking the bones.[29] Other butchers' choppers had two cutting edges, the second resembling the edge of a saddler's knife.[30] Rashi also makes mention of a carving knife.[31] He describes an efficient, saw-like knife with many teeth, similar to knives employed by comb-makers.[32] An unusual combination cited by Rashi is a knife with two cutting edges, of which one is smooth and the other serrated.[33] Rashi knew of two kinds of serrated knives: the one had its teeth pointed toward the handle, the other, toward the tip. He says that if one tests a knife that has its teeth pointed toward the handle by drawing one's fingernail in the direction of the knife's tip, or vice versa, the fingernail will get caught in the knife's teeth.[34] Rashi describes a number of "tradesmen's knives," a large saw, "full of notches," used by woodcutters;[35] the cobbler's knife;[36] a smaller knife for cutting dried figs;[37] and a curved knife for harvesting figs.[38] Finally, there is a brief description of the hair clipper (*shahor*)[39] and a pair of barber's scissors with two blades which can be separated from one another.[40] In Rashi's day there were also special scissors used for cutting woolen garments.[41]

Rashi acquaints us with household gadgets which in many ways remind of those we know today. Flour was sifted through a two-layered piece of material (nifvata), closely woven and tied together at the top so as to resemble a purse.[42] Pulse were stored in small bags (gulki),[43] and were sifted in a funnel-like utensil (kanon), which was wide at the top and had a short, spout-like opening at the other end. The pulse were put into the wide upper opening, the kanon was shaken firmly and the pulse rolled through the spout while the chaff remained in the upper part.[44] There were also sieves made of metal.[45] Beer was kept in barrels or casks[46] which were covered with a special kind of cloth (prunka).[47] Wine was drawn from its barrel with a ladle[48] and was bottled with the aid of a funnel, which was wide on top, with a small, short opening at the bottom. The funnel was placed into the narrow opening of the customer's bottle, and the wine was then poured through the funnel from the measuring vessel into the bottle.[49] A glass pitcher was used for the ritual washing of the hands.[50]

The utensils known to households of Rashi's day were not as specialized as those with which we are familiar, but they satisfied the needs of the medieval Jewish home. Brooms were made of palm branches, probably the material best suited for sweeping sandy floors.[51] Ashes were removed from stoves with a small shovel which resembled a pot cover and had a handle made of thin metal.[52] Such a shovel was also used to separate figs that adhered to each other in clusters.[53] A similar tool, as already noted in the previous chapter, was used to pry bread loaves loose from the floor of the baking oven.[54] These utensils had handles which were attached to the working end of the shovel by a pin that penetrated the shovel.[55] A certain kind of grass was known as an efficient cleansing and polishing agent[56] for metalware. Wooden utensils were polished with the rough skin of a tuna fish,[57] much as we would use sandpaper today. The froth of a liquid boiling in a pot was skimmed off with a ladle.[58] Firewood was stored from season to season in the back yard of the home.[59] Spices were pounded with a pestle; meat was carved on a special meat carving board.[60]

Rashi's commentaries contain references to three kinds of writing materials: a kind of paper made from "grass," probably papyrus;[61] parchments on which, Rashi says, pens made a scratching noise that sounded like "ken-ken;"[62] and wax tablets on which one wrote with a stylus.[63] Rashi describes a kind of primitive paper clip (*atbi*) as a small wooden stick with a notch cut into its top, into which the papers were inserted.[64] Lines were drawn with a special ruler.[65] One writing tool used by scribes was a piece of iron with a point split into two parts, like the nib of a pen.[66] Letters, or any receptacles that had to be securely closed, were sealed with a signet ring.[67]

The extended or composite rods mentioned by Rashi in various connections are of special interest. Housepainters and whitewashers carried with them such composite rods, topped with a rag which was dipped into the lime solution used as whitewash. A very short rod was sufficient to whitewash the lower part of a building, but work on the upper part of the wall made it necessary to lengthen the rod by attaching another rod on top of it.[68] Composite rods were apparently well known and put to many uses in Rashi's day.[69]

Tools described by Rashi include the hammer with its various properties: it draws sparks from the iron[70] and smashes rocks into many particles.[71] An adze could be used to work on iron structures.[72] Also, hammers could widen rings of any size[73] and stretch or expand bars of metal.[74] The sound of a hammer beat was also the signal that the work had been completed; the worker would let the hammer slip off the anvil with his last stroke.[75]

A saw is described as a blade "full of teeth" which may be set in many directions.[76]

Rashi even speaks of a kind of telescope. It is a hollow rod through which, as he puts it, one can see better if it is short; if it is long, one cannot see very far with it.[77]

A novel timepiece took the form of several steps built in such a direction that the time of day could be determined by the length of the shadow thrown on them by the sun.[78]

NOTES

(Biblical and Talmudic passages are printed in italics; abstracts of such passages, and Rashi's commentaries, in Roman type).

1. *Teshuvhot Hakhmei Tzarfat ve-Lother,* ed. Joel HaKohen Miller, 13, 92, 95.

2. Descriptions of this utensil differing from Rashi's description are given by R. Hananel *ad loc.* and by R. Tzadok Gaon (cited in *Ginzei Yerushalayim,* I, p. 6)

3. Rashi on Avodah Zarah 72b:

A man was drawing wine through [a siphon consisting of] a large and a small pipe: Two pipes are cut with ends at a slant. Their ends are fitted to each other at the top and both point downward like this [sic.] One end is placed into a full vessel until it reaches the [vessel's] bottom. The other end is placed in [the worker's] mouth. He sucks [at it] a little until the wine rises [in the pipe]. He then removes the pipe from his mouth and places an empty vessel beneath the flowing wine which is thus transferred from vessel to vessel.

4. For Talmudic context, see Note 85 to Chapter 9.

5. Shabbat 80b [Discussion of quantities which, if carried out of a private domain on the Sabbath, involve a violation of the prohibition against "carrying" on the Sabbath. Here, the material discussed is lime, i.e., the amount of lime needed to whiten the marks of a vessel]:

The teeth-like marks of a vessel:... It has markings resembling small nuts.... The markings were whitened with lime so that they could be seen better.

6. Shabbat 60a [Discussion of laws of ritual purity]:

The most important component: The *arsah* is a long pole to which a horizontal beam, called *jasse,* and a tongue, are affixed. Chains are attached to the beam and they all stand because of the long pole, which is called *flaiel.* The two pans are suspended from the ends [of the chains].

7. *Ibid.*

With a pole: Large scales used in weighing wool, wax and copper. They are made of wood.

8. Bava Bathra 89a [Laws of honest weight]:

Trutina: Scales for silver and gold; they are small.

9. Sanhedrin 107b [Reference to the *aggadah* that Elisha's servant Gehazi hung a lodestone above the golden calves of Jeroboam II and thus suspended the two idols in midair by magnetism]:

A lodestone: It lifts metal without touching it.

10. Betzah 33a [Prohibition against producing heat on the Sabbath]:

From water: Water is placed into a vessel of white glass; [the vessel] is placed into the sun when the sun is very hot. The glass vessel will then produce a flame, and if chaff is brought near the vessel [the chaff] will burn.

11. Sukkah 36b [Discussion of ritual qualifications of an *etrog*]:

[An etrog] grown in a mold so that it has the appearance of another species is invalid: [If it has] the shape of a wheel of a water mill.

12. Shabbat 41a [Discussion of permissibilty of using, on the Sabbath, water that was kept warm in a *miliarion.* Rashi describes this vessel, which the Gemarah merely characterizes as having water inside and coal outside]: *The water is within and the coals are without:* A vessel to which a smaller vessel is attached.... It is a vessel with a small receptacle attached to its side, into which the coal is placed. The water is in the larger receptacle.

13. Shabbat 29a [Discussion of specifications regarding the size of a rag considered susceptible to ritual defilement. The text speaks of a rag less than three fingerbreadths square. Rashi explains the possible use for such a small rag]: *The reference here is to [a rag] less than three [fingerbreadths] square:* It is used for blocking the holes through which the water comes into the [chamber of the] bathhouse.

14. Shabbat 40a [Circumstances under which water heated previously may be used for bathing immediately after the Sabbath]: *If the holes through which a bathhouse is warmed are plugged on the eve of the Sabbath [one may bathe therein immediately after the conclusion of the Sabbath]:* The fire [that heats the water] burns outside and underneath [the bathhouse.]

15. *Ibid.*
Rashi: One stands or sits in the bathhouse and does not put water on oneself but only warms up and perspires.

16. Shabbat 151b [Prohibition against washing a floor on the Sabbath]: *A disciple of Rabbi Meir followed him into the baths and wished to swill the floor for him...:...* The floor of the bathhouse is made of stone.

17. Avodah Zarah 16a [Question of Jews' building a public bath jointly with heathens]: *Bathhouses:* They are built in the ground, very deep down; the water drops down and the people wash themselves while standing upon boards.

18. Shabbat 123b [What tools and untensils may, or may not, be handled on the Sabbath. "The pin of a plough" describes a tool which is made expressly for one purpose only and which, if used for any other purpose, will be damaged as a result, causing considerable financial loss. Such a tool may therefore not be used on the Sabbath for any purpose]: *A fuller's trough is [regarded by the law] like the pin of a plough:* A copper utensil made with many perforations; it is [used] by laundrymen. It is placed above the clothes [to be ironed] and water is sprinkled [through it upon the clothes].

19. Sanhedrin 84b [Discussion of prohibition against performing surgery on one's parents]: *A mahat shel yad may be moved [on the Sabbath] for the purpose of extracting a thorn:* A *mahat shel yad* is a small needle used for sewing clothing.

Shabbat 122b:
A mahat shel yad [may be handled on the Sabbath] to remove a thorn: A mahat shel yad is a small needle used for sewing clothing.

20. Eruvin 53a [A metaphorical passage comparing the intellectual abilities of former generations with those of the present generation]:
But ours is like the eye of a sidkit: A needle used for small rents in garments. It is very fine.

Megillah 19b [statement that when God passed before Moses (Exodus 33:18ff) and the cave of Elijah (I Kings 19:11ff) Moses and Elijah would both have been consumed by the light of God's glory if the cave had had an opening even as tiny as the eye of a sidkit]:
A chink no bigger than the eye of a sidkit: A needle we use, which is very fine and with which small rents in garments are mended.

21. Shabbat 122b [It is permissible to use a sackmaker's needle on the Sabbath in order to unlock a door if the key has been misplaced]:
Sackmaker's needle: A large needle used for sewing sacks; a coarse needle.

22. Hullin 31a [Discussion of permissibility of using an awl for slaughtering an animal]:
What is the law if one used an awl?: The awl of the leatherworker [or cobbler], the blades of which are sharp and cut the threads of the seam [apparently bits of thread left at the end of a finished seam].

23. Berakhot 63a [Needle-stitching described as a trade which is desirable because it is clean and not laborious]:
Needle-stitching: Seams made line by line, like the furrows of a plough.

Kiddushin 82b [Needle-stitching characterized as a clean and easy craft to teach one's son]: A double needle used in making seams... like the furrows of a plough.

24. Makkot 21a [Forms of self-inflicted wounds which are forbidden under Biblical law (Leviticus 19:28). This includes tattooing. The Talmud explains the prohibition against tattooing as deriving from the fact that it imitated a pagan custom; i.,e., the custom among Amorites of tattooing the name of their deity into their flesh]:
He who writes an incised imprint [on his flesh]: He first writes [the design] upon his flesh with a chemical or with red coloring matter. Then he tattoos his flesh [by tracing the design upon it] with a needle or a knife. The coloring matter then enters in between the skin and the flesh and remains permanently visible.

25. See Note 29 to Chapter 9.

26. See Note 29 to Chapter 9.

27. Shabbat 123b [Object which may be handled on the Sabbath]:
A small table knife: A small knife with which one slices bread or meat....

28. Hullin 31a [Knives used in slaughtering animals must be smooth,

without projections which might pierce one of the animal's organs during *shehitah* and thus render the animal unfit for consumption under Jewish law]: *A knife which has no projection [lit., "no horns"]:* They make knives with a kind of horn as ornaments on the backs [of their blades].

29. Pesahim 70a [Knives which can or cannot be used for the slaughtering of Paschal offerings]:
Kufitz: A large knife which is generally not used for slaughtering but for cutting the meat and breaking the bones.

30. See Note 84 to Chapter 9.

31. Shabbat 123b [Tools which may not be handled on the Sabbath]:
A butcher's carving knife: A knife of the meat market with which the butcher carves the meat.

32. Arakhin 23b [Laws pertaining to confiscation of tools as pledges for contributions promised to the Temple. There are two basic tools which must not be confiscated from working men]:
Two tools of every kind: A knife which has notches and works quickly, similar to the knives used by comb-makers.

33. Hullin 15b [Knives which may be used for slaughtering animals]:
A hand sickle: It has two cutting edges, one smooth like a knife and the other serrated.

34. Hullin 17a [Serrated knives may not be used for slaughtering animals]:
Like a saw: With teeth pointing toward [the handle] and those with teeth pointing [toward the tip]. When you draw your fingernail from the end of the knife to its tip your fingernail will be caught in the teeth pointing in the direction of the end, and if you will test it from its tip to its end, your fingernail will be caught in the teeth pointing in the direction of the tip.

35. See Notes 51 and 52 to Chapter 9.

36. Shabbat 123b [Utensils which may not be handled on the Sabbath]:
Harba d'ushk'fei: A cobbler's knife.

37. *Ibid.*
Maktzu'a: A knife for cutting fig cakes.

38. Nedarim 61b [The reference is to a vow taken not to drink wine "until the fig-harvesting knives have been folded up;" i.e.,until the summer has passed]:
Have been folded up: The knives with which figs are harvested and which are then stored away.

39. See Note 71 to Chapter 9.

40. See Note 71 to Chapter 9.

41. Avodah Zarah 75b [Laws regarding utensils purchased from heathens]:

Zugah d'sarblah: Scissors for cutting woolen clothing.

42. Sukkah 20b [Discussion concerning reed mats which may be ritually impure and hence may not be used as a covering for the *sukkah* due to the fact that they can be used for a variety of purposes. One such use is the *nifvata*]:
Nifvata: For sifting flour. The flour is placed upon it; then [the *nifvata*] is folded and tied together at the edges like our *beutels* [purses]:

43. *Ibid.*
Gulki: It resembles the bags into which one puts pulse and small fruits.

44. Betzah 12b [Sifting pulse on a festival]:
Kanon: It is a utensil. One end is wide; the other is made like a short spout. Pulse are placed into the wide opening. When the utensil is shaken, the edible matter rolls through the spout while the waste remains in the utensil.

45. Betzah 23b [The middle part of a pepper mill is susceptible to ritual defilement]:
The middle part: The Sages declared that a non-metal sieve can become ritually impure... but ours, which are made of metal, [can] certainly [become impure].

46. Shabbat 88a [Reference to the *aggadah* that when the Lord was about to give the Law to the Children of Israel He overturned the mountain upon them like an inverted barrel (*gigit*) and said to them that if they would not accept the Law they would be buried beneath the mountain]:
Gigit: A barrel in which beer is stored.

47. Shabbat 48a [Discussion of whether covering a barrel with a turban on the Sabbath in order to keep the barrel's contents warm is any different from covering the barrel with a *prunka*]:
Prunka: A cloth used to cover the *gigit.*

48. *Ibid.* [Utensils which may be handled on the Sabbath]:
Natla: A ladle used for drawing wine from a barrel.

49. Avodah Zarah 72a [Laws regarding wine handled by a heathen]:
[If an Israelite took the funnel and measured wine into a heathen's flask]:
Mashpekh [funnel]: The upper end is wide, tapering off into a short opening at the lower end. It is placed upon the opening of the bottle brought by the customers and the wine is then poured into it from the measure.

50. Hullin 107a [Law concerning the size of the vessel used for the ritual washing of the hands]:
Natla: Vessel made of glass. It was kept to measure the vessel of anyone who was about to perform the [ritual] washing of the hands.

51. Shabbat 124b [Utensils which may or may not be handled on the Sabbath]:
Of palm branches: Like the ones with which we sweep our homes. It must not be used [on the Sabbath] because it smoothes over the holes in the ground [one of the types of activity forbidden on the Sabbath].

52. Exodus 27:3: [Acceccories for the altar in the Tabernacle]:
And its shovels: Small shovels with which ashes are removed; they resemble small pot covers with a handle.

53. Haggigah 20a [Discussion of ritual impurity in utensils]:
And a shovel: An iron tool... used for scraping ashes from the oven, also for separating figs which are stuck together.

54. See Note 77 to Chapter 9.

55. Shabbat 102b [One who inserts a pin through the eyelet of a shovel has violated the Sabbath]:
Inserts the pin into the eyelet of a shovel: A small peg inserted into the handle of a shovel placed into the hole of the iron so as to fasten it properly.

56. Hullin 25a [Discussion of ritual impurity in vessels]:
To rub: To rub [the vessels] with something which polishes them, as is done with a grass called *aspriel* [in Old French].

57. *Ibid.* [Unpolished vessels are considered "unfinished" and hence not subject to ritual impurity]:
To polish with [the skin of a] tuna fish: It is a fish... Its skin is used for smoothing wooden utensils.

58. Shabbat 123b [Utensils which may be handled on the Sabbath]:
A soup ladle: A large spoon used for skimming the froth from [a liquid in] a pot.

59. Shabbat 157a [Timber stored in a shed for the fall may not be used as firewood on festivals]:
With wood from the back yard of the home: Which he placed on a plot in back of his house and intended for the fall. *Muktzeh* refers to a plot in back of the house used as storage space.

60. II Chronicles 24:14:... *[T]hey brought before the king and before Jehoiada the rest of the money and made it into vessels for the House of the Lord, vessels for service and pestles* [alot]...
Alah: Pestle. Mortar and pestle. *Stoessel* in the German language. Used for crushing spices in a mortar.... Some, however, say that *alot* are boards on which meat is carved.

61. Shabbat 78a [Prohibitions against "carrying" on the Sabbath]:
Paper: It is made from grass.

62. Gittin 6a [Laws concerning the writing of a *get* (bill of divorce). It must be written with the woman in mind. Even if the server of the *get* heard only the scratching of the pen and the rustle of the paper while the document was written and this was done with the woman in mind, it is as if he had witnessed the writing of the entire document.]:
The ken-ken of the quill: The preparation of the pen, when one cuts the quill and smoothes it. However, it seems to me that the sound of the quill refers to the [act of] writing [with it] and its sound on the parchment, which sounds like "ken-ken"....

63. Ezekiel 9:2 ... *[A]nd one man in the midst of them clothed in linen, with writing material on his side.*
Writing material: Pinax [In Greek]. Wax-covered writing tablets upon which one engraves with a stylus.

64. Shabbat 98b [Description of the structural parts of a carriage or wagon in the context of the question regarding which parts under the wagon are to be considered "private domain" in the laws dealing with "carrying" on the Sabbath]:
Shmuel said, [the bottom consisted] of laths: It seems to me, however, that *atbi* is a clip as in the "book clasps" [mentioned] in Tractate Menahot, which is called *glouon* in Old French. That is, a wooden stick is split at the top and it then "bites" the pages of a sheaf of papers [to hold them together].

65. See Note 48 to Chapter 9.

66. Sukkah 32a [Laws regarding the ritual fitness of a *lulav* (palm branch used on Sukkot]:
When the palm branch is found split: Himnek: An iron [tool] used by scribes. It has two ends, one of them split.

67. Shabbat 57a [Laws regarding objects which a woman may "carry" on the Sabbath. She may go out wearing a ring without a signet]:
Signet: A device for sealing a letter or anything [else that should be] closed.

68. Shabbat 47a [Sabbath observance]:
As for the joint of a whitewasher's pole: Who plaster and whitewash a house. They have composite rods topped with a rag which is dipped into lime solution. They plaster the house from below with a short rod, but when they plaster the upper part they place one rod on top of another, thus lengthening the rod.

69. Sukkah 4b [Requirements for the minimum size of a valid *sukkah*]:
Solid [attached]: Apostez in Old French. Something lengthened by means of attached parts, to insert one hollow part into another.

70. See Note 36 to Chapter 9.

71. Shabbat 88b [Reference to Jeremiah 23:29: "Like a hammer that breaks the rock into pieces"]:
Like a hammer: Which by its blow shatters the rock into many particles.

72. Shabbat 102b [One who strikes an adze with a hammer on the Sabbath has violated the Sabbath]:
Adze: Like a large iron hammer used [to work on] iron structures.

73. Shabbat 52b [Laws regarding the purification of an object that has become ritually impure. In order for the water of purification to reach every part of a ring attached to the chain of an animal, the ring must not be merely attached but welded to the chain so as to be part of the chain]:
It has been welded together [so as to become one piece]: Beaten with a hammer until the opening around it has been spread and expanded all around.

74. Hullin 25b [An "unfinished" vessel is not susceptible to ritual impurity]:
To beat with a hammer: It has defective parts to be stretched with the hammer.

75. Shabbat 73a [Striking the "finishing blow with a hammer" is one of the primary activities forbidden on the Sabbath]:
To strike with the hammer: It is a sign that the work has been completed. The artisan strikes the anvil once with the hammer, then lets the hammer slip off the anvil as the work is finished.

76. Betzah 31a [Using a saw for the purpose of chopping is forbidden on festivals]:
Megerah [Saw]: It looks like a knife full of teeth and cuts wood very quickly. It is a craftsman's implement.

77. Eruvin 43b [Rabban Gamaliel had a tube through which he was able to see a distance of 2,000 cubits across the land and a corresponding distance across the sea]:
Shefoferet [Tube]: A hollow rod. When it is long one cannot see far with it, but when it is short one sees better.

78. Isaiah 38:8:
Behold, I will cause the shadow of the dial... to return backward ten degrees: The shadow of the dial: Stairs of a sort built opposite the sun to note with their help the hour of the day, similar to a timepiece *(orlogin)* made by the craftsmen.
(Cf. II Kings 20:10: Isaiah said [to Hezekiah]: "It is a light thing for the shadow to decline ten degrees, nay, but let the shadow return backward ten degrees").

CHAPTER ELEVEN

Foods, Cooking and House Furnishings

The many references to foods, food preparation and household furnishings found in Rashi's commentaries demonstrate the scholar's familiarity with what, during the Middle Ages, was considered primarily the domain of women and servants.

The staple foods in the Jewish community where Rashi lived were fish, meat and bread, prepared in much the same manner then as they are today. Small fish, Rashi notes, were coated with flour, then fried[1] in their own fat.[2] Sometimes an egg was added to this coating.[3] In a commentary on a law concerning foods used for *eruv tavshilin* (to sanction the cooking of food for the Sabbath on a festival falling on a Friday), Rashi describes a "salted fish" which was rather soft and was eaten raw, dipped into hot water.[4] The reference in all likelihood is to a herring. Elsewhere, in a digression in a scholarly debate on the subject of forbidden books, Rashi explains that fish were skinned from the gills tailward[5] and then placed on a grill above burning twigs. To protect the fish from burning, Rashi says in a commentary regarding work forbidden on festivals, paper

227

soaked in water was put on the metal grill beneath the fish.[6] Condiments known to Rashi included vinegar and salt.[7] Commenting on a Talmudic passage stating that Rav Papa would not pray in a house where there was fish hash, Rashi says that the odor of the fish disturbed Rav Papa's devotions.[8] In cases of doubt (where fins and scales, the identifying marks of a *kosher* fish, have been removed) fish or seafood prohibited by the dietary laws can be identified by the fact that their heads are pointed and that they have no spine.[9]

In his commentaries on Talmudic laws relating to Sabbath and festival observance Rashi mentions several methods of preparing meat. He describes pot roast as meat cooked in a pot without water or any other liquid except its own fat and juices, and seasoned with onions.[10] Sometimes meat was eaten raw.[11] Spiced meats were hung up for drying.[12] Whole lambs were barbecued on a spit over an open fire.[13] Both lamb and chicken were stuffed.[14] The head and feet of cattle were pickled in vinegar.[15] The hair was removed from a sheep's head by dousing the head with hot water and then covering it with hot ashes.[16] It is interesting to note that Rashi uses the French *bacons* to define the Talmudic term *kotlei hazir* ("sides of pork").[17]

Raw vegetables were served seasoned with wine and vinegar.[18] Vinegar, Rashi notes, was produced from a special kind of unripe grapes.[19] It seems that this vinegar, along with mustard, was used also as a condiment for meat.[20] Rashi describes various kinds of salt and the methods by which they were prepared. Coarse salt *(melah ostrokanit)* was mined from the ground by hand.[21] Fine salt *(melah s'domit,* literally, "Sodom salt") was washed ashore by the sea.[22] The finest salt known in Rashi's day was so fine that it was barely visible and immediately stuck to one's hand.[23] Salt was also produced by diverting sea water into wide, shallow basins. The sun then evaporated the water, leaving the salt crystals.[24]

Oil was extracted from olives which were first softened by cooking[25] and then ground. However, a better quality of oil was obtained by pounding the olives in a mortar. This process, Rashi explained, had the advantage that it left no dregs.[26]

A vegetable to which Rashi gives the Old French appellation *anise* was used as a sweetener but was not eaten by itself.[27] Small, lentil-shaped peas were served as a dessert; they were quite bitter and had to be boiled in seven waters before they lost their bitterness sufficiently to be edible.[28] Grain kernels retained their sweet taste when they were roasted. After roasting, they were ground into flour. Mixed with oil, water, salt and honey, they yielded a sweet dish called *shattita*.[29]

The beverage most commonly taken with meals in Rashi's France was wine.[30] In the view of Rashi's disciples, one was not likely to become intoxicated if the wine was accompanied by a meal.[31] Pieces of ice or hailstones, called *gelda* (probably a corruption of the Latin *gelida*), were placed into the goblet to keep the wine cool.[32] Beer was also known in Rashi's time; it was made from barley, which was soaked in a trough.[33]

It seems that the bread which Rashi knew was baked in the form of flat, round loaves.[34] Some bakers smeared their loaves with grape juice.[35] In connection with the Talmudic law on the taking of *hallah* (the symbolic "priest's share" of the dough, cf. Numbers 15:17-21) Rashi mentions a kind of pancake which was prepared in a well in the baking oven.[36] There were also cookies in bird and tree shapes; these were richly spiced and contained nuts and almonds.[37]

The ovens with which Rashi was familiar were made in a variety of shapes. He mentions a large oven which had its opening on one side as distinct from earlier ovens, which were much smaller, were portable and opened from the top.[38] The small portable ovens were made of clay and had "rings" for two pots;[39] they stood on a tripod-like metal stand. Another type of portable oven had attached to its side little containers, made of clay, which could be used for various purposes, including the rendering of fat.[40] Small ovens were wide at the bottom and narrow at the top, a shape which helped conserve the heat inside.[41] The opening at the top was sealed with lime.[42] Meat to be roasted was suspended in the oven from the top.[43] Ducks were roasted over an open fire with a dish placed underneath to catch the drippings.[44]

Cooking was done in pots placed directly over an open fire or on a tripod.[45] Hot water was kept on hand at all times. It was boiled in a large kettle made of thick copper and suspended over an open fire. Even after the fire had died down, the heat of the kettle would keep the water hot or at least lukewarm for some time.[46] Cooked food was kept warm (particularly over the Sabbath) in a contraption like a haybox, except that in Rashi's day this box was not filled with hay but with cotton wool.[47]

Rashi's commentaries contain few references to milk or dairy foods. Commenting on a statement in Tractate Shabbat that it is forbidden to "set milk for curdling" on the Sabbath, Rashi briefly describes the preparation of cream cheese: buttermilk was poured into a bast receptacle which permitted the whey to drain off but retained the curd.[48]

The homes of ordinary folk in Rashi's Troyes seem to have been furnished rather frugally. Furniture in these homes was mainly functional rather than decorative. The main functional part of a typical bedstead was a rectangular frame of wood with slits and loops through which were threaded the straps of the leather sheet that served as a mattress.[49] This primitive bedstead was portable and collapsible; it could be assembled at bedtime and taken apart again in the morning.[50] Pillows and blankets were stuffed with down.[51]Commenting on a Talmudic discussion on whether a certain type of linen sheet could be worn on the Sabbath, Rashi describes a sheet of felt (*feltrosh* in Old French) which could be folded and used as a pillow or blanket.[52]

More sophisticated bedsteads had four tall corner posts which supported a canopy or curtain.[53] Others had two long vertical rods fastened to the middle of the headboard and the foot end of the bed, respectively. These two rods in turn supported a rod which extended from the head to the foot of the bed and over which a curtain was spread sloping down to the sides of the bed.[54] This curtain was intended to protect the occupant of the bed from flies while he slept.[55] Since the floors of ordinary dwellings were apparently bare soil or sand, not covered with wood,[56] the legs of the beds, which were made of wood, were placed into coasters to protect them from being rotted by the damp ground.[57]

Clothes used every day were not stored in a closet but hung over an arch-like wooden stand.[58] Mirrors seem to have been rather small. In Rashi's view they were sufficiently large to serve their purpose: looking into them while grooming one's hair and beard.[59]

Chairs and benches were backless.[60] People in Troyes mostly sat on "faldstools" or folding chairs, which had a leather seat.[61] A low footstool was used for resting one's feet.[62] Rashi knew of a special low stool used by an invalid who could not move the joints of his leg because his leg muscles had "dried up" or, in more modern terminology, had atrophied. The stool was tied to his rump. He propelled himself forward by leaning on small grips shaped like miniature benches. When he was tired he eased himself backward to rest briefly on the stool tied to his rump before moving on.[63]

Toilet facilities consisted of a privy stool which resembled the "faldstool" except that there was an opening in the leather seat.[64]

As a rule, the homes which Rashi knew were heated by the ovens in which the food was cooked.[65] The nobility, however obtained additional warmth from heaters made of copper.[66]

NOTES

(Biblical and Talmudic passages are printed in italics; abstracts of such passages and Rashi's commentaries, in Roman type).

1. Sukkah 44b [One should not set out for home on the eve of the Sabbath unless he can reach his destination in time to have the Sabbath meals prepared properly]:
I did not find even a fish pie: Small fish fried in flour and in their own fat.

2. Shabbat 118b [Foods to show one's delight in the Sabbath]:
A pie of fish hash: Small fish fried in the fat of their entrails and in flour.

Avodah Zarah 38a [What foods are forbidden if they were cooked by a heathen]:
Fish hash: Fried in a wine marinade, fish fat and flour.

3. Betzah 15b [Laws concerning the cooking of food for the Sabbath on a festival falling on a Friday]:
A fish and an egg upon it: Egg spread on the fish when it was roasted.

4. Betzah 16b [Food that may be used for *eruv tavshilin*]:

Spanish colias: This is a salted fish, rather soft. It is eaten raw, with hot water poured on it. This is the way in which it is cooked.

Shabbat 145b [Preparation of food on the Sabbath]:

Colias: A fish which is rinsed with water before it is eaten because it is so salty.

Avodah Zarah 38a [What foods are not forbidden even if they were cooked by a heathen]:

Salty fish: Eaten as is because they are salty.

5. Sanhedrin 100b [With reference to a passage in the Book of Ben Sirah explaining that it is wasteful to remove the skin of a fish (gildana) which can be eaten even if it is roasted or baked in its skin]:

Gildana: It is customary to skin fish from the gills tailward.

6. Betzah 32b:

One may not break up a potsherd or cut paper [on a festival] in order to fry salt fish upon it: When fish are roasted on a grill, which is called *gradila* in Old French, reeds or straw are cut, or pottery is broken, or paper is cut, and these are soaked in water. The paper is placed upon the grill [beneath the fish] because the metal becomes hot and will burn the fish.

7. Avodah Zarah 35b [Foods that are forbidden when prepared by a heathen]:

Preserved foods: One pickles fish, vegetables, and the heads and feet of animals in vinegar.

Mo'ed Katan 11a [Food preparation permitted during the intermediate days of festivals]:

One may pickle...: Fish and other foods which are preserved in salt and which can be eaten.

8. Eruvin 65a:

R. Papa did not pray in a house that contained fish hash: Rav Papa did not pray in a house where fish hash was cooked, because of its odor.

9. Avodah Zarah 39b [Foods that are not forbidden even if they were cooked by a heathen. These include fish such as pickled herring which has not been minced so that their heads and spines are recognizable]:

All whose heads and spines are recognizable: Because fish are recognizable as permitted or forbidden by their heads. Forbidden fish have a pointed head and no spine.

10. Pesahim 41a [How to prepare the Paschal lamb]:

...[T]hat which is roasted in a pot: Cooked in a pot without water and without any liquid except in its own drippings.

Betzah 11a [Question whether spices may be taken to a mortar on a festival for a special dish when there is a possiblity that the person will change his mind, leave that dish alone and replace it with one that does not require these spices]:

Leave that dish: A kind of dish which requires spices; e.g., meat and onions.

11. Shabbat 145b [Preparation of food on the Sabbath]:
But whatever was not put into hot water before the Sabbath: For instance, dried meat which can be eaten uncooked if necessary.
Shabbat 142b [Preparation of food on the Sabbath]:
...[I]t is fit as raw meat: There are people who like to eat meat in its raw state.

12. Shabbat 140b [Utensils which may be handled on the Sabbath]:
A cord on which meat hangs: Pickled meat which is hung up to dry... the whole length of cord is called *talia.*

13. Pesahim 75a [Preparation of the Paschal lamb]:
...a perforated grill: Made like bolts... and there is much space between the bolts. The spit is placed sideways and the whole lamb is roasted in midair between the two bolts; its meat does not touch the iron [of the grill].

14. Pesahim 74a [Preparation of the Paschal lamb]:
A stuffed [lamb] is permitted: Lambs are stuffed, as are chickens, between their flesh and their bones.

15. Avodah Zarah 35b [Foods that are forbidden when prepared by a heathen]:
Preserved foods: One pickles fish, vegetables, and the heads and feet of animals in vinegar.

16. Hullin 93b [Extraction of the blood from kosher meat. Specifications of the position in which the head of a carcass must be placed so as not to obstruct the free flow of blood from it and to prevent the clotting of the blood inside the head]:
If a head was placed on hot ashes: To remove the hair it is doused with water and then placed into hot ashes.

17. Hullin 17a [According to the Rabbinical interpretation of Deuteronomy 6:11, "And houses full of good things," the Children of Israel during the first seven years of their settling in the Promised Land were permitted to use anything they found in the homes of the Canaanites, including forbidden foods, when there was danger that they would starve otherwise]:
Rabbi Jeremiah bar Abba stated in the name of Rav that even dried pork was permitted: Sides of pork; called *bacons* [in Old French].

18. Shabbat 145a [Preparation of food on the Sabbath]:
If one presses out [pickled] preserves: Raw vegetables pickled in wine and vinegar.

19. Berakhot 38a [Blessings to be recited over various foods]:
Vinegar from stunted grapes: The "last" grapes which never ripen are used for making vinegar.

20. Shabbat 19a [Use on the Sabbath of juice or liquid dripping from foods that were chopped and placed in (or under) a press on the eve of the Sabbath close to the time the Sabbath began]:
Half-ripe grapes: When the grapes still have thin skins the juice is extracted

from them for a meat sauce because it is strong [tasting] and close to fermentation.

Betzah 16b [Laws relating to the dish prepared for *eruv tavshilin*]:
This dish [can be]... pickled...: Pickled in vinegar and mustard and all kinds of vegetables.

21. Menahot 21a [Laws regarding offerings]:
The salt of Istria: Coarse salt which is extracted from the ground by hand.

22. *Ibid.*
Sodom salt: Fine salt which is washed ashore by the sea.

23. Betzah 39a [The moving of objects beyond the "festival limits"]:
The salt of Sodom: Very fine salt. It adheres to the hands and is invisible.

24. Shabbat 66b [Abaye quotes his mother as saying that to cure a "daily fever" one should take 1 *zuz's* weight of salt from a salt deposit]:
A salt deposit: A place where water is allowed to evaporate. Dikes are drawn at the seashore to channel the water into large pools made expressly for this purpose. Once they are filled, the openings are blocked and the sun evaporates the water. The salt remains.

Shabbat 73b [According to Rabba, one who collects salt from a salina on the Sabbath has violated the Sabbath because this involves "gathering in," one of the thirty-nine principal activities forbidden on the Sabbath]:
...[C]ollects salt from the salina: From the water evaporation channels, which are rendered in Aramaic as *haritzei yama.* Water is drawn into them from the sea and the sun evaporates them. Then [salt is left]. And that canal is called *milhata.*

25. Avodah Zarah 75a [How to purify wine or oil pressing utensils that were defiled by a heathen]:
He should scald them with olive water: This is the method of cooking olives in order to make them tender and to extract their oil.

26. I Kings 5:25: *And Solomon gave Hiram... twenty measures of pure oil.*
Pure oil: The olives were not ground with a grinder but crushed with a mortar. Therefore no dregs were produced as would be in the case of ground [olives].

27. Berakhot 39a [The blessing to be recited over aniseed water]:
Aniseed: A vegetable of which a small amount is put into a dish to sweeten it but not to be eaten alone. It is called *anise* in Old French.

28. Betzah 25b [Israel is compared to the lupine. The lupine becomes sweet after seven boilings but although Israel has repented seven times and has been forgiven, it still rebels and makes God bitter toward it again]:
Turmus [lupine]: A small legume resembling a lentil. Its width is that of a small coin. It is very bitter unless it is boiled in seven waters; then it becomes sweet and is eaten as a dessert.

29. Shabbat 155b [Modes of food preparation forbidden on the Sabbath]:

Parched corn: Flour made from dried, oven-roasted grain. This flour is always sweet and it is the "flour of dried grain." A *shattita* dish is made from it by mixing it with oil, water and salt.

Eruvin 29b [Quantities of *shattita* required for the *eruv*]:
Shattita: A meal made of roasted grain dried in an oven and [mixed with] honey.

II Samuel 17:27-29: *Shobi the son of Nahash of Rabbah... and Machir the son of Ammiel of Lodebar, and Barzillai the Gileadite of Rogelim, brought... wheat and barley meal... for David...*

...And wheat and barley meal: And all kinds of pulse dried in an oven while it is still moist. They are always sweet and when they are ground one prepares from them a dish called *shattita.*

30. Shabbat 78a [Discussion of wine in connection with the prohibition against "carrying" on the Sabbath]:
Its [i.e., the wine's] curative purpose is not so common: Because people drink wine not so much to satisfy their thirst as for their meal.

31. *Sefer HaPardes,* p. 48: "As long as one drinks [wine] with a meal one will not get drunk."

32. Mahzor Vitry, p. 129, par. 27: "Therefore one may place hailstones — called *gelda* — into a goblet of wine to cool it, as is done in Germany."

33. Avodah Zarah 8b [Jewish attitude toward idolatrous celebrations]:
From the time when the barley is placed in the trough: Troughs in which barley is soaked to produce beer.

Pesahim 42b [Foods which must not be in the possession of a Jew during Passover]:
Median beer: In Media, beer is made from barley water similar to ours.

34. Pesahim 48b [Laws pertinent to the taking of *hallah*]:
Babylonian loaves which stick to one another: They are wide and round like ours.

35. Shabbat 145a [Laws of ritual defilement]:
If one smooths [the surface of the dough] with grapes [it is not subject to ritual defilement]: A baker who smears the surface of his loaves with grapes by squeezing the liquid from the grapes onto the loaf.

36. Berakhot 37b [Laws pertinent to the taking of *hallah*]:
[Dough baked] in a cavity made in the ground: Made in a well in an oven into which water and flour are placed, similar to a stew.

37. Berakhot 41b [Question whether a blessing must be recited both before and after eating bread taken with the dessert]:
Except for bread taken with the dessert: Bread is served with them. This bread is kneaded with spice like our *ublias.* Some make them in bird and tree shapes. Only a little of it is eaten, and because it contains a large amount of spices, nuts and almonds and only a little of it is eaten, no blessing need be recited after eating... (Blondheim, No. 745, uses the terms *oublies, patisserie*).

38. Betzah 34a [Permissibility of baking in a large oven on festivals, despite the activities involved]:
A large oven: These are like our ovens, with their opening on one side.

Pesahim 31b [Laws concerning loans made by a Gentile to a Jew on his leaven at Passover time]:
Purni: A large oven like ours. But their ovens were small and portable and were opened from the top. Since only small loaves were baked in them the bread was stuck to their sides.

39. Avodah Zarah 35b [Question of whether bread baked by a heathen may be eaten by Jews]:
A large oven: An oven that is large and has its opening on one side. All the ovens mentioned in the Mishnah were small, have two rings and were opened from the top.

40. Shabbat 48b [The ritual defilement of utensils]:
The receptacle on a stove for the oil flask: Such an oven is portable and small receptacles are attached to it. The oil receptacle is for the rendering of fat.

41. Shabbat 38b [Use of an oven on the Sabbath]:
If an oven was heated: Since it is narrow on top and wide at the bottom it conserves heat better than a kitchen stove.

42. Betzah 32b [It is forbidden to fill up cracks in ovens on festivals]:
Smearing the oven: Spreading clay around the oven lid to keep the heat from escaping.

43. Betzah 32b [Rabba orders a servant to roast a duckling for him in the oven]:
Roast a duckling for me in the oven: Their ovens were small and opened from the top. The roast is suspended into it and its opening is then closed...

44. Hullin 111b [Laws regarding the *kashering* of liver]:
Bei dugi: A receptacle to collect drippings just as we use in [cooking] geese. It is called *bei dugi* in Aramaic.

45. Betzah 32b [Activities forbidden on festivals]:
Nor may one prop up a pot: Any act of placing a pot directly over a fire if no tripod is available is referred to as *shefitah.*

46. Pesahim 42a [Passover observance]:
A woman should not knead [dough] with water collected from the kettle: A large copper kettle kept suspended over an open fire. Its copper is thick, and even if there is no fire the water at its walls is warm or lukewarm.

47. Shabbat 34a:
Hot food may be stored away [just before nightfall on Friday in order to keep the food hot]: Placing it into a box filled with cotton wool so that the heat may be preserved.

48. Shabbat 95a:
One who... sets milk for curdling: With a bast receptacle into which the thick

substance [i.e., the buttermilk] is poured. The whey, which separates [from the curd], drains off. This is called *ainkids* in Old French.

(Blondheim spells the word *jonkeirsh* and links it with the French *jonchieres* — *fromages*. HaMetargem renders it as *"Sauermilch")*.

49. Sanhedrin 20b [Mourning customs; the lowering of one's *dargesh* (bedstead) when one is in mourning]:
A dargesh has the strapwork inside: There are slits in its frame; the ends of the straps hanging from the leather sheet are threaded through these and tied.

Mo'ed Katan 27a [Lowering one's bedstead when one is in mourning]:
Its straps from the inside: The straps are inserted from the slits of the bed frame.
Ibid.
The strapwork over the frame: The strapping is placed onto the frame from one side to the other.

50. Shabbat 138a [It is forbidden to put up certain types of beds on festivals]:
A Gallian couch: They take apart their beds and chairs, carry them with them, return with them and put them up again.

Sanhedrin 20a ["Lowering" one's bedstead when one is in mourning]:
A leather hammock: A leather bed with straps attached around the edges of the leather sheet. When the bed is put up, the straps are tied to the frame of the bed, and when the straps are released, [the bed] collapses.

Nedarim 56b [Is a *dargesh* considered a bed if someone vows to abstain from using a bed?]:
A leather hammock: A leather bed with straps [attached] around [the edges of] the leather sheet which are pulled through the frame of the bed. One lies upon it, and when the straps of the leather sheet are untied, it collapses.

51. Shabbat 74b [It is forbidden to pluck the wing or the down from a bird on the Sabbath]:
Pluck the wing: After [the feather] is plucked out, its top is cut off, because it is soft and can be used in pillows and blankets.
And he who plucks the down off the large feather of the wing: Toward the lower end, which is coarse; the hair is plucked from both sides, the shaft is thrown away and the down is put into pillows and blankets.

52. Shabbat 146b [Discussion as to whether a sheet of felt may be regarded as a "garment" and hence worn outdoors on the Sabbath without transgressing the prohibition against "carrying"]:
To wear... sheets: [Sheets of] felt that is called *feltrosh* in Old French; they are folded and used as pillows or blankets.

53. Sanhedrin 68a [Rabbi Eliezer is described as seated in his canopied four-poster bed]:
Four-poster bed: Four posts and a curtain over them.

Sukkah 10a [A *sukkah* is rendered unfit for use if a four-poster bed with a canopy or curtain is placed into it because the curtain then constitutes a "tent" beneath the *sukkah's* covering]:

A four-poster bed: Four posts [corresponding to the] four legs of the bed. They are tall, and rods are placed atop them [extending] from one end [of the bed] to the other, and a curtain is spread over [the rods].

Shabbat 138b [A bridal bed may be assembled and dismantled on the Sabbath because, as distinct from a four-poster bed, the canopy drops from a central rod (see Note 54) and hence does not constitute a "roof" which must not be put up on the Sabbath]:

A bridal bed: This is different from the other curtains, which are spread over a framework with four posters and have a canopy.

54. Sanhedrin 20b ["Lowering" one's bedstead when one is in mourning]:
Curtain-frame: Two long poles are placed in the middle of the bedboards, one at the head and one at the foot. They are forked at the top and are connected by a rod [extending from one end of the bed to the other]. The curtain is spread over [this rod].

55. Mo'ed Katan 27a ["Lowering" one's bedstead when one is in mourning]:
Curtain-frame: Poles affixed to the ends of the bed. A long cross pole connects them, and sheets are spread over the latter as a protection [of the occupant] against flies.

56. See reference to sand floor in Chapter 10, p. 217 and Note 51 to Chapter 10.

57. Shabbat 47a [Activities prohibited on the Sabbath]:
Coasters of a bed: Resembling little feet. They have a receptacle into which the legs of the bed are fitted to prevent them from being rotted [by the damp ground].

58. Sotah 49b [Sumptuary laws]:
One may make a framework of lathes and hang on it anything one desires: Similar to an arch made up of wooden circles, as we do now for hanging up scarves and gold-embroidered veils.

59. Shabbat 149a [Activities forbidden on the Sabbath]:
One must not look into a mirror on the Sabbath [lest one pluck out a hair, which is forbidden on the Sabbath]: Miroir [Old French] because he looks in the mirror [*mar'ah*] solely in order to arrange his hair or his beard.
(Clearly, this is a pun on the French *miroir* and the Hebrew *mar'ah*).

60. Ketubot 111 a-b [An opinion that standing for a long time is not good for the heart]:
Without a back: Beds or soft chairs have backs, but benches and chairs do not.

61. Shabbat 138a [It is permitted to open a folding chair on the Sabbath]:
A folding chair: This is called *traskal* [from the Greek *triskeles*], and *foldenstuhl* in the vernacular. Its seat is made of leather and can be folded. When [the chair] is [to be] removed it is placed next to the wall; when it is needed it is put up again and stands on four legs.

62. Haggigah 12a [Quotation: "Thus says the Lord: The Heaven is My throne and the earth My footstool"]:
A footstool: For his feet, and [also] a chair to sit on.

63. Shabbat 66a [A cripple is not permitted to go out on the Sabbath with his supports and stool]:
Stool: A cripple whose calf muscles have dried up and have atrophied, and who cannot move even his joints uses a kind of low stool upon which he sits. When he moves forward [he does so by leaning on] small grips and so moves his body from the ground, pushes it forward and then comes to rest on his rump, to which the stool is tied.

64. Shabbat 138a (See Note 61)
A privy stool: Similar to the folding chair (*traskal*) except that the leather seat has an opening for toilet purposes.

65. J. Dieffenbacher, *Deutsches Leben im 12. und 13. Jahrhundert*, Vol. II, Sammlung Goeschen, No. 328, Berlin and Leipzig, 1918, p. 39.

66. Shabbat 47a [Utensils which may, or may not, be handled on the Sabbath]:
A portable brazier: A copper vessel in which heat is brought to noblemen for warming [themselves].

Epilogue

One does not erect monuments to righteous men;
their words keep their memory alive.
*(Jerusalem Talmud, Shekalim II:5,
Genesis Rabbah 82)*

Rashi died in the year 1104/05. The last years of his fruitful life seem to have been overshadowed by the tragedies which befell the Jews of western Europe in the course of the First Crusade (1095-99), when hordes of French and German peasants massacred the Jews in the Rhineland. It is quite likely that the hardships and losses sustained by the Jewish communities he knew so well had an adverse effect on Rashi's health. Toward the end of his life he was confined to his bed, too weak to write, so that he was compelled to dictate his responsa to his grandson and to some of his friends.[1]

The compassion and deep sorrow which Rashi felt for his persecuted brethren are apparent in many of his Biblical and Talmudic commentaries. Some of his remarks echo his dejection at the ceaseless sufferings of his people. To Psalm 73:14 ("And my chastisement came every morning") he notes, "We are facing new trouble each morning." His comment on Psalm 38:18 ("And my pain is continually before me") is, "We have become experienced at [suffering] blows and are prepared at all times for disaster." Commenting on a passage in Tractate Sukkah he states that during times of crises which affect the entire world Jews must be on guard more than anyone else.[2] Elsewhere, in connection with a Talmudic description of heathen customs in ancient Rome, Rashi comes to the unhappy conclusion that "Esau is still wielding dominion over Jacob."[3]

Rashi's comments on three oft-cited consecutive verses in the twenty-sixth chapter of Isaiah reflect his search for the meaning of Isaiah's sufferings. Here one sees reflected a mood of resignation and depression, but also Rashi's basic unquestioning acceptance of God's will:

> *Isaiah 26:16-18:*
> Lord, in trouble have they sought Thee;
> Silently they poured out a prayer when Thy chastening was
>   upon them.
> Like a woman with child, that draws near the time of her delivery,
> Is in pain and cries out in her pangs,
> So have we been at Thy presence, O Lord.
> We have been with child, we have been in pain;
> We have, as it were, brought forth wind;
> No deliverance was wrought in the land,
> Neither have the conquerors of the world fallen.

> *Rashi's Commentary:*
> *In trouble have they sought Thee:* They did not question Thy measures.
> *Like a woman with child, etc.:* We saw new troubles all the time and we came to the conclusion that they were harbingers of salvation and deliverance, since we have faith that we will be delivered from the midst of affliction and trouble just like that woman with child.
> *We have been with child, etc.:* As if we had been in childbirth, as if we had been close to deliverance, but there was [only] wind and no salvation.
> *No deliverance was wrought in the land:* In all our sufferings and troubles we do not discern salvation for ourselves.

It is likely that his commentary on Isaiah 53:9 — the famous passage describing the anguish and the horrors experienced by the "suffering servant," who was "despised, and forsaken of men," reflects Rashi's view of the agony which the Jews knew in his own day:

Isaiah 53:9
And they made his grave with the wicked,
And with the rich his tomb,
Although he had done no violence,
Neither was there any deceit in his mouth.

Rashi's Commentary:
He delivered himself to be buried in whatever manner the evil idol worshippers decreed, who inflicted upon them killing, and a donkey's burial [see Jeremiah 22:19, "He shall be buried with the burial of a donkey"] in a dog's grave [i.e., the most humiliating ways in which a corpse could be disposed of]. In keeping with the decision of the evil ones he was willing to be buried [in this manner] and did not deny the [existence of] the living God. In keeping with the decision of the ruling authority he had delivered himself up to every kind of death which [the former] decreed [for him] because he did not want to take it upon himself to do evil and to commit violence, as was done by the idol worshippers in whose midst he lived.

Translated into more straightforward language (Rashi evidently resorted to circumlocutory terms in order not to run afoul of the Gentile censors), this means that the Jews were tortured and killed during the period of the Crusades because they refused to accept baptism and to forsake their own ethical values for those which prevailed among the Gentiles in whose midst they lived.

Until the end, Rashi remained in contact with the Jewish communities which turned to him for spiritual guidance during those trying times. In one of his responsa, he refers openly to a "day of great bloodshed" in which the wife of one of the victims managed to flee to her father, who had survived the massacre.[4]

No monument has ever been erected in Rashi's memory. There was no need for it. He attained immortality by virtue of his life work. He created an indispensable tool for the study of Bible and Talmud, an indestructible key to the great treasury of Jewish law, learning and wisdom. In his own day his commentaries, particularly those on the Tamlud, opened new avenues for Talmudic scholarship in France and Germany and inspired both teachers and students with new zeal for the subject matter they cherished. Following Rashi's death, many of his disciples became students at the Talmudical academies founded in Germany and France by Rashi's sons-in-law and grandsons.

The generations of spiritual heirs that took up Rashi's work adhered to their master's methods as they delved more deeply into his comments, in a constant endeavor to seek and find the meaning of his every stylistic nuance.

Rashi used the compactness of the Hebrew language to the fullest; many an aphorism or *bon mot* that has become a byword in later Jewish parlance derived its original formulation from Rashi's commentaries.[5] His profound sensitivity to the meaning of words helped him make exquisitely careful distinctions between terms which appear synonymous to the untrained, superficial eye, and enabled him to obviate misinterpretations of the Biblical and Talmudic passages on which he comments.[6] In addition, he made his own contribution to the enrichment of the Hebrew language; a very large number of terms commonly used in present-day colloquial Hebrew owe their origin to Rashi. Thus, in the modern State of Israel, physicians, farmers, scientists, poets, artists and businessmen are indebted to Rashi for words that have become part of their everyday professional vocabulary.[7]

The true touchstone of a man's greatness is the extent to which his work survives his death and continues to live among his posterity. Rashi's luster did not grow dim with his passing. Instead, with every new generation that studies the Talmud in the traditional manner, his brilliance has illuminated the farthest corners of the Jewish diaspora until our own present day. It is as if, whenever a student of Jewish law and ethics, be he young or old, famous or still unknown, quotes passages from Rashi's commentary, we can hear the master's own lips whispering to us from his grave.

NOTES

1. Joel HaKohen Miller, *op. cit.*, par. 15, p. 9a:
"I am too weak and my mouth is silenced, to tell of the misfortunes that have befallen me, wave after wave. My hand has therefore become too weak to

write to my friends... the answer in my own hand. I am therefore dictating it to one of my friends and he is writing..."

See also Elfenbein, *op. cit.*, par. 81 and *Sefer HaPardes*, p. 160, par. 242: "I, the undersigned insignificant one, am confined to bed. The time has come to be brief, contrary to custom, for I have become weak and unable to write. I am dictating these lines to my grandson and he is writing them...."

2. Sukkah 29a [Rashi's commentary on a statement that a solar eclipse is an evil omen for those who hate the Jews]:
All manner of outrages come upon the world. Israel must concern itself and say: This omen came more for us than for all the other nations because Israel is more accustomed to being stricken than all the others.

3. Avodah Zarah 11b.

4. Elfenbein, *op. cit.*, par. 215: "Reuben took a wife and was killed on the day of the great bloodshed. He had no children and his wife took refuge with her father, who survived the massacre."

5. a. אימת העליון על התחתון ('The fear of Him who is above is upon him who is below"). From Rashi's commentary on Deuteronomy 32:40: *For I lift My hand to Heaven and say, I live forever.* Rashi explains that this means God has made Heaven the dwelling place (יד ["hand"] is used in the connotation of מקום) of His glory, as the Targum has it, and therefore no one can deliver the idol worshippers from the hand of God. Rashi continues: "For even when the weak person is above and the strong one below, the fear of him who is above is upon him who is below; how much more is this so when the strong one is above and the weak one is below."

b. אימתא דצבורא ("Out of respect for the community"). From Rashi's comment on the prohibition in Sotah 40a against the priests' wearing leather footgear while blessing the congregation.

c. באמת ובלב שלם ("In truth and with a whole heart"). From Rashi's comment on Daniel 2:43:
And whereas thou sawest the iron mixed with miry clay, they shall mingle themselves by the seed of men, but they shall not cleave to one another, even as iron does not mingle with clay: They will marry other nations but they will not cleave to them in truth and with a whole heart.

d. באה שבת באה מנוחה ("Sabbath came — rest came"). From Rashi's comment on Genesis 2:2:
And on the seventh day God finished His work which He had made: Sabbath came — rest came.

e.. עני חשוב כמת ("A poor man may well be considered as one who is dead"). Rashi cites this statement from Nedarim 64b in his commentary on two Biblical verses: Genesis 29:11 and Exodus 4:19.
Genesis 29:11:
[And Jacob kissed Rachel] and wept: [Rashi explains that Jacob wept because he had no possessions. He had given them all to Esau's son Eliphaz, who had been ordered by Esau to kill Jacob. Eliphaz found himself in a dilemma. On the one

hand, he could not bring himself to kill Jacob. On the other hand, he felt he could not disregard his father's order. Jacob thereupon suggested a way in which Eliphaz would be able to let Jacob live without being a disobedient son to his father]: Take all I have [and then you can say that] I am dead because a poor man may well be considered as one who is dead.

Exodus 4:19:
[The Lord told Moses to return to Egypt] "for all the men are dead [who sought thy life]": Who were these men? Dathan and Abiram. [In fact] they were [still] alive, but they had come down [in the world] because they had lost their property and a poor man may well be considered as one who is dead.

f. ניבא ואינו יודע מה ניבא "He prophesied without knowing what he was prophesying."
(From Rashi's comment on Genesis 45:18):
[Pharaoh tells Joseph to bring his family from Canaan to Egypt] *and I will give you the best of the land:* The district of Goshen. He prophesied without knowing what he was prophesying [because the Children of Israel would carry away the best of the land when they would leave the land of Egypt].

g. צדקה אין לה קצבה "There is no limit to charity" (From Rashi's comment on Gittin 52a, on the subject of tithing).

6. a (1) Genesis 8:13:
And behold, the face of the ground was dried up [חרבו]: It had become like clay, for its surface had been somewhat hardened.
(2) Genesis 8:14:
The earth was dried [יבשה]: It became hard as is its natural state.

b. (1) Genesis 19:9: [The people of Sodom came to break in the door to Lot's home]:
Door [דלת]: [The framework] which swings round on hinges to close and open.
(2) Genesis 19:11 [The two angels whom Lot had taken in struck the others at the entrance to Lot's home with blindness so they could not find an opening to enter]:
Opening: [פתח]: The hollow space through which people go in and out.

c. Genesis 29:17:
But Rachel was of beautiful form [תאר] *and fair to look upon* [מראה]: *Form:* This denotes the shape of her face. To look upon [*Appearance*]: This denotes the beauty of her features.

d. Exodus 21:25:
...wound [פצע] *for wound, bruise* [חבורה] *for bruise:*
Wound: An injury which draws blood, the accused having crushed the flesh of the other. *Bruise:* A wound in which the blood is congealed but does not come out, only the flesh on that spot becomes red.

7. a. שדול ("persuasion," from שדל, "to entice")
From Rashi's comment on Exodus 22:15:

And if a man entice a maiden: "Entice" meaning persuasion.

b. עדשן ("a freckled person")
From Rashi's comment on Leviticus 13:29:
Skin that has white and dark spots: Freckled.

c. שתוק ("silencing")
From Rashi's comment on Judges 3:19:
And [Eglon] said: Keep silence: This [word] still means "silencing." (In modern Hebrew, שתוק is also used to denote paralysis).

d. תכופות ("continuous" or "successive")
From Rashi's comment on II Samuel 12:31:
And he brought forth the people that were therein and put them under saws: A saw: A knife with successive notches.

e. תחבשת ("bandage" or "dressing")
From Rashi's comment on Isaiah 1:6:
[The wounds have] not [been] dressed: Not dusted by a physician with a powder containing dressing.

f. נתבלבלו ("confuse")
From Rashi's comment on Isaiah 51:16:
The heavens vanished like smoke: Another interpretation: The heavens were confused.

g. רסוס ("spray")
From Rashi's comment on Ezekiel 46:14, a reference to the meal offering:
To moisten the fine flour: Another interpretation: To make the flour fine (מרוסס) and to mix it.

h. שאיפה ("ambition")
From Rashi's comment on Amos 2:7:
Who pant after the dust of the earth: The meaning is: who have the ambition to possess....

i. הסכמה ("agreement")
From Rashi's comment on Nahum 1:12:
[Though Israel's enemies be] in full strength and likewise many: [Though they are] in full agreement.

j. תמיכה ("support")
From Rashi's comment on Psalm 16:5:
Thou hast placed my hand unto the best part: Another interpetation: Thou hast supported my lot. Derived from the word תמיכה, "support."

k. מאסר ("prison" or "arrest")
From Rashi's comment on Psalm 66:11:
Thou didst bring us into the hold: Into a narrow place as if into a prison.

l. ממזג ("mixed wine")
From Rashi's comment on Proverbs 23:30:
They that go to try mixed wine: Wine that has been mixed.

m. מתעקם ("is bent")

From Rashi's comment on Ecclesiastes 12:6:

Before the silver cord is snapped asunder: This is the spinal cord which is white like silver; at death its marrow is lost. It becomes empty, dry and bent.

n. נתוך ("melting")

From Rashi's comment on II Chronicles 34:21:

For great is the wrath of the Lord that is poured out (נתכה) upon us: As the wrath is fire, the expression "melting" (נתוך) is appropriate in this verse.

THE FAMILY OF RASHI

Simon the Elder

Daughter = Isaac

Nathan

Samuel

Solomon (Rashi) 1040-1105

Meïr = Jochebed
about 1065-1135

Rachel (or Bellassez) divorced by Eliezer (or Jocelyn)

Miriam = Judah (Ribam) Azriel

Samuel (Rashbam) about 1085-1158

Jacob (R. Tam) about 1100-1171

Isaac (Ribam) left 7 children

Solomon

Solomon

Yomtob

Miriam (?)

Judah

Isaac

Dolce = Eleazar of Worms
d. 1196   d. 1230

Samuel

Simhah of Vitry

Samuel = Miriam

Isaac (Ri the Elder) about 1120-1195

Elhanan d. 1184

Samuel

Judah Sir Leon of Paris
1166-1224

Selected Bibliography

TEXTS

Berliner, Abraham, *Raschi (Salomonis Isaacidis) Pentateuchum Commentarius*, Berlin, 1866.

—————————, *Raschi, der Kommentar des Salomo B. Isak ueber den Pentateuch*, Frankfurt a.M., 1905.

Breithaupt, Joh. Friedrich, *Commentarius hebraicum in Pentateuchum, R. Salomo Jarchi, Raschi, dicti (Commentarius hebraicus in Prophetas, maiores et minores, et in Hiobum et Psalmos, latine versus, cum duobus vetustissimus codicibus*, Gotha, 1710.

Hofes Matmonim sive Anecdota Rabbinica Continentia, ed. Berl Goldberg, Berlin, 1844.

Lehmann, Manfred, *The Commentary of Rashi on the Pentateuch* based on a Yemenite manuscript, N.Y. 1981.

Likkutei HaPardes, Daniel Bomberg Printing Press, Venice, 1519.

Mahzor Vitry, ed. Shimon Hurwitz, Berlin, 1889-93.

Melo Hofnayyim, ed. Abraham Geiger, Berlin, 1840.

Pentateuch with Targum Onkelos, Haphtaroth and Rashi's Commentary, tr. into English and annotated by Rev. M. Rosenbaum and Dr. A.M. Silbermann, in collaboration with A. Blashki and L. Joseph, New York, n.d.

Piyyutei Rashi, ed. A. M. Haberman, Jerusalem, 1941.

Sefer HaOrah, ed. Salomon Buber, Lemberg, 1905.

Sefer HaPardess, ed. H.L. Ehrenreich, Budapest, 1924.

Sefer Issur veHeter, ed. Yakov Freiman, Berlin, 1936.

Sefer Rashi, tr. into Arabic by Jospeh ben David, Dzerba, 1941.

Siddur Rashi, ed. Yakov Freiman, Berlin, 1911.

Teshuvot Hakhmei Tsorfat ve-Lothir (Responsa of the scholars of France and Lorraine), ed. Joel HaKohen Miller, Vienna, 1881.

Teshuvot Rashi, ed. Israel Elfenbein, New York, 1943.

BIOGRAPHIES AND BIOGRAPHICAL ARTICLES

Aptowitzer, Victor, *Introductio ad Sefer Rabiah*, Jerusalem, 1938, pp. 395-407.

Bacher, Wilhelm, "Raschi," in *Jahrbuch fuer Geschichte und Literatur*, 1906. pp. 86-106.

Beerman, Max and Doktor, Max, *Raschis Leben und Wirken*, Worms, 1906.

Berliner, Abraham, *Raschi*, Vortrag im Verein fuer Juedische Geschichte und Literatur zu Berlin, Berlin, 1906.

Cohen, Arthur, *Raschi, ein populaerer Vortrag*, Basel, 1906.

Efrati, Moshe Zevi, *Rashi, Rabbi Shlomo Yitzhaki, Hayyav U-Mif'alo, Devarav Ve-Imrotav*, Tel Aviv, 1957.

Falk, Felix, *Le Rabbin Salomon Fils d'Isaac de Troyes (1040-1105)*, Geneva, 1909.

Glenn, Menahem, *Rashi, der Folkslerer* (Yiddish), New York, 1940.

Gordin, Aba, *Rashi (Rabbenu Shlomo Yitzhaki)*, Tel Aviv, 1961.

Gross, Henri, *Gallia Judaica*, Paris, 1897, pp. 226-230.

Hakohen, Mordekhai, *Toledot Rashi*, Jerusalem, 1955.

Hazan, Leib, "Rashi, Rabbenu Shlomo Yitzhaki, Zemano, Hayyav u-Feulato," in *HaTekufah*, Tel Aviv, 1940.

Indelman, Elhanan, *Rashi*, New York, 1956.

Liber, Maurice, *Rachi, un Rabbin de la France de Nord au XIe siècle*, Paris, 1905; English translation, *Rashi:* (tr. Adele Szold), Philadelphia, 1906, 1938, 1948; New York, 1970.

Lipschuetz, Eliezer Meir, *Raschi, sein Leben und sein Werk*, Warsaw, 1914.

Marx, Alexander, *Essays in Jewish Biography*, Philadelphia, 1947, pp.61-86.

Mulder, Samuel Israel, *Over de Verdiensten van R. Salomo ben Izak*, Amsterdam, 1826.

Ne'eman, Pinhas, *Rashi, Mefaresh HaTorah*, Jerusalem, 1946.

Rothschild, Samson, *Rabbi Schlomo ben Isak, ein Lebensbild*, Worms, 1924.

Schloessinger, Max, *Rashi, His Life and His Work*, Baltimore, 1905.

Simon, Ernst, *Rashi, Sippur Hayyav*, Tel Aviv, 1957.

Spivak, Itzhak, *Rashi, Rabbi Shlomo Yitzhaki, Tekufato, Toledotav U-Fa'olo Hayyav*, Tel Aviv, 1940.

Taubenhaus, Efraim, *Rashi, Hayyav U-Fa'olo, Tel Aviv, 1955.*

Twersky, Yohanan, *Rashi*, (Hebrew), Merhavia, 1946.

Unterman, Itzhak, *Rashi, zain lebn, shaffung un oyftu* (Yiddish), Philadelphia, 1940.

Weiss, Isaak Hirsch, "Toledot Rashi," in *Beth Talmud II*, Vienna, 1882, pp.

33-40, 65-73, 97-101, 129-138, 161-166, 193-206, 225-231, 257-264, 289-297.

Wellesz, Julius, *Raschi*, Budapest, 1906.

Winoker, M., *Toledot Rabbenu Shlomo Yitzhaki*, Berditchev, 1906.

Zeitlin, Solomon, "Rashi," in *The American Jewish Year Book, 5700,* Vol. 41, New York, 1939, pp. 111-140.

Zunz, Leopold, "Salomon ben Isaak, genannt Raschi," in *Zeitschrift fuer die Wissenschaft des Judentums,* 1823, pp. 277-384. This essay was translated into Hebrew and annotated by Samson Bloch, *Vita R. Salomon Isaki.* First edition Lemberg, 1840; Second edition Warsaw, 1862.

SPECIALIZED STUDIES

Baer, Itzhak, "Rashi Ve-HaMetziut HaHistorit shel Zemano," in *Tarbiz,* 1950, pp. 320-333.

Blumenfield, Samuel M., *Master of Troyes,* New York, 1946.

Fraenkel, Jonah, *Darko shel Rashi Be-Ferushav LaTalmud HaBavli,* Jerusalem, 1975.

Freiman, Aron, "Manuscript Supercommentaries on Rashi's Commentary on the Pentateuch," in *Rashi Anniversary -Volume,* New York, 1941, pp. 73-114.

Hailperin, Herman, "Nicolas de Lyra and Rashi: The Minor Prophets," in *Rashi Anniversary Volume,* New York, 1941, pp. 115-147.

——————————, *Rashi and the Christian Scholars,* Pittsburgh, 1963.

Jacobsohn, David, "Education in Rashi's Time," in *Jewish Education,* Vol. 12, No. 2 (September, 1940, p. 79ff.)

Katan, Moshe, *La Vie Privée en France au XIe siècle d'après le Commentaire de Rachi,* Paris, 1949.

Kleinman, Saul, *Yalkut Rashi,* St. Louis, Mo., 1942.

Leibowitz, Nehama, *Iyyunim Hadashim B'Sefer Shemot,* Jerusalem, 1973, pp. 495-524.

Loew, Immanuel, "Pflanzennamen bei Raschi," in *Birkat Abraham: Festschrift zum siebzigsten Geburtstage A. Berliners,* III, Frankfurt a/M., 1903, pp. 231-254.

Maschkowski, Felix, "Raschis Einfluss auf Nicholas von Lyra," in *Zeitschrift fuer Alttestamentliche Wissenschaft,* Giessen, 1891, pp. 268-316.

Michalski, Abraham, "Raschis Einfluss auf Nicolaus von Lyra in der Auslegung der Buecher Leviticus, Numeri und Deuteronomium," in *Zeitschrift fuer alttestamentliche Wissenschaft,* Giessen, 1915, pp. 218-245; 1916, pp. 29-63; 1921, pp. 300-307.

Neumann, J., "Influence de Rachi et d'autres commentateurs Juifs sur les Postillae Perpetuae de Nicholas de Lyra," in *Revue des Études Juives,* Vol. XXVI, pp. 172-182; Vol. XXVII, pp. 250-262.

Passamaneck, S., "Rashi and Marine Architecture," in *Jewish Quarterly Review*, Vol. 67, No. 4 (1977), pp. 218-225.

Rosenthal, Erwin I.J., "Rashi and the English Bible," in *Studia Semitica*, Vol. I (1971), pp. 56-85.

Rosenthal, Judah M., *The Commentary of Rabbi Solomon ben Isaac (Rashi) on Song of Songs*, New York, 1958.

Shereshevsky, Esra, "The Significance of Rashi's Commentary on the Pentateuch," in *Jewish Quarterly Review*, Vol. 54, No. 1 (1963), pp. 58-79.

_____, "Rashi and Christian Interpretations," in *Jewish Quarterly Review*, Vol. 61, No. 1 (1970), pp. 76-86.

_____, "Some Aspects of Everyday Life in Rashi's Times," in *Jewish Quarterly Review*, Vol. 65, No. 2 (1974), pp. 98-114.

Zeitlin, Solomon, "Rashi and the Rabbinate," in *Jewish Quarterly Review*, Vol. 31, No. 1 (1940), pp. 1-58.

MISCELLANEOUS WORKS ON RASHI

Berliner, Abraham, *Zur Charakteristik Raschis*, Breslau, 1900.

_____, *Beitraege zur Geschichte der Raschi-Commentare*, Berlin, 1903.

_____, *Blicke in die Geisteswerkstatt Raschis*, Frankfurt a.M., 1905.

Epstein, Abraham, "Schemaja, der Schueler und Sekretaer Raschis," in *Monatschrift fuer Geschichte und Wissenschaft des Judentums*, 1876, Vol. XLI, p. 257-263, 296-312.

Raphael, Itzhak, *Ta'arukhat Rashi BiY'rushalayim*, Jerusalem, 1940.

Rosenblatt, Samuel, "Rashi's Gift to France," in *The Jewish Outlook*, September, 1940, pp. 7-9.

RASHI'S IMPACT ON LANGUAGES

Avineri, Itzhak, *Thesaurus Linguae Hebraicae Auctore Rashi (Rabbi Solomon Izhaki)*, Vols. I-IV, Tel Aviv, 1949.

Berliner, Abraham, *Kuntrus HaLo'azim*, Cracow, 1905.

Blondheim, David S., "Gloses Françaises dans les Commentaires Talmudiques de Raschi," in *Études Lexicographiques*, Paris, 1937.

Darmesteter, Arsène and Blondheim, David S., "Les Gloses Françaises dans les Commentaires Talmudiques de Raschi," I, *Texte des Gloses* Paris, 1929.

Elstof, E., "Rashi's Knowledge of the Triliteral Root in Hebrew," in *Journal of the Manchester Egyptian and Oriental Society*, Manchester (Eng.), 1927, 1929.

Englander, Henry, "Rashi's View of Weak ע"ע and פ"ן Roots," in *Hebrew Union College Annual*, Vol. VII (1930), pp. 399-437.

_____, "Rashi's Vowel Terminology," in *Hebrew Union College Annual*, Vol. XII-XIII (1937-8), pp. 505-521.

_____, "Grammatical Elements and Terminology in Rashi," in *Hebrew Union College Annual*, Vol. XIV (1939), pp. 387-429.

_____, "A Commentary on Rashi's Grammatical Comments," in *Hebrew Union College Annual*, Vol. XVII (1942-3), pp. 427-498.

Gruenwald, Moritz, *Das Altfranzoesische aus Raschis Bibelcommentar*, Belovar, 1883.

Grunwald, Max, *Etwas ueber Raschis Einfluss auf die spaetere hebraeische Literatur*, Berlin, 1905.

Hirschfeld, Leo, *Raschi und seine Bedeutung fuer die Erhaltung der muendlichen Ueberlieferung*, Frankfurt a.M., 1906.

Kronberg, Nehemias, *Raschi als Exeget mit besonderer Ruecksicht auf das Sprachwissenschaftliche in seinem Bibel Commentar*, Halle a/S., 1882.

Onderwijzer, A.S., *Raschies Leven en Werken*, Amsterdam, 1901.

Pereira-Mendoza, Joseph, *Rashi as Philologist*, Manchester (Eng.), 1940.

Shereshevsky, Esra, "The Use of Prepositions and Conjunctions in Rashi's Commentary," in *Jewish Quarterly Review*, Vol. 57, No. 3 (1967), pp. 200-211.

_____, "Inversions in Rashi's Commentary " in *Gratz College Anniversary Volume*, Philadelphia, 1971, pp. 263-268.

_____, "The Accents in Rashi's Commentary," in *Jewish Quarterly Review*, Vol. 62, No. 4 (1972), pp. 277-287.

FESTSCHRIFTEN

Bitzaron (Rashi Issue), Vols. XI, XII, Av-Elul, 1940.

HaDoar (Rashi Issue), Shevat, 1940.

Rashi Anniversary Volume, American Academy of Jewish Research, New York, 1941.

Rashi, His Teachings and Personality; Essays on the 850th Anniversary of His Death (Hebrew and English), S. Federbusch, New York, 1958.

Rachi, Ouvrage Collectif, ed. Manes Sperber, Paris, 1974.

Sefer Rashi, Kovetz Torani Mada'i. Yotze l'or l'zekher m'loth t'sha meot shanah l'huledet Rashi, ed. Rabbi Y.L. Fischman, Jerusalem, 1941.

Sefer Rashi, ed. Rabbi Y.L. Hakohen (Fischman) Maimon, Jerusalem, 1955.

Sefer Rashi, LiSh'nat huladeto ha-t'sha meot, Buenos Aires, 1940.

GENERAL WORKS CONTAINING REFERENCES TO RASHI

Berkovits, Eli[ezer] L., *Was ist der Talmud?* Berlin, 1938.

Chones, S.M., *Toledot HaPosskim*, Warsaw, 1910.

Freimann, Aron and Hildesheimer, Meir, *Birkat Abraham; Festschrift zum siebzigsten Geburtstage A. Berliners*, Frankfurt a.M., 1903.

Guedemann, Moritz, *Geschichte des Erziehungswesens und der Cultur der Juden in Frankreich und Deutschland*, Vienna, 1880.

Heilprin, Jehiel ben Solomon, *Seder HaDoroth*, I, Warsaw, 1886.

Urbach, E.E., *Ba'alei HaTosafot*, Jerusalem, 1955.

Zacuto, Abraham ben Samuel, *Sefer Yuhasin HaShalem*, ed. Zvi Philipowsky, London-Edinburgh, 1857.

Index

*Note:*Pertinent subject headings that occur in the Notes at the end of each chapter are included only if there is no specific reference to them in the text of the chapter.

I. GENERAL INDEX

255

II. INDEX OF BIBLICAL AND TALMUDIC SOURCES

A. BIBLE

D. MIDRASHIC LITERATURE